"Gottlieb and DeLoache's first edition of *A World of Babies* earned the right to be called a classic of anthropology. Although one might expect the second volume of *A World of Babies* to be a simple update of the same studies, Gottlieb and DeLoache have instead done the unexpected – they present an entirely new volume with seven new studies of parenting practices. Taken together, these books set the example of how anthropology, when done well, can open minds to the possibility that there is more than one way to do just about anything, including parenting. I can think of no better way to become a more thoughtful, insightful, and therefore better parent than reading both editions of *A World of Babies*."

Meredith F. Small
Cornell University, author of *Our Babies, Ourselves*

"I cannot effuse enough about the second, fully revised edition of *A World of Babies*! The first edition has been a mainstay in my classroom for over a decade, and I have frequently given it as a gift to new parents. The creative, innovative, quasi-fictional design of both editions – 'imagined childcare guides' authored by ethnographers studying in a broad range of cultures, writing as if they are imparting knowledge to new parents as a childcare expert, such as a grandmother, midwife, or diviner – makes *A World of Babies* an enjoyable and impactful read for students and new parents alike. At a time when it may seem like there is no 'right' way to raise a child . . . it is refreshing to read a book which concludes that, in fact, there are *many* 'right' ways to raise children."

Christa Craven
College of Wooster, author of *Pushing for Midwives: Homebirth Mothers and the Reproductive Rights Movement*

"This is a fantastic book! I am going to use it right away with both my large undergraduate class and advanced graduate seminar . . . It [has] an impressive array of authors, each with deep knowledge of the culture for which they are preparing their 'advice.'"

Patricia Greenfield
UCLA, author of *Mind and Media: The Effects of Television, Video Games, and Computers*

"*A World of Babies* provides terrific and vivid personal examples reminding us of the importance of family, culture, history and context in children's lives in today's globalizing world."

Thomas S. Weisner
UCLA, co-author of *Higher Ground: New Hope for the Working Poor and Their Children*

"This very accessible yet soundly scholarly book reads like a novel describing the same event from different perspectives, thereby shedding light on the socio-culturally constructed nature of what we might think of as 'objective' and self-evident 'truths' about early child development. A 'must read' for students and researchers in the area of developmental psychology as well as a 'great read' for anyone interested in the world of babies."

Alexandra M. Freund
University of Zurich, co-editor of *The Handbook of Life-Span Development: Social and Emotional Development*

"Starting with a most captivating and comprehensive overview of the worldwide challenges facing 21st century parenting, alongside their seven, fictitious, 'composite person' *community* authors, who could (if real persons) appropriately dispense 'how to' infant care advice, yet, again, Professors Gottlieb and DeLoache manage to spin their baby-care magic for both students and professionals alike . . . the seven new (and one updated) chapters provide, as did the first edition, a sparkling set of 'manuals' but with an even greater degree of wit, clarity, and intimate cultural knowledge, spreading cross-cultural insights that at times shock, amuse, and entertain, but always shed further light on the diverse . . . ways both biology and culture find expression in how we care for our babies."

James J. McKenna
University of Notre Dame, author of *Sleeping with Your Baby*

"Clever, refreshing, indeed witty way to engage readers . . . not only in the study of children, childhoods and socialization, but also in the conduct of ethnographic field research and the ways in which we present our work."

Myra Bluebond-Langner
University College London, author of *The Private Worlds of Dying Children*

"The editors, in the second edition of *World of Babies*, have made a great book out of a very good one. The work is unique in combining perspectives not normally found in a single case study . . . we learn much about the enormous diversity in cultural practices vis-à-vis babies and about the contemporary forces that provoke change and resistance to change."

David F. Lancy
Utah State University, author of *The Anthropology of Childhood*

"This lively, well-written book is authoritative, but not in the usual way. It's not going to tell you how to give birth or raise your child. Instead, it will tell you many ways to do it, each blending a deep cultural tradition with the modern world. It's the perfect antidote to the worst parenting myth: *There is one right way, and if I don't find it my child will suffer.* Treat yourself instead to *A World of Babies,* and encounter a wide world of ways."

Melvin Konner
Emory University, author of *The Evolution of Childhood*

"They had me at page 1: Encountering a few of the differences in beliefs held around the world about raising babies made me eagerly read for more. Students of child development at all levels of education need this book to help them gain perspective on their own culture's childrearing practices. Practices that appear 'natural' and unquestionable are in fact deeply rooted in physical, cultural and economic realities . . . The book is brilliant. I can see this book generating extensive discussion and provoking endless consideration of the role of nature and nurture in child development."

Roberta Michnick Golinkoff
University of Delaware, author of *How Babies Talk*

"This thoughtful and engaging book should be read not only by anthropologists and psychologists but by all expectant mothers. It makes American childrearing seem distinctly exotic. At the same time, it shows how much all mothers share. The effect is both liberating and moving."

Tanya Luhrmann
Stanford University, author of *When God Talks Back*

PRAISE FOR THE FIRST EDITION:

"If you ever find yourself assuming that there's just one right way – your way – to bring up babies, read this book. It's highly enjoyable and such a good idea that I only wish I'd thought of it myself."

Penelope Leach
author of *Your Baby & Child, From Birth to Age Five*

"Every American parent should reflect on these cultural essays."
Jerome Kagan
Harvard University, author of The Nature of the Child

"Having a baby is a life-enhancing and mind-extending trip into new lands, much like the marvelous anthropology of child rearing in this book. Take its expedition and it may help clarify the values and contexts of your own parenting, and bring the world's children into the clearer focus of our knowledge and concern."

Catherine Lutz
Brown University, author of *Schooled: Ordinary, Extraordinary Teaching in an Age of Change*

"Read these pages. This is a very moving book[,] and a revealing one."

Jerome Bruner
New York University, author of *Child's Talk*

"Judy DeLoache and Alma Gottlieb's book is just delightful. What a treat to read about the early child rearing practices in the seven cultures around the world. The universals and the individual differences are just wonderful. This book should be a treat for all parents everywhere."

T. Berry Brazelton
Harvard University, author of *Touchpoints: Birth to Three*

"Put away your volumes of Dr. Spock and enter a world where there is no final wisdom about what is best for baby; only as many variations on the theme as there are ways of imagining what it means to create a new human life."

Ruth Behar
University of Michigan, author of *Translated Woman*

A World of Babies

Imagined Childcare Guides for Eight Societies

Fully Revised Second Edition

Should babies sleep alone in cribs, or in bed with parents? Is talking to babies useful, or a waste of time? *A World of Babies* provides different answers to these and countless other child-rearing questions, precisely because diverse communities around the world hold drastically different beliefs about parenting. While celebrating that diversity, the book also explores the challenges that poverty, globalization, and violence pose for parents. Fully updated for the twenty-first century, this edition features a new introduction and eight new or revised case studies that directly address contemporary parenting challenges, from China and Peru to Israel and the West Bank. Written as imagined advice manuals to parents, the creative format of this book brings alive a rich body of knowledge that highlights many models of baby-rearing – each shaped by deeply held values and widely varying cultural contexts. Parenthood may never again seem a matter of "common sense."

Alma Gottlieb is Professor Emerita of Anthropology and Gender and Women's Studies at the University of Illinois at Urbana-Champaign. She conducted long-term fieldwork in Beng communities (1979–93) and now connects with young Beng people through social media. A full-length ethnography of Beng childrearing practices appeared as *The Afterlife Is Where We Come From: The Culture of Infancy in West Africa*; she has also written a *Beng–English Dictionary* (with M. Lynne Murphy) and *Under the Kapok Tree: Identity and Difference in Beng Thought*. With proceeds from two memoirs of their lives with the Beng (*Parallel Worlds* and *Braided Worlds*), Gottlieb and fiction writer Philip Graham have co-founded the Beng Community Fund, a non-governmental organization that funds development projects in Beng villages.

Judy S. DeLoache is the Kenan Professor of Psychology Emerita at the University of Virginia. She has published extensively on cognitive development in infants and young children. She has served as President of the Developmental Division of the American Psychological Association, and as President of the Cognitive Development Society. Dr. DeLoache's research was funded by a Scientific MERIT Award from the National Institutes of Health and the National Science Foundation. She is a Fellow of the National Academy of Arts and Sciences. In 2013, Dr. DeLoache received the William James Award for Lifetime Distinguished Contributions to Psychological Science from the American Psychological Society, as well as the Distinguished Research Contributions Award from the Society for Research on Child Development.

A World of Babies

Imagined Childcare Guides for Eight Societies

Fully Revised and Updated Second Edition

Edited by

Alma Gottlieb
University of Illinois at Urbana-Champaign

and

Judy S. DeLoache
University of Virginia

CAMBRIDGE
UNIVERSITY PRESS

University Printing House, Cambridge CB2 8BS, United Kingdom

Cambridge University Press is part of the University of Cambridge.

It furthers the University's mission by disseminating knowledge in the pursuit of education, learning, and research at the highest international levels of excellence.

www.cambridge.org
Information on this title: www.cambridge.org/9781107137295

First published 2017
Reprinted 2017

Printed in the United Kingdom by Clays, St Ives plc

A catalogue record for this publication is available from the British Library.

Library of Congress Cataloging-in-Publication Data
Names: Gottlieb, Alma, editor. | DeLoache, Judy S., editor.
Title: A world of babies : imagined childcare guides for eight societies / edited by Alma Gottlieb, Judy S. DeLoache.
Description: Fully revised second edition. | Cambridge ; New York : Cambridge University Press, 2017. | Includes bibliographical references and index.
Identifiers: LCCN 2016014777| ISBN 9781107137295 (Hardback) | ISBN 9781316502570 (Paperback)
Subjects: | MESH: Child Rearing–ethnology | Socialization | Social Values | Cross-Cultural Comparison
Classification: LCC GN482 | NLM WS 105.5.C3 | DDC 649/.1–dc23 LC record available at https://lccn.loc.gov/2016014777

ISBN 978-1-107-13729-5 Hardback
ISBN 978-1-316-50257-0 Paperback

We dedicate this book to the grandbabies of our worlds –
Dean and Mona Graham,
and Waverly Aimone and Wilder Lewis Clore

Contents

Contents

Note to the Reader

Before you read any of the chapters in this book other than the first one, it is important to understand two things about them.

First, each chapter is written in the style of a childcare manual from one of eight societies around the world. The "author" described in each chapter's "About the Author" section is semi-fictional; such a created persona (based, however, on individuals or composites of individuals from these societies) permits the creation of a "manual" in the style of famous authors of childrearing books such as those by Dr. Benjamin Spock, Berry Brazelton, Penelope Leach, and others. We hope this format provides information about infant care practices in different societies in a lively and memorable way.

Second, the chapters are solidly based on ethnographic field research conducted in the societies they discuss. You will learn what anthropologists and other scholars have written about what people in these communities believe about the nature of babies, and how best to care for them.

The book is thus a mix of scholarly research and literary narrative – quasi-fictional "authors" presenting factual information.

Note to the Reader

[illegible]

... and how best to care for them.

[illegible]

CHAPTER 1

Raising a World of Babies

Parenting in the Twenty-first Century

Alma Gottlieb and Judy S. DeLoache

- Should babies sleep alone in cribs, or in bed with their parents?
- What's the best way to bathe newborns?
- Should parents talk to babies, or is it a waste of time?

In this book, you'll find answers to these and many other questions about how to care for infants and young children. In fact, you'll find several different answers to each one, not only from different societies around the world but even within the same society, as a result of both social complexity and social change. Whether the practices you read about here are longstanding or recent, and whether they are widely accepted or hotly contested, many differ significantly from what the majority of contemporary middle-class, White, North American or European parents do. Here are just a few examples of diverse views you'll encounter in these pages.

- In the Faroe Islands (an autonomous province of Denmark), babies always nap outdoors for a few hours every day – to avoid indoor germs, accustom the baby to cold temperatures, develop the immune system, and toughen children for a difficult life. Elsewhere in Europe, babies of Muslim immigrant families from Guinea-Bissau now living in Portugal are always allowed to nap uninterrupted – in case Allah might be sending angels delivering messages to the dreaming infant.

- Most middle-class North Americans bathe their infants inside their homes on a daily basis – socializing them early into a life that values privacy. In the West Bank and Gaza, Palestinians bathe their babies outside, with local children gathered around the basin in which the baby is bathed – socializing them early into a life that values the community.
- The Beng of West Africa talk regularly to their babies – who are cherished as reincarnations of ancestors and, as such, deemed to be able to understand all the languages of the world. In contrast, Somali adults in East Africa typically do not address babies and toddlers at all, because children in this authoritarian society are not permitted to respond to adult communications.

As these brief ethnographic summaries suggest, people in diverse communities hold dramatically different beliefs about the nature – and the nurturing – of infants. This book celebrates that diversity. At the same time, this book also addresses the challenges that violence, poverty, and rapid social change pose to parents in raising their children. For example, how should Israeli mothers answer questions about World War II that their children bring home from kindergarten after their teachers introduce a three-day unit for Holocaust Remembrance Day – inaugurated by a loud siren that disrupts their playful classroom at 10 a.m.? How should Palestinian mothers raise their sons to fight for statehood, while urging them to resist the call to throw stones at Israeli tanks or plan bomb attacks in Israeli cafés?

Attending simultaneously to the divergent goals of understanding cultural differences, as well as the larger political and economic contexts of globalization, poverty, and war facing so many families, calls for a creative approach. Accordingly, each of the eight chapters in this collection is written as though it were an "advice manual" for new parents in a particular society. This approach offers two distinct advantages. For one thing, the advice manual format makes for engaging reading. For another, the combination of eight distinct and sometimes contradictory "manuals" undermines the universalist assumption that underlies the "manual" genre itself – as we explore later in this Introduction.

UNDERSTANDING THE WORLDS OF BABIES

This book is an entirely revised edition of an earlier collection of essays written in the style of childrearing manuals (published in 2000). The new edition speaks directly to conversations gaining momentum across the US and elsewhere. In recent years, US interest in childrearing strategies has skyrocketed, with the proliferation of TED talks and popular books that have advocated "other" childrearing practices inspired by places as diverse as China and France. These books and talks have produced heated debates about whether mainstream, middle-class, Euro-American practices are too laid-back and forgiving compared to parenting practices elsewhere. Their authors' willingness to "parent in public" by airing personal thoughts and decisions about childrearing has encouraged a new generation of parents to consider both the virtues and the deficits of different parenting approaches.

With such texts and podcasts readily available, parents today increasingly realize that beliefs and behaviors differ substantially from one place to another. However, that awareness does not necessarily bring acceptance. Understanding and appreciating the ways of other people present a challenge precisely because our sense of how to do things we consider to be of great importance is so deeply ingrained. This is especially true for the task of raising children.

Every group thinks that its way of caring for infants and young children is the obvious, correct, and natural way – a simple matter of common sense. However, as the anthropologist Clifford Geertz once pointed out, what we complacently call "common sense" is anything but common. Indeed, what people accept as "common sense" in one society is often considered odd, exotic, or even barbaric in another.

Oddity cuts both ways. Although our readers will no doubt be surprised, perhaps even shocked, by some of the ideas and practices described in these pages, many parents who follow those practices would find our readers' values and behavior – *your* values and behavior – equally surprising.

Each of the eight childrearing "manuals" we present here is intended as a "common sense guide to baby and childcare" – echoing the title of the original edition of the best-selling childcare guide by "the world's most famous baby doctor," pediatrician Dr. Benjamin Spock. Since 1946, seven editions of that book have sold over 50 million copies – second in sales only to the Bible. Unlike the advice offered in that and other "how to" guides, however, the nature of the advice contained between the covers of this book varies dramatically from one chapter to another, underscoring the variability of how children are understood and raised in different communities.

Our primary aim is to illustrate how the childrearing customs of any community, however peculiar or unnatural they may appear to an outsider, make sense when understood within the context of that society, as well as within its broader geopolitical context. Childcare practices vary so much across time and space precisely because they are firmly embedded in divergent physical, economic, and cultural realities.

Challenges of Caring for Children

The remarkable diversity of infant and childcare practices is all the more remarkable when we consider that, to a substantial degree, these diverse practices largely represent strategies for dealing with similar challenges. Human infants are distinguished from many other animals by, among other things, extreme helplessness at birth and a very long period of dependence on others for survival and development. A crucial role undertaken by their parents is ensuring their survival, health, and safety. Parents or other caregivers furthermore typically assume a major role in encouraging their children to develop desirable personal characteristics and social relationships, acquire technical skills, and adopt the values and beliefs that will enable them to participate fully in their society. In the following pages, we focus first on the general challenges involved in keeping infants alive and healthy and then on the practices that promote cultural learning.

Helping Babies Survive and Thrive

The first challenge to rearing children is successfully navigating pregnancy and childbirth. People in the communities represented in the chapters that follow posit culturally distinctive models and practices of conception and pregnancy to enhance the likelihood of a successful birth.

Infant Mortality

The likelihood of surviving infancy depends on basic economic resources. In industrialized societies throughout the world today, the rate of infant mortality is very low – only two to five children of every thousand die, making it likely that few of these parents worry constantly about their children perishing. Parents in many areas of the world today face a far more grim reality. As of 2015, many countries in the global south have very high infant mortality rates, including three countries in which fully 10–11 percent of all babies die. A great majority of these deaths could be averted by access to professional medical care. Here, we address the more proximate causes, while reminding the reader of the geopolitics of the past half-millennium of European colonizing of the world that contributed to the current tragic state.

Nutrition

Economic factors play a major role in whether infants have a diet sufficient to promote their survival and development. Medical researchers assess the incidence of "undernutrition," and the more serious condition of "malnutrition," by measuring the proportion of children who are significantly below the standard height ("stunting") and weight for their age. Although these statistics have improved significantly over the preceding twenty-five years, in 2013, 161 million children under five years of age were estimated to be "stunted." That same year, 99 million children under five years were classified as "underweight." In both cases, nearly all of these children lived in Asia and Africa.

Such nutritional deficits frequently take a fatal toll. As of this writing (2015), approximately 3.1 million children die from hunger each year, even though the world's farmers produce enough food to feed the world's population. The unequal distribution of global resources that causes tragic inequities in food availability remains a major political issue of our planet.

Adequate maternal nutrition is necessary for the development of the fetus, and most societies encourage pregnant women to pay attention to their diets for the sake of their unborn children. Yet the specific rules and recommendations for expectant mothers about which foods they should seek out and which they should avoid vary greatly around the globe.

In many places, traditional reasons for forbidding certain foods based on various symbolic notions have now been replaced by practical considerations. For example, in the Faroe Islands (an autonomous province of Denmark), industrial pollution from fertilizers, distant mining, and fossil fuel combustion has contaminated the local waters with high levels of mercury and PCBs. These poisons accumulate in the fatty parts of fish and whales – and in the bodies of pregnant and nursing women who eat them, posing a particular threat to healthy fetal brain development. Pregnant Faroese women are now advised by government-sponsored maternity nurses to avoid eating these traditionally rich sources of protein.

People in societies around the world adopt a wide variety of strategies for providing adequate nutrition to developing infants. Throughout human history until the last few decades, breastfeeding was the *only* way to supply young infants with a reliable source of sustenance. Although their biological mothers have most often provided infants' primary source of breastmilk, "wet nursing" – the practice of having an infant breastfed by someone other than his or her own biological mother – has been practiced in both Western and non-Western settings, and in both ancient and modern times. In the ancient world, from Mesopotamia and Egypt to Greece and Rome, wet nurses commonly fed wealthy women's babies. In western Europe, the practice became common in elite families in the eleventh and twelfth centuries and lasted through the eighteenth century: infants of wealthy mothers were nursed by peasant women, who in turn handed their own babies to others for their sustenance. In 1780, this practice was so common in Paris that, of the 21,000 infants born in the city, only about 700 were breastfed by their own mothers. In some European countries, wet nursing did not cease entirely until World War I, when poor women could, for the first time, make more money working in factories than from serving as wet nurses.

Elsewhere, infants who are breastfed primarily by their mothers may occasionally be nursed by other women as well. In many Muslim societies, infants who are breastfed by the same woman become "milk kin." Having suckled at the same breast is considered to create a bond between children as strong as that between biologically related siblings. In these societies, a marriage between "milk kin" would be considered incestuous.

Before the relatively recent introduction of "infant formula," there were several disastrous attempts to substitute something for breastmilk as infants' main source of nourishment. For example, in seventeenth- to eighteenth-century Iceland, infants were typically fed cow's milk rather than human breastmilk. So many babies died that women bore as many children as they could, in an effort to offset the shockingly high losses.

In the current era, breastfeeding occupies an increasingly contradictory space in the public imagination. On the one hand, scientific research overwhelmingly testifies to the nutritional superiority of breastmilk over any other substance for the human infant. The American Academy of Pediatrics and the World Health Organization both recommend exclusive breastfeeding, with no supplements, for virtually all infants for the first six months of their lives. These two organizations also recommend continuing to breastfeed (supplemented by solid foods) for another six months or eighteen months, respectively.

Yet the proven nutritional superiority and health benefits of breastmilk have come to be ignored in many places. In the United States, while the percentage of infants who begin breastfeeding at birth has increased significantly from recent public health campaigns, only 49 percent of all infants are still breastfed at six months – although there is substantial variation by region, economic status, educational level, and ethnic background. For example, 71 percent of six-month-old infants are still breastfeeding in California and Oregon compared to only 2 percent in Mississippi. Beyond the US, the figures are even lower: globally, fewer than 40 percent of infants under six months of age are exclusively breastfed.

In industrialized countries, commercially produced "infant formula" can support healthy growth and development, although with a somewhat higher rate of infections and other medical problems, both short and long term. In many countries in the global south, however, formula-feeding presents far graver health risks. Some 750 million people around the world – approximately one in eight people – lack access to safe water. In such places, infant formula is inevitably mixed with polluted water in unsanitary containers. Furthermore, impoverished parents often dilute the formula, to make the expensive powder last longer. Under such circumstances, parents' sincere efforts to promote the health and well-being of their babies can be tragically undermined.

The decision of when to introduce solid food – and what, and how – differs greatly from one society to another, for reasons including both local availability of alternatives to breastmilk, and cultural norms. In Palestinian communities detailed in this book, for example, infants from three months on receive food pre-chewed by their mothers and other female relatives. With this practice, the decision to introduce solid food becomes a social one shared among women.

Weaning decisions are not just individual or even community-based; government policies can also have an enormous impact on when a mother weans her child from the breast. In northern

European nations that offer generous, paid maternity leaves, women have the luxury of exclusively breastfeeding their infants for four to six months. In this volume, our manual for the Faroe Islands of Denmark chronicles such a case:

From between four and six months of age, you should start introducing solid foods to your infant. Most families make their own food for their infants – for instance, by putting cooked vegetables in a blender. Because you have a long maternity leave and will therefore be home more than your husband, you'll probably be the one to make this food most of the time.

In nations lacking such government support, many working mothers may find it impossible to continue breastfeeding their babies exclusively (or at all) once they return to their jobs. Some women in industrialized settings may also find it impossible to continue breastfeeding because of lack of workplace facilities to pump breastmilk. From local norms (and, sometimes, laws) that assume that women's breasts should never be bared in public, scolding and other shaming practices further discourage many women from breastfeeding in restaurants, shops, parks, and other public spaces. Frustration over such constraints led one American journalist to call for a return of wet nurses, to help working mothers continue their working lives.

Broader issues of global import also affect micro-level feeding decisions. In this volume, our chapter on China discusses dangerous levels of food contamination due to lack of government oversight, with accompanying risks to infants. Chinese mothers who prefer to use infant formula are cautioned to buy or import formula from the West. Such scenarios underscore the extent to which globalization also includes fatal flows of poisonous substances.

Illness

Whether or not an infant survives also depends on the resources that are locally available for treating disease. Strategies and resources to prevent, diagnose, and cure illness vary dramatically around the globe. At the pragmatic level, they depend on whether medical clinics are available and affordable. At the cultural level, they also depend on what parents believe are the underlying causes of given ailments. What you do for a case of diarrhea may differ depending on whether you think your baby has "caught a bug" or has been "caught by a spirit."

In many societies today, including those featured in this book, parents have exposure to both traditional healers and modern medicine. If they can afford it – a big *if* – many will use both. For example, if she can pay for transportation to the closest clinic, a Beng mother of a sick child in Ivory Coast might consult not only a village diviner but also a clinic nurse or doctor. As insurance against medical risks, she might secure for her baby both a cowry shell bracelet and – if she can find the money for it, and if it is available locally – a tetanus shot.

Yet modernity not only offers beneficial new treatments for disease, it also brings new exposure to sickness. One of the bitter ironies facing many immigrants to the US is a general decline in health and an uptick in dangerous conditions such as obesity and diabetes due to changes for the worse in their diet – as chronicled in our chapter on Somali-Americans in Minneapolis.

Supervision

Babies also need protection from mishap and accidents. Strategies for safeguarding children depend on the nature of local risks. Cars whizzing by on a busy street, an open cooking fire in the middle of the family compound, and poisonous snakes all require different approaches to keeping babies and toddlers safe. Very different strategies are needed to protect against risks that are less visible but still perilous, such as the machinations of witches or malicious spirits who are said to harm or steal babies – or the equally mysterious workings of bacteria that might be killed by vaccines. Ideas about such invisible risks do not necessarily fade in modern, industrialized settings. In the Faroe Islands of Denmark, for example, mothers who are addressed in our imagined manual receive mixed messages about the relevance of such folk beliefs:

> You might . . . teach your child about our traditional belief in the "hidden people," or *huldufólk*. Most young people do not believe in these supernatural beings any more, but older people still share

stories in which they claim to have seen them . . . [and] people are still careful not to move large boulders in which they reportedly live. But you don't want to scare your children when you tell them these stories: they should be entertaining and are important to remember only as a part of our history.

Other risks to babies' health and survival may depend on the work that their mothers perform to earn a living, and how the infants are supervised. In societies in which all healthy adults work in the fields, tend livestock, or engage in hunting and gathering, babies are typically cared for during the day by older siblings, cousins, or other children. As long as the child babysitter can bring the baby along to the mother's workplace to be nursed, the infant can thrive (Figure 1.1).

However, this caretaking arrangement is less viable in other settings, where extreme poverty makes it difficult or even impossible for working mothers to care effectively for their

Figure 1.1 In many communities around the world, older siblings commonly take responsibility for younger siblings. In this Balata refugee camp in Nablus (West Bank), a Palestinian baby is being well cared for by an older sister.
Photograph by Bree Akesson.

infants. Such is the case in the *favelas* of northeastern Brazil, for example, where many mothers perform domestic work for wealthy families. Because their employers see the house cleaners' children as dirty and contagious, young infants often remain at home with an older child, or even alone in a hammock. Deprived of their nursing mothers' milk, these babies do not get adequate nourishment; some eat nothing all day, and an alarming number die.

Relationships

Right from birth, forging satisfying emotional attachments is a fundamental part of the human condition. In many Western societies, it is generally assumed that infants will form close attachments to their parents, but not with many others – possibly only with immediate family members. By contrast, adults in many other societies place a premium on integrating infants into a larger group. In Beng villages in Côte d'Ivoire, this effort begins right away: A member of every household in the village is expected to call on a newborn baby within hours after the birth to welcome the tiny person into the community.

Elsewhere, the expectation that a child will be cared for by a group of people beyond the biological parents supports a variety of adoption practices. On the Micronesian island of Ifaluk, the adoption of infants is very common. Because they retain close ties with their biological parents, the adoptees feel they are an integral part of two families.

Such an "additive" approach can work well in a small community. Yet with globalization, adoptions now occur well beyond the local community. Increasingly, children are being adopted outside their racial, ethnic, and national boundaries. The challenges of such interracial and international adoptions are just beginning to be charted, with the most vexing cases involving unwitting participation in human trafficking schemes. For example, some children from impoverished families in countries such as Uganda, Ethiopia, and Guatemala are misidentified as "orphans" to be put up for adoption by international agencies, with parents misunderstanding the structure and outcome of the process.

The caretaking arrangements of many rural African societies foster a different set of ties. Older siblings (who may be as young as six or seven) typically care for their infant and toddler siblings for much of the day while their mothers work, resulting in a strong bond between the siblings. In industrialized societies, young children who attend formal daycare programs often develop strong relationships with their daycare teachers, as well as with a number of other unrelated children.

Beyond connections with relatives and neighbors, many societies also encourage ties with the departed. Those who view infants as reincarnated ancestors may endeavor to maintain a relationship between their flesh-and-blood child and the ancestor's spirit. In Kenya, the Baganda naming ceremony for an infant features someone calling out a series of names belonging to various deceased relatives of the baby. When the child smiles, it is taken as a sign that he or she is a reincarnation of the ancestor just mentioned and wishes to be called by that name.

Elsewhere, connections with spiritual beings may continue actively throughout life. For instance, in Australia, pregnant Warlpiri women may dream that they conceived their child in a place associated with a certain spirit that has given life to the baby. Once born, the child has a lifelong tie to the land associated with that spirit and, as an adult, can always have a say in matters relating to that piece of land. With current movements of people well beyond their homelands, will such spiritual ties continue to have meaning? Will they serve as sources of comfort, longing, or distress? Perhaps the Portuguese concept of *saudade*, that complex notion combining regret, desire, and nostalgia for a place or time, may become the clarion call of our age.

Meanwhile, as the world grows more interconnected, developmental psychologists have increasingly considered the implications of cultural differences for children's lives. For example, early advocates of "attachment theory" assumed the model to have universal relevance regardless of local family structure or parenting practices. Now, psychologists acknowledge "the different faces of attachment" that are produced by the variety of cultural values and political institutions (local and global alike) that structure parents' ideas of what sorts of emotional attachments *should* be sought for their children – and what sorts *may be possible*, given constraints.

In this volume, Shirdon poignantly chronicles the ways that, in Somali-American households in Minneapolis, apartment living results in a much smaller group of people to interact with infants and toddlers than would have been the case back in Somali villages or urban neighborhoods. This new American setting, with its restricted linguistic and social interactions, is now resulting in diagnoses of autism in twice as many young Somali-American children as in the general US population. As the Somali-American case suggests, models of attachments need updating to take into consideration the global flows of people to new living spaces that often create new contexts for social interaction – sometimes enriched, but all too often impoverished.

Life Skills

Most parents have clear ideas about how to prepare their children for successful lives as adults. Children everywhere need opportunities to acquire life skills that will enable them to become fully functioning members of their particular society. In traditional societies, young children typically learn how to do work by serving, in effect, as apprentices – whether watching a parent weave at the loom, washing laundry and cooking, hunting, or weeding, hoeing, and harvesting on the farm (Figure 1.2).

In the contemporary world, the life skills that many children must learn for a successful life have changed drastically. In Lisbon, migrant Mandinga and Fula parents from Guinea-Bissau have adapted a traditional naming ritual for infants in ways that acknowledge these changes. In our imagined manual for these parents, a Guinean mother living in Portugal advises:

> Back home [in Guinea-Bissau] on this special day, babies are shown those things that will be important throughout their lives, depending on their gender and caste: a cooking pot or hoe for a girl, for example, or leatherworking tools for a baby from a leatherworking family. But . . . this part of the ritual . . . doesn't make sense in Lisbon, where children have so many options available to them. Which objects will be important to your child depends entirely on what he or she ends up doing in life. Who are we to make assumptions about that in this new country?

Figure 1.2 In Côte d'Ivoire, this Beng toddler and young girl are already proficient at pounding food in a large mortar. Beng girls play an important role helping their mothers prepare meals for their large families.
Photograph by Alma Gottlieb.

Implied in this set of comments about new work opportunities is the set of broad-ranging, literacy-based skills offered by a modern education. Whereas earlier generations were educated by their communities for a life path that was narrowly delimited, current generations are exposed to myriad job options. Our chapter on a Quechua community living in a small town in rural Peru highlights the difference that schooling can make for newly educated peasants. "Study hard!" becomes the rallying cry motivating young people to get ahead, not just for themselves, but to improve the quality of life of their families.

Yet for too many, this equal-opportunity model remains more a dream than a reality. The combination of class, race, religion, immigrant status, and national origin puts refugees such as the Somali-Americans profiled in this book at an enormous disadvantage. In this context, those Somali-Americans who become successful business owners in the face of such long odds seem especially remarkable, whereas those who fail to overcome the enormous obstacles often become, troublingly, stigmatized with designations ranging from "autistic" to "terrorist."

We now consider an extended example illustrating many of the points we have made about childcare and culture.

Where Should the Baby Sleep?

Although sleeping is a necessity for everyone, never do we spend so much time asleep as when we are babies. People in all societies accommodate infants' need for sleep, but they do so in very different ways – and sometimes for different reasons.

Across most of the world today, and throughout most of human history, infants have spent the night in the company of others. In early childhood (and sometimes into the later childhood years), sleeping has been a social, not a solitary, affair. Most commonly, infants sleep with their mothers, although others might play this role. In many contemporary urban, middle-class families in China, a baby sleeps with his or her paternal grandmother, who serves as the primary caretaker and brings the baby to her daughter-in-law to nurse.

Co-sleeping is rarely motivated by lack of space. Even when families live in multi-room dwellings, parents in co-sleeping societies take their infants into bed with them. One virtue is that the mother can easily breastfeed whenever the baby awakens – often without fully awakening herself. Children continue to sleep with their mothers or other older relatives for varying lengths of time – from one or two years for Mayan babies in

Guatemala to, until recently, into the teen years in Japanese families.

A very different practice characterizes the sleeping pattern in North America (and some other Western nations). In middle-class, Euro-American families, the most common pattern is for infants to sleep in their own beds, and often in their own rooms – a practice long approved and recommended by the vast majority of American pediatricians. In fact, recent public health campaigns in US cities have warned against the risks of unexplained deaths (sudden infant death syndrome, or "SIDS") from infant–parent co-sleeping – the concern being that a parent might accidentally roll over onto the infant and smother it (Figure 1.3).

However, members of some groups in the US prefer other sleeping arrangements. In a recent study, 28 percent of Asian parents reported sleeping in the same room with their children, compared to 8 percent of White parents. Moreover, despite recent critiques of how "attachment theory" has been mischaracterized in popular discussions, a recent trend in "attachment parenting" has taken hold in some slices of urban, educated Euro-America, for whom it is now fashionable for infants and parents to co-sleep (among other "attachment"-promoting practices). However, it remains difficult to estimate the extent of this trend, since infant/parent bed-sharing remains stigmatized in mainstream discourses (both medical and popular) – a situation that, doubtless, leads some parents to conceal their bed-sharing habits, making it likely that bed-sharing is under-reported in the US.

To make matters even more confusing, the above-mentioned public health campaigns against co-sleeping rely on warnings by US-based pediatricians that bed-sharing increases the risk of SIDS – yet, other scientific researchers have reached the opposite conclusion. For example, biological anthropologist James McKenna has concluded that the risk of SIDS is actually lower for infants who share their parents' bed, so long as the parents are non-smokers unimpaired by alcohol or medication, and in safe circumstances (without loose pillows or blankets). This stark contrast between models of bed-sharing as both *increasing and*

Figure 1.3 In New York City, a public health campaign launched in 2008 put posters in subways to urge parents not to sleep with their babies.
Photograph by Alma Gottlieb.

decreasing the likelihood of SIDS, as interpreted by pediatricians versus biological anthropologists (respectively), gives us pause.

In effect, these divergent beliefs and practices belie different values on the part of parents. In a study comparing attitudes of middle-class Euro-American mothers and Mayan mothers, for example, the American mothers viewed co-sleeping as, at best, strange and impractical – at worst, suspicious or even immoral. In contrast, the Mayan mothers regarded physical closeness at night as part of normal caring for children. When told of the middle-class American practice of infants sleeping alone, the Mayan mothers were shocked at what they considered mistreatment and felt sorry for the babies – echoing adults in many other societies who view the nightly isolation of many middle-class American infants as parental neglect.

Why do so many people disapprove so deeply of where other people choose to have their babies sleep? Co-sleeping strengthens ties between baby and mother, but parents evaluate this result differently: as a benefit in the eyes of co-sleepers, but a source of concern by others, who worry that co-sleeping will make their infants overly dependent. Societal goals of **interdependence** are well served by parent–infant co-sleeping, whereas those of **independence** are not.

In short, a question so seemingly simple as where to put a baby to sleep conceals layers of cultural beliefs. And unlike some other childcare practices, sleeping decisions seem fairly stable. In the US, some of the most devoted bed-sharing families are found in immigrant communities hailing from bed-sharing societies, as we have learned from over three decades of conversations with Indian-American students. Sleeping decisions may be one form of "cultural intimacy" that has a great deal of staying power even in the face of globalization and social change.

LEARNING TO CREATE THE WORLDS OF BABIES

As we have been suggesting, the care and raising of infants are generally considered far too important to leave to personal preference. In every society, new generations of parents are expected to follow a set of practices that replicate basic values that are widely approved, while adapting to new conditions. How do parents acquire these culturally approved caretaking practices?

Advice for Parents

Part of what every one of us knows about being a parent comes from our own early experiences. For better or worse, we all acquire at least a good chunk of our model of how parents behave toward their children from how we were cared for. Even those who deliberately reject aspects of their parents' (or other caretakers') childrearing style in raising their children nevertheless find themselves basing their behavior on their own childhood experiences. After having children, many of us have had the sudden, sometimes disquieting insight, "Oh, no, I sound just like my parents!"

In most societies until recently, children also learned about childrearing not only through what their parents did with them, but also from observing other adults. Living in close proximity to others – whether in extended family groups, small bands, or villages – children could observe at first hand how other adults treated their children. What they mostly saw was other people behaving pretty much as their own parents had acted – that is, following common cultural norms. Such daily observations become part of children's knowledge base. Seeing mothers carrying their babies around in homemade cloth slings all the time, a child forms the idea that carrying babies is a natural part of mothering. Another child, seeing mothers transport their infants in a succession of backpacks and front packs, strollers, and car seats, assumes the naturalness of manufactured baby carriers. When these children eventually become parents, they simply "know" how these things are done and rarely reflect critically upon that knowledge.

However, opportunities to observe and learn about traditional childcare practices in stable communities have recently been diminishing. In many nations across the global south, parenting practices are changing – sometimes gradually, sometimes dramatically. As a result of global capitalism, some groups are gaining new access to economic resources and are experiencing upward mobility, while many more are experiencing the opposite. In yet other places, long-term political strife and unrelenting poverty are causing tremendous upheaval and suffering. In extreme cases, refugee camps created to accommodate those fleeing unrest in Syria, Afghanistan, and other unstable places are creating new social forms whose parenting challenges are just beginning to be charted. In this book, the chapter on Palestinians in the West Bank and Gaza focuses on one case of this troubling scenario.

For their part, urban industrialized societies also offer fewer opportunities for learning early in life about parenting by directly observing other people and interacting with infants. Nowhere is this more evident than in the US. With high levels of occupational and geographical mobility, family members are increasingly isolated from one another. Young couples may have no mothers, grandmothers, or aunts close by to advise them about the birth process, or what to do when the baby cries or is ill, or when one can expect the infant to begin walking and talking. Advice communicated by telephone or, increasingly, via the Web is useful, but a poor substitute for on-the-spot assistance.

The high value placed on family privacy, combined with the modern pattern of newly married couples moving into their own homes, further diminishes the possibilities (for both children and parents) of directly observing and learning from how others care for their infants. Moreover, the smaller size of today's families in many places around the globe makes it likely that a new parent will have less experience with babies than did new parents of previous generations.

Over the past century, North Americans and western Europeans have made up for this decreased level of hands-on experience with children in a variety of ways. Many parents sought advice about child behavior and development from pediatricians. The second most common source of information was books.

A massive amount of information is now available for Western parents to answer their questions and allay their concerns about children and childrearing. Bookstores in the US and the UK typically boast shelf after shelf of books devoted to advice on parenting. In addition to manuals covering child development in general, a wealth of books – as well as magazine and newspaper articles – offer advice on specific topics targeted to specialized audiences. A pregnant woman can easily find books and articles on the benefits of sound nutrition and yoga, as well as programs for communicating with her unborn baby. Books abound to help new parents learn how to encourage their babies to sleep through the night, how to succeed in breastfeeding, or even how to accomplish toilet training in twenty-four hours. New terms proliferate to describe (or criticize) parenting styles – current ones being "helicopter parents" and its obverse, "free-range parents." One blogger dubs the current glut of childcare advice, the "Parenting Industrial Complex." The fact that advice for parents is such big business suggests the existence of a very eager readership.

With any popular literary genre, there must be a good fit between the basic cultural orientation of author and reader – a shared set of assumptions about the nature of the world that facilitates communication. Childcare manuals are very much cultural products that reflect the dominant values and beliefs of their authors and intended audience. Indeed, it could hardly be otherwise: No parenting manual that flies in the face of the locally accepted cultural beliefs and practices of its target audience could possibly achieve great success and influence.

At the same time, some of these best-selling parenting manuals have also served as agents of change. For example, Dr. Benjamin Spock is credited with relaxing the emphasis on rigid scheduling that pervaded American infant care when he began writing in the 1940s. In the next generation of pediatrician advice givers, Berry Brazelton was acknowledged for drawing attention to the active role that infants play in their own development. Currently, many parents appreciate Penelope Leach's sensitive efforts to examine parenting from the perspective of children, even infants.

How can these manuals both reinforce common cultural practices and in some cases transform them? Some of the more influential books have proven influential in subtle ways – by first appealing to what readers already know, while playing down the revolutionary aspects of the advice to come. The opening lines of Dr. Spock's best-selling childcare guide read: "Trust yourself. You know more than you think you do."

Although parents today continue to consult childrearing books, an even greater assortment of childrearing advice is now readily available to anyone with an Internet connection. Shortly before completing this book, we asked a student assistant to estimate how many websites and blogs offer discussions about parenting. She reported the impossibility of the request, as thousands of such sites have proliferated. Our own daughters-in-law may be typical of their generation in that, when confronted with a new parenting challenge, their first impulse is to check the Web.

Despite the dizzying array of perspectives on childrearing offered online, many bloggers communicate confidence that whatever works for their child should work for others. That confidence – like that of book authors before them – is itself rooted in largely unconscious assumptions about the nature of children and the goals of parenting.

Now, imagine a childrearing manual from another part of the world. A Berry Brazelton who had been born in a Beng village in Côte d'Ivoire and had become a diviner (rather than a pediatrician) would emphasize how critical it is for babies to form close and loving ties with their grandparents. Indeed, he would advise parents to teach their children how to dish out ribald insults to their grandparents as a sure-fire way to help the children feel free and familiar with their much older relatives.

Or suppose Penelope Leach were a Palestinian resident of the West Bank instead of a Cambridge University-educated psychologist. Would she still suggest that mothers be content whether they have boys or girls? Or would she instead advise mothers to keep trying to have a boy in order to gain greater respect in their community?

And so we come to this book.

ABOUT THIS BOOK

The First Edition

The first edition of this volume developed from a seminar on cross-cultural views of infancy and young childhood that we co-taught at the University of Illinois several years ago. Our interest in designing this course sprang from our shared fascination with the nature and challenges of childhood, coupled with our perception of the contrasting strengths and weaknesses of our two disciplines – psychology and cultural anthropology.

A revolution in psychological research on infants during the previous two decades had produced a burst of new knowledge about development in the first years of life. However, until relatively recently, the majority of this research had been conducted with Euro-American infants. For their part, cultural anthropologists were keenly aware of the enormous diversity in human behavior; however, most had paid relatively little attention to parenthood and even less to infancy. Joining forces to co-teach a course meant putting our two disciplines into active conversation.

Each student chose a society to research throughout the semester and wrote a series of short papers about specific aspects of infant care in that society. Along with many readings in anthropology and psychology, we assigned an excerpt from one of the editions of Dr. Spock's classic parenting guide, as well as a short anthropological article that playfully spoofed Spock's book by purporting to offer childrearing advice for West African parents. Throughout the semester, as we discussed various societies around the world, the "Spock model" sparked many stimulating class discussions: What advice would an infant-rearing manual from another society offer parents?

For their final papers, our students drew from their research about their target society to write an imagined childcare guide for the society they had investigated. The papers proved brilliant, and we resolved to work with their authors to expand them for publication. And so, the first edition of *A World of Babies* was born. This new edition updates the content of the original edition with seven new case studies while retaining the fundamental structure and "advice manual" approach of the book.

The Creative Approach

Not coincidentally, the original idea for *A World of Babies* as a set of imagined childcare guides came from a writer (Philip Graham). Both the original and the current editions offer a set of imagined childcare manuals that use the writer's narrative techniques to chronicle actual parenting practices. The advice offered in each manual is based on extensive ethnographic research conducted by the chapters' authors, each drawing on the rich fund of data that they have gathered (supplemented by historical background and other reliable ethnographic accounts).

Most importantly, each manual purports to have been written by a member of the society that is the focus of the chapter. The invented "authors" that the real authors have created are the sorts of persons who actually give advice to parents in these societies – ranging from a grandmother and a diviner to a schoolteacher, a refugee mother, and a maternity nurse. In some cases, the actual authors of the chapters have modeled the manual's fictional author on a single individual they have known. In other cases, our contributors have created a composite persona combining aspects of several individuals they have known. In all cases, the imagined manual authors are based on a type of actual member of the society in question. These individuals are realistically portrayed by our chapter authors, all of whom are seasoned fieldworkers who have conducted at least a full year, and in many cases several years, of field research with members of the communities they profile here, mostly working in one or more local language(s). Moreover, one of our authors (Sirad Shirdon) is a member of the (Somali-American) community that she writes about here.

Complementing this research base, four additional fictions are necessary to appreciate the manuals. First, the reader must imagine that each society contains a childrearing expert who would be motivated to write such a manual. For the societies represented in this collection that have a long tradition of literacy, this is already likely. For example, many Chinese mothers now actively seek out parenting books written by foreign authors whose titles are recommended on Chinese websites, and many European governments now provide parenting brochures to all women who give birth in state-sponsored hospitals or birthing centers, or who use the services of state-sponsored nurse-midwives. For societies less steeped in literacy, childcare advice is typically dispensed by older female relatives. In all cases, the choice of a fictional manual author for our chapters is based on how advice is actually communicated to parents in these societies.

A related fiction is that the majority of the members of the eight societies we explore would have any need or desire for a written childcare guide, or would be able to read them even if they did. All these societies are undergoing rapid social change, and our manuals are directed to that subset of literate new mothers in these societies who might especially appreciate guidance in raising their babies. Such social change can come from several forces, including migration; political, economic, and military upheavals; demographic shifts; and religious challenges. Our manuals take such changes into account for their impact on raising children.

For example, in our chapter on Israel, with its manual fictively authored by a kindergarten teacher, new Russian immigrant mothers are advised on how to raise their young children so they will be able to integrate easily into Israeli society. In our chapter on Peru, an imagined mother–daughter duo advises new mothers how to raise their children for a life organized around formal schooling conducted in Spanish, rather than farming activities conducted in Quechua. In our chapter on Somali-Americans, a refugee mother advises pregnant Somali-American women to use a birthing ball during labor, both to ease childbirth and to avoid the obstetric complications that often result from the severe form of female circumcision (infibulation) that many women undergo in Somalia.

A third assumption we made in producing this book is that the fictive authors of our "manuals" would be aware of the cultural logic underlying their societies' practices. Yet, as anthropologists such as Claude Lévi-Strauss and others have long observed, few people have such conscious insights regarding their own daily habits. Think about why American mothers nowadays routinely dress their baby boys in blue and baby girls in pink (although the opposite pattern prevailed in the early twentieth century), or why European and American parents devote little effort to encouraging their young infants to sit upright. If you cannot immediately give the reasons for these preferences, we've made our point.

Finally, from the series of fictions we have just identified, it should be clear that the eight imagined childcare guides presented here are in no way intended to advise actual members of these societies. Rather, our manuals are intentionally directed to Western-educated readers who are interested in learning about childcare practices elsewhere. The success of the first edition of the book offers evidence that the creative format of the book can communicate information in a particularly compelling and immediate way.

Our writing experiment, while unique in its particular invention of a new genre, has ample precedent in other experimental writing by scholars. In creating this genre, we chose the childcare guide format to communicate information about the numerous cultural differences in childrearing around the globe because it permitted our authors to use narrative techniques while accurately describing the beliefs and practices of the societies they profiled. Moreover, childrearing advice manuals have existed in other times and places, from Renaissance-era Italy to ancient and modern China. And over the course of the past century, Western parents turned increasingly to the infant and childcare manuals that became a veritable growth industry.

We offer our imagined childcare guides, then, as ethnographic/literary constructions that rely on the very common genre of the *How to* manual to present some very uncommon *How to*'s. In juxtaposing a familiar format with a set of decidedly unfamiliar information, we hope to demonstrate a simple but powerful truth: that many models of childhood exist, and that every such model is shaped, albeit invisibly, by a combination of deeply held values and widely varying social, political, and economic contexts.

The *faux*-authoritative tone of our "manuals" directly addresses an imagined indigenous reader looking for helpful advice. The eight guides presented here playfully mimic the authoritative tone of parenting guides dispensing advice as if it were universally applicable. By adopting this approach in the manuals that follow, we hope to dispel any assumption of an Everybaby – or an Everyparent – who somehow exists outside culture. As we hope the foregoing has made clear, the "world of babies" is truly many different worlds.

What's New in this Edition, Updated for the Twenty-first Century

In the sixteen years since the first edition of *A World of Babies*, children's lives have changed dramatically in many places around the world. Some changes such as general health indicators are positive, while others such as the recruitment of child soldiers have proven catastrophic. We have highlighted both types of changes in this collection. For readers familiar with the first edition, we point out three basic differences between it and the current version.

First, this edition contains seven entirely new chapters and one updated chapter from the first edition in order to focus on challenges of parenting in the twenty-first century. Our eight case studies sample a good cross-section of the world's societies: two in **Europe** (southern Europe – Portugal; northern Europe – Faroe Islands/Denmark); two in the **Middle East** (Israel; Palestinian Territories – West Bank/Gaza); one from **Asia** (People's Republic of China); one from **North America** (US); one from **Latin America** (Peru); and one in **Africa** (Côte d'Ivoire – West Africa; as well as immigrants from the West African nation of Guinea-Bissau now living in Portugal, and immigrants from the East African nation of Somalia now living in the US).

A good cross-section of the world's religions also appears in these new chapters, including Confucianism (People's Republic of China), Christianity (Catholicism – Quechua/Peru, Portugal; Protestantism – Faroe Islands/Denmark), Islam (Somali-Americans; immigrants from Guinea-Bissau; Palestinians), Judaism (Israel), and an indigenous religion (Beng/Côte d'Ivoire). By design, Muslims are heavily represented in the new edition. In our post-September 11th world, Islam has become a primary focus for thinking about global issues by public policy makers, political leaders, journalists, and ordinary citizens alike. Representing a diverse set of Muslim families' childrearing practices is a considered decision on our part, aimed to counter the essentialist Othering that occurs all too easily by non-Muslims concerning Muslim families' lives. At the same time, we present a chapter on Israeli Jewish childrearing practices to provide a more balanced perspective on the fraught region that is the Middle East.

The residents of our chosen societies support themselves in a variety of ways, from hunting/gathering, fishing, and farming, to teaching school, operating small businesses, and providing in-home health care. Most importantly for our purposes, these eight societies represent a wide spectrum of beliefs and practices with respect to infants, and members of each are forging new ways to raise children while accommodating the demands of life in industrialized and globalized societies. Together, these chapters suggest that childrearing is always conducted in a cauldron of religious, economic, and political contexts.

That said, our selection of eight societies is just that – a selection motivated by a variety of factors, prominent among them being the availability of scholarly investigation.

Second, parents living in the societies we highlight here engage in multiple ways with the contemporary challenges of modernity. The first edition of the book had a largely "indigenous" orientation, with most chapters chronicling local, small-scale groups. This new edition instead mostly emphasizes larger-scale societies and/or groups located in urban or semi-urban settings, from China to Europe. More specifically, the chapters especially address the following issues that (among others) confront families aiming to survive and thrive in the twenty-first century:

- What impact do globalization and migration have on parents' and children's lives?
- How can parents raise stable, healthy children in extraordinary contexts of violence and war?
- What are the particular childrearing challenges for Muslim and Jewish families living in the twin shadows of post-September 11th Islamophobia and anti-Semitism?

- How should new parents and grandparents manage intergenerational conflicts over childrearing agendas in contexts of rapid social change?
- What difference does systematic government support of families, via family-friendly policies and services, make for the well-being of parents and children?

Third, as noted above, all authors of this new edition's chapters are ethnographic specialists who undertook extensive ethnographic fieldwork in the communities about which they are writing. There, they conducted research conversing in one or more local language(s), using research methods ranging from formal questionnaires to immersion in everyday life in a particular society.

As we have engaged actively with the globalizing forces that partly (but by no means fully) mitigate cultural difference, the field of developmental psychology has itself engaged with cultural difference far more systematically than was the case when we published the first edition of this book. Indeed, some psychologists have recently coined the ironically oriented acronym, WEIRD, to refer to the fact that, until recently, the majority of their research subjects have been overwhelmingly **W**estern, **E**ducated, from **I**ndustrialized societies, **R**ich, and living in **D**emocratic nations. The ironic use of "weird" to refer to precisely the group of people who were previously taken as normative reminds psychologists of the statistically unrepresentative nature of their earlier research pool when compared to the world's diverse populations. This critique is transforming the field with unprecedented cross-cultural studies of childhood that will account more realistically for human diversity. For its part, since the first edition of *A World of Babies*, the field of cultural anthropology has attracted many scholars interested in children's lives. We feel gratified if the first edition of *A World of Babies* contributed in some small way to these two welcome disciplinary changes to our respective fields. We offer this new edition as a further continuation of the very fruitful conversation that we see our two disciplines now enjoying.

Organization of the Book

Eight chapters chronicling particular childrearing regimes follow this Introduction. Each chapter begins with brief background information on the community in question, to provide some context for the childcare practices described. Our authors discuss local cultural routines as well as major historical events, basic economic and political structures (both micro and macro), urban landscapes, and legal challenges.

A brief biography of the fictive author of a childcare "manual" for that community or nation follows each introduction. That manual then offers advice to (imagined) prospective and new parents (especially mothers) on a wide range of topics. Some, but not all, parenting issues cut across all chapters; the variability arises partly from differences in local contexts of childcare in these societies, and partly from the nature of the research conducted by each author. For example, some chapters focus on the first two years of life; where circumstances compel, and scholarly data allow, others extend the discussion into the middle years of childhood.

Each chapter also emphasizes particular themes that are especially relevant in local contexts. For example, our chapter on Peru has much to say about bilingualism (in Quechua and Spanish), while our chapter on the People's Republic of China focuses on sometimes competing, sometimes complementary childrearing agendas endorsed by two generations of women who are negotiating rapid social change, as the mother-in-law joins the household to care for the soon-to-be-born child of her pregnant daughter-in-law – a member of the urban middle class who works full-time as a teacher.

Beyond such particularities lies the unifying fact that members of all eight societies featured in this volume have undergone, and are continuing to experience, major social changes. Some of the values and practices recorded in earlier published ethnographic work are barely discernible. Our fictive manuals address imagined modern readers who want to raise their children in ways that partly follow the ways of their grandparents and ancestors, and that partly accommodate the radically new circumstances of the twenty-first century that earlier generations could not have anticipated.

We invite you now to discover eight worlds of babies.

CHAPTER 2

Never Forget Where You're From

Raising Guinean Muslim Babies in Portugal

Michelle C. Johnson

INTRODUCTION

This chapter addresses the lives of Muslim migrants from Guinea-Bissau to Portugal who now call Lisbon *home*. A small nation in West Africa (south of Senegal and northwest of Guinea), Guinea-Bissau gained its independence from Portugal in 1974 after an eleven-year war of liberation, becoming the Republic of Guinea-Bissau in 1975. Approximately half the country's population of 1.4 million is Muslim, most of whom are ethnically either Fula or Mandinga.

In Africa, Fula people (also called Fulani, Peul, or Fulbe) inhabit a broad east–west belt of savanna region at the southern edge of the Sahara Desert, and live across several countries, including Burkina Faso, Chad, Mauritania, Senegal, Gambia, and Guinea. In Guinea-Bissau, the Fula are the second largest ethnic group (approximately 290,000 people) – about 20 percent of the population – living primarily in the northern and eastern savanna regions. They speak Fula (which belongs to the West Atlantic group of Sudanic languages) as well as the dominant languages of the countries in which they live. Traditionally,

Fula were nomadic cattle herders; today, a minority are still fully nomadic, traveling seasonally with their herds. Others live with no cattle in villages or towns, with many making their living as farmers, merchants, or Qur'anic scholars and healers. The majority of Fula today blend these two lifestyles, engaging in farming and keeping some cattle (or camels, goats, and sheep). No matter where the Fulani live or how they make their living, cattle remain central to their identity: the cow is said to be the "father of the Fulani." A Fula proverb states, "If the cattle die, the Fulbe will die."

As for the Mandinga, they trace their origin to the Mande heartland in present-day Mali, but now live in several countries throughout West Africa, including The Gambia, Guinea, Guinea-Bissau, Mali, Senegal, and Sierra Leone. They speak related languages and make their living as farmers, merchants, or Qur'anic scholars and healers. In Guinea-Bissau, they are the fourth largest ethnic group (about 200,000 people) and make up 13 percent of the population. Although most Mandinga in Guinea-Bissau live in villages in the northern region of the country, they also constitute a large population in the capital city of Bissau.

Because their origins lie elsewhere, both Fula and Mandinga peoples in Guinea-Bissau are considered "outsiders," even though they have lived there for centuries. As such, both groups share a diasporic identity: they emphasize their oneness with (respectively) Fula or Mande peoples throughout West Africa, and their difference from indigenous peoples in their "home" country. Both their societies are hierarchical, with people born into groups of nobles, artisans, and descendants of former slaves, whose members do not intermarry. For members of both ethnic groups, Islam is central to their identity: to be Fula or Mandinga is to be Muslim. By contrast, members of the indigenous ethnic groups of Guinea-Bissau live on the coast, are egalitarian, and practice African indigenous religions or Christianity, or both.

Although Fula and Mandinga individuals look different from one another, have distinct cultural traditions, speak unrelated languages, and were at war with one another in the past, Islam has brought them together – especially those living side-by-side in Bissau and Lisbon as Guinean Muslims. Despite being proud of their inclusion in Islam's global community, or *umma*, Guinean Muslims have retained many aspects of the local, indigenous religions that they likely practiced before converting to Islam, including ritual practices and beliefs with respect to ancestors, spirits, and witches. This is true even for those living in urban areas in Africa and Europe.

Migration from Guinea-Bissau to Portugal is a recent phenomenon. Beginning in the 1950s, elites of mixed African and Portuguese descent left the country to study in Europe. A larger wave of migration followed Guinea-Bissau's independence from Portugal in 1974. Guinean Muslims were part of the largest wave of immigration from Guinea-Bissau to Portugal, which occurred in the 1980s and 90s. A civil war in 1998 sparked another wave of migration to Lisbon that continued as conditions deteriorated in Guinea-Bissau through the early 2000s. Recent Guinean Muslim migrants to Portugal are distinct from earlier, more privileged groups, in that most migrated directly from villages rather than from the capital city of Bissau. As such, they remain rooted in "tradition," which they imagine as originating in rural Guinea-Bissau.

In Portugal's capital city of Lisbon, Guinean Muslims live either in apartments in the center of the city or in Lisbon's many exurbs. Some exurban neighborhoods are inhabited almost entirely by African immigrants from Portugal's former African colonies, who often organize themselves by country of origin, ethnic group, or religion (see Figure 2.1). Many men earn their living either as construction workers or as merchants, selling items from home (such as kola nuts and tobacco) to nostalgic, fellow Guinean immigrants. The more prosperous among these men own shops in central Lisbon or in the exurbs, while others sell their goods on the streets, in the plazas near train stations, or around Lisbon's central mosque. Many Guinean Muslim men also work as healer-diviners and see clients – African and Portuguese alike – for problems concerning work, health, and personal relationships. Most Guinean Muslim women work as wives and mothers, as well as clothing merchants or house/office

Figure 2.1 Guinean children take a break from playing, to pose for a photograph in a Guinean neighborhood across from Lisbon, on the southern bank of the Tejo River.
Photograph by Michelle C. Johnson.

cleaners. Others own or work in Guinean restaurants or assist their healer-diviner husbands by booking appointments or translating for clients.

When Guinean Muslims migrate to Portugal, they simultaneously join two new diasporas: people from Portugal's other African colonies, and a transnational community of Muslims. Approximately 15 million Muslims live in Europe today, only 30,000 of whom are in Portugal. In the 1970s, the majority of African Muslims in Lisbon were Mozambicans of Indian descent, but by the 1980s, Guinean Muslims (Fula and Mandinga peoples) officially outnumbered them. Many Guinean Muslims attend Friday prayer sessions and Muslim holiday celebrations at Lisbon's central mosque, but others – especially women – prefer to pray at home. Many – especially women – also belong to immigrant associations, whose members gather to hold life-cycle rituals, concerts, and fashion shows, and to celebrate Muslim holidays. Immigrant associations also serve as rotating credit associations, loaning money to help members start a business, return to Guinea-Bissau, or make the pilgrimage to Mecca that is required for all Muslims who are able to go.

No matter where they live, everyday life for Guinean Muslims is characterized by gender separation, with men and women performing distinct, complementary roles. In rural areas in Africa, men herd animals or farm cassava, millet, and peanuts, while women perform household chores, care for the children, and farm rice and corn. In the urban settings of Bissau and Lisbon, both women and men often work outside the home. Men have more time to socialize, drink tea, and gather in public spaces than women do.

The Qur'an permits men to marry up to four wives, and polygyny is common among Guinean Muslims in both Guinea-Bissau and Portugal. Having two or more wives makes it possible for rural men to farm more land and have more children. For their part, co-wives provide one another with help, companionship, and opportunities for economic pursuits. When Guinean Muslim men in Lisbon have multiple wives, they typically live with only one wife in Lisbon while the other(s) continue(s) to live in Guinea-Bissau. Some of their children born in West Africa, however, may eventually be sent to Lisbon for education, to be raised by their mothers' co-wives. Nowadays, young Guinean Muslim men and women in both Africa and Europe are becoming more critical of polygyny, and some now prefer to marry monogamously. Although marrying outside one's ethnic group is almost unthinkable in Guinea-Bissau, that norm, too, is changing in Europe, with ethnic out-marriage becoming somewhat more common in Portugal, although still discouraged.

Guinean Muslims in Lisbon acknowledge their unity as Guineans but remain proud of their ethnicity. They prefer to speak their indigenous language (Fula or Mandinga) among themselves and to their children, although most also speak Kriolu, Guinea-Bissau's lingua franca. Guinean Muslims also continue to cook and eat their traditional dishes, and they consider Guinean foods central to their identity and well-being in Portugal. They also continue to practice many indigenous cultural traditions, especially life-cycle rituals, which form the basis of community and association gatherings and are deemed central for teaching children to "never forget where they're from." Although Muslim and non-Muslim Guineans often inhabit different worlds in Lisbon, they come together occasionally as Guineans, such as during elections. Furthermore, they are united by shared experiences of suffering: nostalgia for home, anti-Islamic sentiment, and racism. Once classified as either "Fula" or "Mandinga," they are now called *pretos*, or "blacks" – Africans in a foreign land.

NEVER FORGET WHERE YOU'RE FROM: RAISING GUINEAN MUSLIM BABIES IN PORTUGAL

About the Author

My name is Awa – like the name the Christians called "Eve." I was born in a Mandinga village in Guinea-Bissau. As a child, I studied at the village Qur'anic school. When I got older, I attended Portuguese school in town until my teacher left and was never replaced. Unable to finish my studies, I married soon after my circumcision and initiation. My husband, who is also Mandinga, worked for a development organization in town. We had a son and a daughter together before he married my co-wife, who has also given him two children.

When a civil war broke out in the capital city of Bissau, life became difficult all over the country. My husband decided to try his luck in Portugal, as many Guineans have done. It took a year for him to get a passport and plane ticket, but he eventually made it to Lisbon. Two years later, he brought me – the senior wife – and my children to Lisbon, where we have been living for thirteen years. My co-wife remained in Guinea-Bissau to care for our house and her children. Here in Portugal, we rent an apartment in a neighborhood outside Lisbon where many other Guinean Muslims live. My husband is a successful healer-diviner with many clients, both African and Portuguese. Although my most important job is to care for our family, I also work part-time as a cook in a Guinean restaurant. Life in Portugal is hard, but we manage, thanks be to Allah. We are proud to be Muslims: my husband attends mosque regularly, and I belong to the oldest and largest Guinean Muslim women's association in Lisbon.

Because of my experience raising children in both Guinea-Bissau and Portugal, association members asked me to write this guide. I hope it will be useful to Guinean Muslims who face the challenge of raising their children in Portugal. The customs that I write about here are especially familiar to Mandinga parents, but they also will make sense to Fula parents. Although our peoples have had their differences in the past, Islam unites us, and this is especially true as we struggle together in Lisbon.

The advice I offer here is intended for new parents, but it may also be helpful for experienced parents who travel between Portugal and Guinea-Bissau. You might also find it useful if you have been living in Portugal a long time and want to keep your beliefs and customs in mind when raising your children in Europe. After all, your children are, and will always be, Guinean Muslims, even though their home is now Portugal; it is your job to help them never to forget where they're from.

My advice here focuses most on pregnancy, birth, and early childhood, but I also offer some guidance about children up to the age of seven. While this guide is designed to assist both mothers and fathers, due to the nature of our culture, mothers will find it most helpful. For this reason, I address most of my guidance to women.

It is true that you must always remember to respect and listen to our elders, the wise women who gave birth to us, since they know things that young people do not yet know. Nevertheless, you probably realize that despite their wisdom and experience, elders do not always understand the struggles of life in Lisbon. I hope that this manual will help Guinean Muslim parents find a common ground between our traditional ways and how to survive in our new home. Although many women of my generation who now live in Lisbon were born in Guinea-Bissau and remember well what life was like there, most of our children were born in Portugal, and many have never even been to Guinea-Bissau. Portugal is the only home they know, and we need to understand and accept that.

MAKING A BELLY

If you are reading this manual, then you probably recently discovered you are making a belly. Take note: you are on your way to a changed status forever. Having a baby is your initiation into true womanhood and adulthood. If you were circumcised and initiated back home, you had your first taste of womanhood. But this was only the first step; a Guinean Muslim is not fully an adult until he or she becomes a parent.

Although pregnancy is an exciting time for both you and your husband, it is also a dangerous, unpredictable time, and you must remain stoic. This goes without saying back home in Guinea-Bissau – where, according to White people's numbers, 91 out of 1,000 infants born alive will die, and 790 out of every 100,000 mothers die in childbirth. Give thanks to Allah that you have made a belly here in Portugal, where only 4 out of 1,000 babies die, and 8 out of 100,000 mothers die in childbirth. Nevertheless, don't let these better odds give you too much confidence; humans are never in control in matters of life and death. Allah fixes the time and place of your death at your birth, and this is true no matter where you live.

Allah's will aside, there are some things that you can do to help ensure your own and your baby's health and safety. Avoid calling attention to your belly, and don't admit you have one for as long as possible. As the months pass, your belly will grow, and your female relatives and friends will probably comment on it. They might even try to pry the news from you or trick you into telling them. Resist this pressure. Hiding and denying your belly will protect you from spirits and people with big mouths who may be jealous and want to harm you or your baby. If someone points out your growing belly, just respond, "This belly? There's nothing in here but rice!" or simply say, "Life is sweet in Lisbon." No one can deny that Guineans often get fat in Lisbon, where rich foods like sugar and oil are plentiful. We say that "A good Muslim does not lie," but rest assured that Allah won't punish you for your desire to protect yourself and your baby during this vulnerable time.

While you are making a belly, you must have frequent sexual relations with your husband. A belly is made when the sexual fluids of a man and woman – which we call "blood" – mix during sexual intercourse, and Allah breathes life into the fetus during the third month of this mixing. We say that a man's blood forms the baby's hard parts, such as the bones and fingernails, and the woman's blood forms the soft parts, such as the skin and internal organs. Frequent sex while you are making a belly will provide a steady supply of both types of blood to the baby. Although having sex three times a month is ideal, once a month is still sufficient to ensure the proper development of your baby. In theory, you should stop having sex after the seventh month, as the Qur'an forbids it. But don't worry too much if you break this taboo; you certainly would not be the first! Many women have told me that their husband's penis broke their water. These women were faithful Muslims whose babies turned out just fine. Allah is very forgiving!

Still, following a few important taboos will protect you and your growing baby. First, do not eat eggs. Although my grandmother never explained it this way, a clever friend of mine who studied anthropology in the university once commented that eating eggs while pregnant would be like auto-cannibalism. No doubt, our wise ancestors had this symbolism in mind when they created this rule, even if most of us don't understand the logic, nowadays. In addition, you should not eat fruit that has fallen onto the ground. If you break this taboo, your child will, likewise, "fall" from your womb, to be born prematurely. Why? Well, Islam teaches us that humans should eat only what we choose (that's why Muslims don't eat carrion); fallen fruit has a different sort of destiny.

In addition to these important rules, you should also avoid the meat of animals with claws or fangs, such as rats, crocodiles, or monkeys. This last set of taboos is easy enough to follow in Lisbon, where these animals are not readily found. But if you return to Guinea-Bissau at any time while you are making a belly, you must be familiar with these taboos and follow them. You should also avoid the meat of the dove, since this interferes with making milk to breastfeed your baby. Finally, do not bathe near water sources, such as rivers or wells, at night, since spirits hang out there. While this is less of a problem in Lisbon, where we bathe indoors, you should avoid swimming pools or beaches, just in case. Most importantly, pregnancy is not the time for you to take a lover; you should not have sex with anyone else but your husband during this time, as sex with another man would lead to the improper mixing of bloods, and this might cause your baby to be born with a disability.

As time passes, it will become harder for you to hide your pregnancy. People might no longer ask, but simply assume that you have made a belly – no longer believing that it's just a rice belly. They might even be so bold as to predict the sex of your baby. If you've had other bellies, you might already know which kind of belly you have. If this is your first, you will soon learn that male and female bellies behave differently. It might take you a few pregnancies before you can predict with any accuracy, since exactly how male and female bellies behave varies from woman to woman. One woman might know she has a male belly if she vomits when she sees someone naked. Another might know she has a male belly if she never feels thirsty. One thing is usually true for all women: If you suddenly find yourself getting along better with men than with women, then you probably have a male belly. If you get along with everyone, there is a good chance that you have a female belly.

Guinean Muslims are not the only ones who delight in predicting which belly a pregnant woman has. Just for fun, ask an older, white Portuguese woman to find out which belly you have. All she'll need is a needle and thread, which she'll make into a pendulum. If the needle swings forward to backward, you have a male belly; if it moves in a circular motion, you have a female one. Your doctor will also ask if you want to know the sex of your baby, which he or she can see from the ultrasound machine. If you agree to this, the machine might simply confirm what you already know based on the behavior of your belly, or your White friend's prediction.

You may hear many different views about which sex is better to have. Your husband and his relatives will probably want a boy. In your own heart, you might wish for a daughter, who could help you with chores and become a loyal life companion. Keep in mind that what matters more than the sex of your baby is that Allah bestows blessings – what we call *Baraka* – on your little one. Boys and girls are equally good, and women who give birth to an equal number of them in alternating fashion are said to birth "sweetly." If you are blessed with this ideal birth pattern, don't be alarmed when other pregnant women ask you for your blessings; it is your right and duty to give them.

If your documents for residing legally in Lisbon are not yet in order, be sure to address this issue before your baby is born. Of course, if you and your husband are Portuguese citizens, then your baby will be set. If not, and you don't have residence permits, then you need to start the process of obtaining one as soon as possible. You'll need a valid passport, some photographs, and proof that you've been living in Lisbon for five years. Even if you and your husband are legal residents, you'll need to get these documents if you want to get Portuguese citizenship for your baby. Either way, you'll need to show up in person at the immigration office they call the Serviço de Estrangeiros e Fronteiras. As you have probably heard from others, the process is horrible, but trust me: standing in line for hours, making sense of complicated paperwork, and explaining the details of your life over and over will all be much harder with a crying baby! Ask a friend who has navigated the process before, and who speaks and reads Portuguese well, to accompany you for support.

THE STRUGGLE

Although it may sound obvious, it is important to acknowledge that giving birth in Lisbon is different from giving birth at home – especially if you are from a village, as are most Guinean

Muslims in Lisbon. Back in Guinea-Bissau, although hospital births are on the rise, the majority of women still give birth at home. But here in Lisbon, your birth will surely take place in a hospital. If you grew up in Guinea-Bissau, you probably fear hospitals and may even consider them a place where one goes to die. It's time to change your attitude. A hospital birth is a blessing; if anything goes wrong, the doctors and nurses have the knowledge, skill, medicines, and technology to help you and your baby. Nevertheless, I will highlight some of our traditional birth customs and their consequences that might improve your hospital birth experience. While some are impossible to follow in Lisbon, you might manage to practice a few. In any case, simply knowing about them might bring you some comfort as you attempt to find a middle ground between your past experience and your present realities.

As you may know, Guinean Muslim women back home give birth in the kneeling position with the help of two birth assistants: the first supports the birthing woman's head and the other sits at her feet to catch the baby. The baby catcher asks Allah for the baby to be born. If she fails to do this, the baby might refuse to come out, and may also refuse Islam. Your own birth scene will be very different in Lisbon. The nurses will be your primary birth assistants, though you may invite one other person for support. The hospital staff will assume that you'll choose your husband. The thought of this may make you or your husband uncomfortable, since giving birth in front of men is not our way. Simply explain to the staff that you would prefer a female relative or friend to help you instead.

Chances are that your nurses won't understand our culture and will know little, if anything, about Islam. You and your friend or relative will have to do a few things that the nursing staff won't be able to do, such as asking for the baby to be born. You might be in so much pain during the struggle that this plea will come naturally to you. As all women know, childbirth is painful, and one can never be fully prepared for the intensity. Try to remember your initiation: as a young girl or teenager, you suffered the pain of having your clitoris excised, probably without even wincing, let alone screaming. The stoicism you learned from that experience prepared you, at least in part, for the pain of childbirth. You were probably just as afraid then as you will be when you give birth, but do your best to conceal your fear, and be confident that you can endure the pain. The doctor and nurses might ask you if you want medication to ease the pain; whether or not you take it is your choice. But keep in mind that if you use medication to ease the pain, the process might seem less sweet to you in the end, as true sweetness must entail suffering.

At the same time, take a moment to praise Allah that you are an African woman; our struggle is usually easier and faster than that of White women. Although we don't know why for sure, this might be due to the foods we prepare from scratch ourselves not having all those chemicals that supermarket products have; or it could be because of the farm work we do back home, which makes our bodies strong. In any case, if you choose to struggle without pain medication, don't be surprised if you find yourself screaming. This is fine, as long as you don't shame yourself in the process. Make sure that your screams are appropriate. Scream for God's help, yelling: "Waay! Allah, help me!" or "Aah, my mother!" A mother will always help her daughter, no matter where she is, and no mother can resist a daughter in labor. Screaming anything else is shameful and should be avoided, even though you're in Portugal. If community members find out that you screamed inappropriately, you might never hear the end of it.

The doctor and nurses might ask you questions and talk to you while you are struggling, telling you when to push and when to wait. Be polite and cooperate as best as you can, but listen to your body: when you feel the urge, push. When your baby is born, the doctor and the nurses will probably announce the sex of your baby and congratulate you. While it is only natural for them to celebrate, you must remain stoic, as the struggle is not over. The placenta – what we call "the thing that kills" – still has to come out.

Back in Guinea-Bissau, our birth attendants make sure that a birthing woman does not speak during the period between when her baby is born and the placenta coming out. If you speak, the placenta might refuse to come out, which could put your life in danger. It will probably feel strange for you to remain completely silent during this time, especially since everyone else will expect a reaction from you, but just toning down your reaction and keeping as quiet as you can will show respect for the placenta. With a little luck, the doctors and nurses will blame your lack of emotion on exhaustion and will leave you alone to rest during this critical time.

Back home, when the placenta refuses to come out, women pound rice or millet, and the rhythmic sound calls it out. If your placenta is late in coming, pray to Allah for it to come, or try calling it yourself by tapping your right hand against the hospital bed to mimic the rhythmic sound of pounding. If the placenta still does not come, rest assured – the doctor will give you medicine to help. Accept it, praising Allah that you are in Portugal and not in Guinea-Bissau, where you would most likely die.

We Guinean Muslims have many ideas about the umbilical cord and the placenta, and what we should do with them. At home, a birth attendant would stretch the umbilical cord to the baby's knee and cut it with a knife or razor blade. She would then tie it tightly, reinforcing the knot with thread. If she cuts a baby boy's cord too short, we'd say he might grow up to be impotent. In your case, the doctor in Lisbon will cut the cord, and you won't have any time at all to worry about the length. But you can still say, *Bisimilaahi ar-rahmaani, rahiimi* – "In the name of God, the beneficent, the merciful" – as a general safety precaution.

A good Guinean Muslim knows that bodily substances such as hair and fingernail clippings should always be buried in the ground, where our bodies go after we die. This is also true of the placenta and umbilical cord – which, back home, are carefully placed in the ground near where the baby was born. Burying these helps establish a connection between the baby and his or her new home. This is why, when someone asks a Guinean Muslim, "Where are you from?" he or she often responds, "My umbilical cord is buried in Bafata," or wherever else they were born. Burying the placenta and umbilical cord also keeps them safe from witches, who might find and "work" with them, causing harm to babies.

These beliefs present one of the biggest challenges to hospital births for Guinean Muslims, no matter where we are. Even in Bissau, the hospital no longer allows mothers to take the placenta and umbilical cord home for burial, as the doctors claim that this practice is unhygienic. In Portugal, I don't know of anyone who has asked to take these home but the hospitals most likely would not allow it, either. Still, don't worry about this: your baby's placenta and umbilical cord will be incinerated in the hospital, making it impossible for witches to "work" with them in order to harm you.

Even if the hospital allowed you to perform our traditional practice of taking home the placenta and umbilical cord for burial, there is little advantage to doing this in Lisbon. Let's face it: those of us who were born in Guinea-Bissau simply don't feel the same attachment to Portugal as we do to the Land of Our Ancestors. While this sentiment is perfectly normal, it does raise some important concerns: How will our children connect to the physical place they will call *home*? How will they develop a sense of who they are without this powerful connection? Don't lose any sleep worrying about these questions now; they are complicated ones, and you have enough on your mind. For now, rest assured that your baby's life is not in danger just because the placenta and umbilical cord were not buried in Lisbon. Remind yourself that you are doing the best you can in this new land.

POSTPARTUM CARE

After giving birth, you must be extra attentive to your newborn's – and your – vulnerable bodies. You should devote some time to treating your baby's umbilical cord stump so that it falls off quickly. Back home, women use a mixture of palm oil and homemade salt, though some people in towns use rubbing alcohol, if they have it. In Lisbon, the nurses will handle this while you're in the hospital, and they'll certainly use rubbing alcohol. When you go back to your apartment, you can either continue using the alcohol or try palm oil and salt. The nurses probably told you to treat the cord stump twice daily, but that is not nearly often enough. Do your best to treat it at least six times a day, or as often as you can, and it should fall off after two or three days. When the cord stump falls, you can either bury it as you do hair and fingernail clippings, or you can take it to a leatherworker at Rossio near the train station in downtown Lisbon. Have him sew it into an amulet, then tie it around your baby's waist for health, beauty, and protection from spirits and witches.

You must pay extra attention to hygiene during the post-partum period. In Guinea-Bissau, new mothers boil the leaves of the *bolonkuduba* tree in water and bathe with the mixture twice daily for three days. As you won't find these leaves anywhere in Lisbon, you'll have to settle for hot water alone. Continue to bathe with only hot water for one month, as this will help expel the blood of childbirth from your body. This blood comes in two types: *yele fiɲo*, or "black blood," and *yele koyoo*, or "white blood." While black blood flows easily from the body, white blood is more stubborn, especially if you gave birth to a boy. If this blood collects in your belly or head, it can lead to sickness or insanity, and who knows if the Portuguese have medicines to help?

Portuguese views about bathing after birth are completely different from ours. If the doctor or nurses tell you to ice your belly or to take cool baths to promote healing, smile politely and nod in agreement, but be mindful that following this regimen could actually endanger your life. Along with chemicals in their food, their fear of hot water might be another reason that Portuguese women seem to tire more than African women do during and after childbirth.

After giving birth, you must stay inside for at least a week. You might prefer to follow the more strictly Islamic forty-day confinement period, especially if this pleases your husband. Whichever you choose, during your confinement you will be called *jibakutoo* – "one who has just given birth." Enjoy the new title and consider your confinement an opportunity to rest, heal, and get to know your new little one. Of course, the confinement period is also meant to protect you, as some unexpected things pose a serious danger to women who have just given birth. Certain protective medicines that Guinean Muslim men and women wear around their waists, under their clothes, are especially dangerous. They contain secret, powerful Qur'anic verses or plants from the bush back home that are too strong for new mothers' vulnerable bodies. Avoiding these medicines is tricky business, since you can't see them. Staying at home ensures that you avoid unplanned contact with anyone who might be wearing them, and Guinean visitors will know to remove these medicines before coming to visit you.

When a baby is born in a village back home, every person comes to greet him or her, shaking the little one's hand and welcoming the newcomer to the world. Don't be surprised during the confinement period if your apartment becomes a central meeting place for the entire Guinean Muslim community in Lisbon. Be prepared to receive more visitors than you have received in years, especially if you belong to a Guinean Muslim women's association in Lisbon. Women in these groups pride themselves in visiting new mothers and bringing them foods and gifts. Enjoy the attention and admiration of your newborn, as well as the opportunity to catch up on the latest gossip. During your confinement, visitors won't expect you to offer them food and the green tea we call *ataaya*. They understand that as a new mother in a foreign land, you do not have the luxury of co-wives to take over routine tasks for you. Later, your visitors can drink tea or have a cup of the strong coffee the Portuguese call a *bica*.

Your birth experience will remind visitors of their own experiences with childbirth, so don't be surprised if people offer lots of suggestions, and even some criticism. If this begins to annoy you, remind yourself that these women are more experienced than you are, so you have much to gain from their knowledge and wisdom.

On the other hand, if you don't receive as many visitors as you had hoped, or if people don't stay as long as you wished they would, remember that this is Portugal, not Guinea-Bissau. People are busy with work and school schedules and live far away from one another, so it's hard to find time to visit as people do back home, and transportation is expensive. If you ever feel lonely during your confinement period, rely on your mobile phone to "visit." Ask your husband to keep lots of money on it during this period. If he is reluctant, explain to him that the supportive conversations with other women will keep you happy and will minimize any other demands that you might be tempted to make. What husband wouldn't want that?

Don't be surprised if visitors insult your baby, calling the little one "ugly" or "worthless." Even if Guinean Muslims in Portugal don't view direct compliments to babies in Lisbon as life-threatening, as our people do back home, compliments are still rude and should be avoided, just in case. But immigrants who have lived in Lisbon for a long time might forget about this custom and slip up, commenting unthinkingly on how beautiful or fat your baby is. To anticipate such remarks, ask a healer-diviner ahead of time to prepare some protective medicine that you can have sewn into an amulet and tie onto your baby. This will protect your little one from these people's big mouths. On the other hand, don't worry if Portuguese people, especially older ones, compliment your baby; they simply love babies and don't share our beliefs. Rest assured that their compliments are completely harmless.

DEALING WITH COMPLICATIONS

So far, I have emphasized what to expect during a problem-free, successful pregnancy and birth. In doing so, I have probably made it all seem easy. Sometimes it is, but at other times there are complications. Making a belly might be harder than you think, even if your menstrual cycle is regular and you have no obvious medical problems. Infertility can be very stressful for couples, considering the immense pressure from everyone – especially your husband and his relatives – to have children. Living so far away from your in-laws might relieve this pressure a bit, but you might be surprised by their ability to find ways to pester you, even from such a great distance. They are in-laws, after all!

In schools and clinics today, we learn that fertility problems can be due to either women or men, but among Guinean Muslims, we women are still most often blamed. Be prepared for this and try to understand their perspective. It is only natural for your husband and his relatives to become frustrated and feel shame, especially if you have been married for a couple of years and are still childless. If your husband speaks of taking another wife back home (if he doesn't already have one), encourage him to first try some herbal or magical remedies to increase his sexual vigor and aid in conception. He can find these at African shops at the Mouraria Commercial Center, and in several other neighborhoods on the outskirts of Lisbon where African immigrants live. He can also obtain them privately from a healer. If remedies from home don't work, ask your doctor to refer you to someone who specializes in helping women get pregnant. If your husband is reluctant, encourage him to have faith and work with you to solve this problem, keeping an open mind to explore all options. We Guinean Muslims could learn a thing or two from European couples on this matter: they face the problem together and support one another in the process.

Sometimes the problem is not in making a belly, but keeping one. It is common for bellies, especially first bellies, to ruin, so don't be too discouraged if this happens to you. Just remind yourself that it couldn't be helped, that it was Allah's will. Suffer the loss in stoic fashion like a good Muslim, and have faith that there will be other bellies. Share the news with community members, and they will shower you with blessings for another pregnancy and many healthy children. If more than two or three of your bellies ruin, then you might have a serious problem on your hands. This might be due to something other than Allah's will, so dedicate some real time, energy, and money to discovering if this is the case.

Begin by making an appointment with your doctor, as there might be an easy medical solution. You want to explore all possibilities, and it makes sense to start with the simplest one.

If the doctor's advice and remedies have no effect, then your problem might be a traditional one, what we call a "problem of the land." In this case, European medicines will be useless. Problems of the land come in many types. Witches are a real danger for Guinean Muslims, and you're not safe from them just because you are living in Europe. Although it is true that in Lisbon there are fewer witches – what we call "people with a head" – there are still plenty of them, and in any case it only takes one to cause damage. Just like spirits, witches move easily between Guinea-Bissau and Portugal; in fact, the elders claim that witches can fly between the two countries a billion times faster than an airplane!

Alternatively, your problems might be caused by the spirits we call *iran*. Just as Allah made people from clay, He created angels and spirits from fire. *Iran* stick behind women they desire as spouses, and are jealous of their human husbands and children. They ruin women's bellies by hitting their babies, born or unborn, with giant machetes, ending their lives in a single blow. If you suspect that your fertility problems might be *of the land*, schedule a consultation with a healer-diviner. If you don't already have one, ask a trusted friend for a reference. Although you might have seen ads for healer-diviners in the local newspapers, or you might have seen their business cards tucked under the windshield wipers of parked cars around Lisbon, the best way to find a good one is by word of mouth. The best healer-diviners don't believe in advertising, and you want one who has had the right training and is serious about his work, not a false one who is simply interested in eating your money. For a small fee, the healer-diviner will look into your problem with the most appropriate divination method, such as sand, cowry shells, or the kind of dream divination we call *lastakaro*. He'll identify the cause of your problem and what you need to do to keep a belly. If your problem is due to witchcraft, the healer-diviner will give you medicine to wash with, or that you can have sewn into an amulet to wear during your pregnancy. This medicine is stronger than witches. If the healer-diviner confirms that you have an *iran* stuck behind you, he'll help you try to get rid of it, or at least protect your babies from it. He might discover that the *iran* is only jealous of your male children, in which case he'll give you medicine and blessings for a female belly.

You can also try some strategies that Guinean Muslim women have developed over the generations. *Iran* are persistent, but they are easily fooled. If you manage to evade the *iran*'s efforts and give birth to a healthy baby, give the little one a *bono* name. These names are very common in Guinea-Bissau, and you've probably encountered a few people in Lisbon who have them. There are a few different types. An insulting name – such as Kalabantewo, meaning "thief," or Sunkutungo, meaning "garbage" – will fool the *iran* into thinking that your baby is not worth taking. If your husband is less than enthusiastic about this type of *bono* name, be patient and try to understand his perspective. Our men try very hard to appear to be good Muslims in Lisbon's transnational Muslim community, and they have their reputations to protect. Your husband probably considers blaming infertility, ruined bellies, and infant death on anything other than Allah's will as "un-Islamic" and as a threat to His oneness. But remember that your husband wants a healthy baby as much as you do, so it's better to work with him than against him. He might prefer the type of *bono* name that takes the form of a prayer, such as Allahbatu, meaning, "Wait, Allah," or Tenbulo, "Stay in My Hand." Whichever type you choose, remember that *bono* names stick for life. If your baby survives, the name will be a part of your and your little one's identities forever: It identifies you as someone who lost a child and your child as someone who tempted fate. If this makes you feel a little proud, this is only normal: you fought a Guinean Muslim mother's hardest battle against *iran* spirits, and you won.

Beyond using *bono* names, women back home who are afflicted by *irans* also slap their babies' faces so they cry, and they dress them in dirty clothes – all to make them undesirable to the spirits. If a woman who has lost several female infants prays or obtains medicine for a boy and gives birth to a girl anyway, she might dress the baby in boys' clothes and give her a boy's name to try to confuse the *iran* into not taking her. She might even go a step further and act like a madwoman in public, in an attempt to chase away the spirit. What spirit would desire a madwoman? Although it is good for you to be familiar with these strategies that are so much a part of our culture, you probably won't need to go to such extremes in Lisbon – a *bono* name will most likely do the job. I realize that if White Portuguese people hear about these practices, they would probably dismiss them as silly superstitions. But then, many of them still have some magical practices of their own – like giving babies the pre-baptismal names of Inácio or Inácia, sewing garlic into their clothes, or fastening rosemary to their beds – to protect them from witches. So you don't need to feel embarrassed about seeming "traditional" in the "modern" city, since so many Portuguese think about these things the same way.

There is, of course, an even simpler way to grow your family: consider foster-raising a child. We Africans have a tradition of this, and it fits quite nicely into our new lives in Europe. Fostering a child will be especially easy for you if you have co-wives back home in Guinea-Bissau. Talk with your husband about the possibility of bringing one or more of his children back home to live with you in Lisbon. If he can afford it, your husband would probably love the idea of having more of his children in Lisbon, and the benefits to your co-wives are countless. However painful it is to be separated from one's child, no Guinean Muslim mother in her right mind would pass up the chance for her child to be educated in Europe. If she appears reluctant at first, remind your co-wife of this fact, and ease her mind by telling her how well you will care for her child. Who knows what great things this child will end up doing for the whole family? As the child's biological mother, your co-wife would be a primary beneficiary of the child's success. But do keep in mind that Europeans aren't fond of our practice of polygyny, and they don't understand the difference between fostering and adoption. It is best to keep the specifics of the arrangement to yourself. Your Portuguese friends will assume that you're the biological mother of the child, and you'll just confuse them if you try to explain otherwise. In any case, as the child's mother's co-wife, you are a "little mother" to the child, after all.

BREASTFEEDING YOUR BABY

While it is encouraged in Europe, breastfeeding is still considered one of two choices, and many Portuguese women who start out breastfeeding end up weaning their babies when they are still very young – from three to six months old, I hear. This is not the case for Guinean Muslims: it is your duty to breastfeed your baby for at least two years. By breastfeeding, you provide your baby with much more than simply the best nourishment for a growing body. Breastfeeding is actually a form of communication between mothers and babies, and breastmilk plays an important role not only in our families and marriages, but even in the development of our identity as Muslims. Breastfeeding is also one of the ways our children acquire their unique personality traits and habits – such as talkativeness, or the tendency to eat quickly or slowly. Our Fula sisters are even more adamant about this aspect of breastfeeding than we Mandinga are.

Breastmilk is a "kinship glue" that creates a special bond between people. Children of one mother, who nursed from the same breasts, have a close, trusting relationship due to the milk that linked them. Children of one father, who nursed from different women, are more distant and competitive with one another. Two unrelated babies who drink from the same breast become what we Muslims call "milk kin." Because they share this powerful substance, we consider them too close to marry each other. If someone who is unable to breastfeed her own baby asks you to breastfeed the little one for her, consider this request carefully. Although we Guinean Muslim women often help each other in this way, you must weigh the rewards of helping a friend in need with the danger of limiting your child's pool of potential marriage partners. Although this might be more of a concern for women in small villages back home, it is still something to be aware of in Lisbon, especially if you want your child to marry another Guinean Muslim from your own ethnic group. You might agree to breastfeed only those babies that your own children can't marry anyway, such as those we call "joking cousins," or a cousin whose parent nursed from the same breast that you or your husband did. That way, you can offer help without limiting your baby's choice of future marriage partners.

Finally, breastmilk plays an important part in shaping your baby's religious identity. This can be a blessing or a curse for you. If your baby grows up to be a good Muslim, people will compliment you, saying, "Your breastmilk was good," or "Your son or daughter drank Islamic piety straight from your breast." On the other hand, if your baby grows up to be a bad Muslim or if (may Allah forbid it) he or she rejects Islam, you might be accused of having bad milk, of not having breastfed long enough, or of having failed to breastfeed properly. Worse yet, people might assume that you yourself are a bad Muslim, and your baby got this trait through the milk.

If you are starting to feel nervous just reading this, know that you are not alone; the link between breastfeeding and Muslim piety creates a lot of pressure for Guinean Muslim women. You will probably find it difficult to remain pious – to pray, attend mosque, and fast during Ramadan – during your childbearing years, when you are working so hard to care for your children. Do your best and bear this in mind: even looking the part of a Muslim woman can help. Buy a headscarf from the merchants outside the central mosque and wear it to community events and Islamic holiday celebrations. Pray when and where people can see you. Buy a set of Muslim prayer beads and use them when your baby is napping or when a visitor is holding the little one. Of course, don't drink alcohol or eat pork or any food that might contain pork products, like yogurt. This is extremely difficult in Portugal, where pork is everywhere and in everything, even if you can't see it, but know that your efforts will bring you considerable peace of mind: if your child does not grow up to embrace Islam, community members might be less likely to blame you.

Before Guinean Muslims back home breastfeed their babies for the first time, they squeeze out the colostrum, or "water," from their breasts. We say that colostrum is thin and weak, like amniotic fluid. Although we consider it worthless to our babies, Europeans insist that it is good for newborns, and your doctor and nurses will expect you to give it to your baby. Happily, this worthless water will not actually harm your little one. Before you breastfeed your baby for the first time, wash your breasts with warm water, starting with the right breast (since the right is auspicious for us). Touch your nipple to your baby's mouth three times, saying *Bismilaahi, ar-rahmaani rahiimi* each time. Then tell your baby to *suusuu*, meaning "suck." If you do this, your baby should breastfeed easily, and Islam will be in the little one's heart and not just in his or her head.

Avoid sleeping with your husband until your baby has begun walking, at which point you can start to wean him or her. If you become pregnant at any time before this period, you must wean your baby right away. The milk forming in your breasts while you are making a belly belongs to the child inside you, and it is dangerous for the older baby to drink milk that doesn't belong to her. If your baby is reluctant to wean, try these helpful strategies. Yell at him or her, "Let go of the breast!" and threaten to put hot pepper on your nipples. If you can, leave for a few days and have a close relative or friend babysit. If your toddler still refuses to wean, you can seek magical remedies from a healer-diviner. If your husband objects, simply remind him that these remedies are Qur'an-based. This all may sound harsh to you, but know that the consequences of milk stealing from a belly are much harsher: your older child could fall seriously sick and even die.

If you do not become pregnant while you are nursing, you won't need to think about weaning for at least two years. You may have heard about methods of deciding when to become pregnant – what White people call "birth control." If you want to learn about these, I suggest you go speak with a nurse in a clinic. Don't expect me to tell you anything here, since the methods we sometimes use are secret, and anyway, the elders always say that pregnancy is Allah's will. You probably know how delicate this subject is for us Guinean Muslims. I know that plenty of both Christian and Muslim Guineans back home, especially in the capital, use White people's birth control methods. But since God always plays a role in making babies, women who take that pill, or use those gadgets they call IUDs, still occasionally get pregnant. Back in Bissau, I know several children named "IUD" and "Pill" – after the method that was supposedly going to keep their mothers from becoming pregnant. This is proof that, when it comes to making babies, God is in control, not human beings. So, feel free to try one of these White people's methods, if you must, but remember that it is not foolproof. If Allah wants you to make a belly, you will.

Another issue that separates us from the White Portuguese is where we feed our children. While it's fine to breastfeed your child for three or four years, keep in mind that this is Europe, and White people are often uptight about breastfeeding older children. Make sure your child knows better than to ask for the breast in public, or people will stare at you.

EARLY CHILDHOOD RITUALS

So far I have focused on caring for your baby's bodily needs and protecting the little one from harm. But it is equally important for new parents to attend to the development of their baby's identity, both ethnic and religious. You might have assumed that these identities are automatically acquired: after all, if your husband is Mandinga or Fula, then your baby will have his name and will also be Mandinga or Fula. While everyone knows that to be Mandinga or Fula is also to be Muslim, it is a bit more complicated than this. This natural, given aspect is only part of the process of becoming who one is; it puts your baby on the path to his or her identity, but it is your and your husband's duty to ensure that your baby takes that path. This can only be accomplished through three rituals, which all Guinean Muslim parents must hold for their children, no matter where they are living: the name-giving ritual, the writing-on-the-hand ritual, and circumcision.

The Name-giving Ritual

As you now know, becoming parents has made both you and your husband full-fledged adults. For you, the price of this status change was obvious: you carried your baby for ten months (Europeans insist that pregnancy lasts nine months, but we know that it lasts ten), and you suffered the pain of childbirth. What about your husband? Babies are born with a debt owed to them by their fathers, a debt that can only be paid by holding the name-giving ritual, which we call *kulliyo*, or "head-shaving." While the daily care of babies is primarily a mother's responsibility, responsibility for the name-giving ritual falls upon the baby's father. It is your husband's duty to plan and finance the ritual, and to hire the necessary participants, such as a holy man and some of the traditional musicians we call *jaloolu*.

Back home, we normally hold the name-giving ritual about a week after a baby's birth. A married couple almost always has a spare sheep or goat, and animals are easily borrowed. In Lisbon, the situation is more complicated. Here, we can't keep animals, and borrowing money brings shame in the immigrant community. It is one thing to complain to your friends that life in Europe is hard, but quite another to admit that you are unable to pay for your own baby's name-giving ritual!

There is also the issue of timing. If you have the money to hold the ritual, and the seventh day of the baby's life falls on a weekend, then consider yourself blessed and name your baby then. If you don't have the money, or if the day for the ritual falls on a work day, then consider postponing your baby's naming until you have the cash, and schedule it for a day that won't interfere with school and work schedules. Some people in Lisbon actually wait years and name all of their children on one big day, as this is more economical and doubles, or even triples, the celebration. Although this may sound tempting, keep in mind that putting off a father's debt to his child is risky. Some people will criticize you, insisting that a "big party"-style ritual completely misses the point. The name-giving ritual is about fulfilling your duty as a Guinean Muslim parent: giving your baby a good Muslim name and paying your husband's debt; it is not about building your own names in the immigrant community by displaying your status, wealth, and success.

Of course, which kind of name-giving ritual you hold for your baby is entirely up to you, but be prepared to accept the consequences of your choice.

If you do postpone the naming for any reason, you must still hold a replacement ritual – what we call a *nyangbo* – one week after your baby's birth. In Guinea-Bissau, a father buys a chicken especially for this purpose and shows it to the baby. Then he slaughters it and places it under the baby's bed until the chicken dies. In Lisbon, live chickens are hard to find and even harder to transport, so simply purchase some properly butchered *halal* meat outside the mosque instead and show it to your baby, explaining its purpose to the little one. Keep in mind that the *nyangbo* does not cancel your husband's debt to his child; it merely postpones it until he can hold a proper name-giving ritual at a later time.

Before staging the event, invite your best friends to help you with the cooking, and remind them that you'll be happy to return the favor. On the day of your baby's naming, expect guests to gather at your apartment by mid-morning. If your apartment is small, you might be tempted to rent a larger space for this purpose, but I advise you to resist the temptation. The blessings that are given at the name-giving ritual are particularly powerful, and you want them to stay in your home and benefit you and your family (see Figure 2.2).

Spread out some prayer rugs in the front room, and seat the older men on them. Divide the remaining guests into the other rooms according to gender and age, as you would back home. Dress your baby in his or her best matching outfit and beg the little one to cooperate; this is his or her big day, after all! Back home on this special day, babies are shown those things that will be important throughout their lives, depending on their gender and caste: a cooking pot or hoe for a girl, for example, or leatherworking tools for a baby from a leatherworking family. But you can skip this part of the ritual, since it doesn't make sense in Lisbon, where children have so many options available to them. Which objects will be important to your child depends entirely on what he or she ends up doing in life. Who are we to make assumptions about that in this new country?

Figure 2.2 A Guinean Muslim elder blesses a newly named baby boy at an infant-naming ritual, in an immigrant neighborhood outside Lisbon.
Photograph by Michelle C. Johnson.

Next, the holy man will shave your baby's head almost completely in the case of a boy, leaving a small tuft of hair in front. While girls' heads are also shaved like this in Guinea-Bissau, this is Europe, and people may mock your baby girl: ask the holy man to have mercy on your daughter and remove only a small lock of hair instead. Take whatever hair is removed and either bury it outside in the ground, or have it sewn into a protective amulet for your baby.

Back in Guinea-Bissau, one of the most important aspects of the name-giving ritual is the sacrifice of a goat or sheep, which takes place at the same time that the baby is named. This is practically impossible in Lisbon, of course, since we couldn't easily obtain live animals. In any case, apartments lack spacious courtyards to perform animal sacrifices, and what would your Portuguese neighbors think if you killed a sheep or goat on the streets of Lisbon? You don't want to make life any harder for African immigrants than it already is. Instead, buy some *halal* meat and cook it. When the holy man announces your baby's name aloud, your husband can relax: his debt to his baby is officially paid. Next the holy man whispers the baby's name in his or her right ear, telling the little one who he or she is. He then whispers "God is great" three times and invites the baby to take up the path that God has chosen for him or her. Finally, the holy man bestows blessings on the child for a long and prosperous life. At this point, all of your guests will join you in tapping their foreheads, saying: "Amen, may God make it so." Take a few moments to take all of this in – you and your husband will recall it as one of the happiest moments of your new lives as parents.

Finally, you must serve your guests a meal and brew tea for them. Provide a single large bowl with plenty of rice and sauce, one for each room, to be shared among the guests. Don't worry if you lack enough spoons for everyone; good Guinean Muslims never forget how to eat with their right hands! Before the guests depart, give each person a few kola nuts, if you've managed to buy some from a Guinean merchant in downtown Lisbon, and some leftover uncooked meat. Now you and your husband can finally feel at ease: his debt is paid, your baby has a name, and the little one is further along on his or her path to becoming a true Muslim. Unless you have another baby soon, you can relax a bit, as you won't need to hold another big ritual for six years.

The Writing-on-the-Hand Ritual

This ritual is the next milestone in the development of your child's identity as a Guinean Muslim. When children are named, they are shown the path that God has chosen for them; when they have their hands written on, they are placed on that path. Prepare to hold this ritual for your child at age seven, the time when he or she should also start Qur'anic school. When you enroll your children in European school, you write on papers; when you enroll them in Qur'anic school, you write on their hands. But in having your child's hand written on, you are doing much more than just enrolling him or her in Qur'anic school: this ritual prepares children for studying Islam's most sacred text by opening their heads, cooling their hearts, and steadying their spirits. Like the name-giving ritual, the writing-on-the-hand ritual requires some planning, but the good news is that the burden doesn't fall on just one parent; you and your husband can work together.

In many ways the day will remind you of your child's name-giving ritual: guests will gather in the morning in different rooms according to their age and gender, and the elders will recite the Qur'an in the front room. Select a holy man with a good reputation to perform the hand writing ritual, and provide him with the old-fashioned but essential supplies: ink, a wooden slate used in village Qur'anic schools back home, and a fountain pen. During the ritual, the holy man will dip the pen in ink and write the opening *Al-Fatihah* prayer of the Qur'an on your child's right palm. He will then add a pinch of salt to the ink and instruct the child to lick the mixture from his or her hand three times. Next he'll point to each letter of the Arabic alphabet and tell your child to repeat it. This puts a lot of pressure on both your child and you and your husband. Rest assured; we have a way of lessening it. As your child says each letter, you and your guests must join in. You won't be able to distinguish your child's voice from the rest of the voices, and you'll see how relaxed and confident your child is as a result. Aside from easing the pressure, this trick also teaches our children that they are never alone: they can always count on the support of the wider community. During the recitation, everyone present will place gifts of euro bills and kola nuts on the child's head. Later, you can claim the money to help offset the cost of holding the ritual.

Your next task will be to distribute a bit of the rice flour dish sweetened with honey that we call *munkoo* to everyone present. Pounding enough rice to make *munkoo* is not easy in Lisbon, since you'll have to use a small version of the traditional mortar and pestle, which is all that we can transport from West Africa to Lisbon. Call on all of your female relatives and friends well ahead of time so that you can make enough *munkoo* for the ritual. Finally, provide your guests with a meal of rice and sauce before they depart.

The writing-on-the-hand ritual marks an important transition in your child's life. Before the age of seven, children don't know the difference between right or wrong, and adults can't hold them accountable for their actions. During this time of innocence, children have no contact with angels – those beings that mediate between people and Allah. After the ritual, your child will enter into a lifelong relationship with angels, who will record his or her good and bad deeds on giant wooden slates and report them to Allah on Judgment Day. On the day of the writing-on-the-hand ritual, Allah pardons your child's sins. This opportunity for a clean start applies to you and your relatives, as well: when the holy man writes the first half of the *Al-Fatihah* on your child's palm, Allah pardons the sins of one hundred of your relatives. When he writes the second half, Allah pardons the sins of one hundred of your husband's relatives.

The writing-on-the-hand ritual brings new responsibilities to both you and your child. From now on, your son or daughter must be mindful of the consequences of his or her behavior. You and your husband must do your best to keep the channels of communication open between your child and the angels: do not wake your son or daughter from sleep unless absolutely necessary, as this disrupts any messages that Allah might be sending to him or her via angels through dreams. You must also not allow female nudity or dogs in your apartment; in their own way, both these are problematic and scare away angels.

You might hear some conflicting opinions in Lisbon about the writing-on-the-hand ritual. Muslims from Saudi Arabia and even some Guinean Muslims who have studied the Qur'an or made the Mecca pilgrimage claim that it is an African custom that has nothing to do with Islam. Those Guineans who want to be more like Saudi Muslims will tell you that what matters more than the ritual is that you send your child to Qur'anic school. You can listen to these viewpoints, but consider this as you and your husband attempt to form your own opinion: our holy men and healer-diviners point out that children who have had their hands written on are less likely to drink alcohol than those who have not. This magical safeguard is especially important in Lisbon, where the difficulties of immigrant life, combined with the influence of non-Muslims, often drive our children to drink, eat pork, and fall from Islam.

Circumcision

This is the last of the three rituals that are crucial for the proper development of your child's Guinean Muslim identity. It is also the most difficult of the three to plan, since there are many variations. It is also much more complicated in Europe, where it is not commonly practiced for either boys or girls and quite controversial. The ritual consists of two parts: the "little initiation" – cutting a boy's foreskin or a girl's clitoris; and the "big initiation" – the educational and celebratory aspects that accompany the cutting. While we used to practice these two rituals together, they have been pulled apart, and nowadays both parts are changing. My goal in this manual is not to provide you with clear answers, proper practice, or even advice. Instead, I hope to give you some important information about circumcision, and to alert you to the controversy. You and your husband will have to sort it out from there and make the decision that is best for you and your child.

If you gave birth to a boy, then praise Allah: your path is simple and easy, even more so now that you're in Lisbon. Your son is a Muslim, so he must be circumcised. Allah commands that a boy be circumcised in order to pray, slaughter animals, and fast during Ramadan. If your son is not circumcised, neither God nor other Muslims will consider him a Muslim. If you were in Guinea-Bissau, you would face more choices: you would have to decide whether to have your son circumcised at puberty, as was common in the past, or earlier, as is more common now. You would also have to decide how and where the event would take place: in the "bush" as part of a proper initiation ritual, in the hospital, or some combination of the two.

The situation is less complicated in Lisbon: your only option is to have your son circumcised in the hospital. If you have him circumcised as an infant, you can wait to hold a coming-out ceremony when he is older, around eight years old. Or you can simply wait until then and hold the ceremony immediately after the healing period. Whatever you decide, coming-out ceremonies in Lisbon are much simpler than in Guinea-Bissau, where people spend weeks dancing with the initiates, feasting, and running from the masquerade figure we call *Kankuran*, who protects the initiates from witches. To celebrate your son's circumcision in Lisbon, simply invite members of the community to your apartment, dress your boy in his finest, big, Muslim clothes, take a few pictures of him, and serve your guests a delicious meal from back home. Ask someone to beat homemade calabash drums; if you don't have them, even overturned plastic basins will get people dancing. (We Guinean Muslims have never paid much attention to the Muslims who forbid drumming as "un-Islamic.") Guinean Muslim mothers in Lisbon are fortunate not to have to worry about our sons' safety in the bush, or worry that they might suffer from hunger, elders' beatings, or pain (the hospitals use anesthesia). As you are spared such worry, you can focus entirely on the joy of your son's coming-out: he is circumcised and is now a true Muslim.

If you gave birth to a girl, then brace yourself: the path ahead of you is much more difficult. You might find yourself wishing that you had given birth to a boy! Just as hospital circumcisions for girls are not an option in Guinea-Bissau, they are also not an option in Portugal. You don't have to live in Europe long to learn that female circumcision is very controversial; indeed, people are arguing about it all over the world. Many people even call it "female genital mutilation" and consider it a form of violence against women. These activists are demanding that the practice be stopped, and in 2012, the United Nations passed a resolution to ban the practice worldwide. All this makes it very difficult for Guinean Muslim women, especially those who were born and circumcised in Guinea-Bissau, and now must decide whether or not to have their daughters – born in Portugal – circumcised. Our grandmothers' grandmothers practiced this ritual, and the majority of Guinean Muslim women today have a hard time seeing it as violent or harmful. You know that, to us, it is a sacred tradition that allows women to be real Muslims and to participate as fully in Islam as men do.

Like boys, girls used to undergo the "little initiation" and the "big initiation" at the same time, at the start of puberty. This was one major step in the gradual change from girlhood to womanhood, and the "suffering" involved prepared a girl for marriage and the pain of childbirth. Today, girls in Guinea-Bissau are circumcised earlier – some when they are still infants – since the cutting is simpler, and there are fewer arrangements and decisions to make. But this change doesn't really matter, as the cutting itself is more important than the other activities that traditionally have accompanied it. When a girl's clitoris is cut, she is made clean so that God can hear her prayers.

Here in Lisbon, many Guinean Muslim men, especially those who want to be more like Saudi Arabian Muslims, now oppose female circumcision. This is strange for women, since our men used to claim that it was "women's business" and leave us alone. Now they claim that Allah does not mandate the practice and that women, because they study the Qur'an less than men do, simply don't know this. In their minds, circumcision is an African custom and has nothing to do with Islam. It is true that in Saudi Arabia women are not circumcised, and no one would ever claim that they are bad Muslims. And not all African Muslims circumcise women: the Wolof people in Senegal don't, and they are very pious Muslims. Still, some of our women are convinced that our men oppose the practice simply to look more cosmopolitan. Our men claim that when we circumcise our daughters, we make African men look like bad Muslims.

If you already feel confused, know that you are not alone. In sorting it all out and making an informed decision, you have many things to consider. Aside from your daughter's Muslim identity, you must also think of her future marriageability. Men might claim to oppose the practice, but the reality is that very few if any of them want their sons to marry uncircumcised women. You must also think of your daughter's sexuality. Women have a stronger sex drive than men do. Circumcision will tame your daughter's sex drive, so she won't end up following her husband around all the time, demanding constant sexual attention. If you do prefer to have your daughter circumcised, you'll need to decide whether to send her back home or to have her circumcised in Lisbon. People claim that there are Guinean Muslim women in Lisbon who are trained traditional circumcisers, but I have never met one, nor do I know of anyone who has actually had her daughter circumcised by one.

The reality of the situation is that many Guinean Muslim girls born in Lisbon are not being circumcised, because their mothers either can't make up their minds or can't work out the details. Yet, if you decide to send your daughter home to Africa, there are many risks: she'll have to miss school and will surely fall behind. Plus, you'll have no say about the form of cutting: just the hood of her clitoris might be cut, as we have done traditionally, but it's also possible that her entire clitoris and inner labia might be removed, as some people claim our Fulani sisters are beginning to do. The biggest problem is timing: once your daughter becomes sexually active, it is too dangerous to have her circumcised, as the wound may never stop bleeding. I know I am leaving you with many possibilities and unanswered questions, and much uncertainty, as a young mother in a foreign land who already has enough to worry about. The only advice I can offer is this: proceed carefully, make the decision that is best for you and your family, and leave the rest to God.

THE ROLES OF THE MOTHER, THE FATHER, AND THE COMMUNITY

As parents, you and your husband share the primary responsibility of loving and caring for your children, but mothers and fathers have separate (and complementary) duties in raising them. As a mother, your relationship with your children should be carefree and relaxed, and you will feel very close to them. As a new mother, you might have already experienced a powerful emotional weakness toward your baby, who has suddenly become the most important person in your life. The elders claim that this is why women back home don't climb palm trees as men do: they feel such a love for their children that they don't have the courage to risk falling to their death and leaving them without a mother. This is actually not a weakness at all, but rather a completely normal and highly valued part of motherhood: without it, you would be a bad mother. Your primary responsibility as a mother is to care for your children's everyday needs. You are their principal advocate in life: nothing can ever match the love and support of a mother.

To the father: although you will share your wife's pride in your children, your behavior toward them is considerably different from hers. It's not that you don't love your children; of course you do, but you should express it much less. Whereas your wife should show devotion, attachment, and affection toward your children from the very beginning, you must maintain an emotional distance from them. You are your children's principal authority figure, and keeping your distance will force them to respect and obey you. Although it is normal for you to want to indulge or play with your children on occasion, you must not do so too much, or they will never listen to you when you are serious and want them to do something. Much of your verbal interaction with your children should be in the form of giving orders. Your role as principal authority figure is even more important in Lisbon, where your children are exposed to a way of life that is very different from yours. They might observe, for example, that Portuguese children openly show disrespect to their parents by arguing with them or even yelling at them. You must work even harder than normal to instill in your children from a very young age respect not only for their parents, but for anyone who is older than they are.

To you both: the advice that I have offered in this manual is far from complete. Remember to include your relatives, friends, co-wives, and community members in making important decisions regarding the health and education of your children. If you are not already involved, start going to Friday prayer and Islamic holiday celebrations at the mosque, or join an immigrants' association. Raising good Guinean Muslim children is much easier back home, where they grow up with other Guinean Muslim children; in Portugal, you will have to work much harder to create a supportive community for your children, and you have many new challenges ahead of you. If you attempt to hide problems or big decisions from community members, they will be offended, and they will probably hear about your problems through others, as news travels fast in our immigrant community, especially with mobile phones. It is best to avoid any trouble by talking openly to people in the first place. Keep in mind that parenting is too much work for one or two people alone. Back home, we always said that it takes an entire community to effectively raise a child; although it may be harder, it's even more important to follow this saying for those of us living far from home, in Europe.

CHAPTER 3

From Cultural Revolution to Childcare Revolution

Conflicting Advice on Childrearing in Contemporary China

Erin Raffety

CULTURAL CONTEXTS OF CHINESE CHILDREARING

There is arguably no country in the world that has experienced more dramatic family change over the last century than the People's Republic of China. At the outset of the twentieth century, China was an agrarian society, with just a few populous cities. The great majority of its people lived in the countryside and depended on large, extended families to farm for a living. In fact, one might say that the entirety of social life in premodern China was ordered around the kinship system, through which people defined their economic, political, and social identities.

Many families were organized around strong patrilineages. Families literally worshipped their forefathers and passed down businesses and titles from generation to generation. Marriages were important for fostering careful and important alliances between families – alliances through which both goods and prestige were exchanged and established. In this patriarchal system, women were particularly vulnerable: when they came of age, they were forced to leave their birth families, often moving far away to make a new life in their husbands' households, under the supervision and jurisdiction of their mothers-in-law. By contrast, men remained in their natal homes for life, becoming heads of the household as they came of age, directing both internal and external family activities, and carrying on the family line by raising sons.

At the turn of the twentieth century, a group of political activists (the Nationalists, led by Sun Yat-Sen) rebelled against some of these traditional ways, challenging gender roles as well as the political and economic bases of the family structure. A few decades later, in 1949, following the Communists' defeat of the Nationalists in a civil war, the massive Communist Revolution began to reform Chinese society toward collective ways of life. "Collectivization" was initiated at the levels of the municipality and the town by redistributing land between and among families. Eventually, everyone was organized into formal units termed "communes," "brigades," and "work teams." In dividing lineages – often intentionally – these new, government-created formations strained family allegiances.

Especially during the decade known as the "Cultural Revolution" (1966–76), the Communists attempted to transfer people's loyalties from the family to the state by destroying two primary sites of ancestor worship – lineage halls and ancestor shrines – and by increasing women's rights and roles beyond childbearing and childcare. To an extent, the Communist regime expanded the role of women in society, increased opportunities for impoverished peasants, and released people from the confines of some of the limitations of traditional patriarchal family roles. For instance, in the collectives, women often worked alongside men, gaining valuable "work points" for their production teams, and many people of low socio-economic status were assigned key leadership roles in the Revolution's new government structure. However, many of the traditional strictures of patriarchy remained, even when the government applied force. For example, despite women's increased participation in the workforce, women labored at tasks that were often classified as less valuable than men's tasks, and traditional discriminatory practices such as "brideprice," as well as unequal domestic roles and burdens within family life, remained.

From Cultural Revolution to Childcare Revolution

Under his early Communist reorganization of society, Mao Zedong encouraged a high birth rate to strengthen the nation. More children meant more "work points" for the production team, so couples found it advantageous to have as many children as possible. However, as early as the mid-1950s, Mao began to feel ambivalent about the benefits of a large population and broached the topic of state "birth planning." Nevertheless, for reasons internal to political processes, the government did not take significant action to restrict population growth for another three decades. In the 1970s, this inattention contributed to one of the largest-scale famines in modern history. By then, Mao could do little to reverse the effects of "overpopulation," and its severity contributed to his decline in power and prestige.

In the 1980s, Mao's successor, Deng Xiaoping, sought to reinvigorate China's political stature and economy by privatizing key industries and opening the country to foreign investment. As part of China's "modernization" process, he implemented the country's infamous "one-child policy." In fact, it was never truly a one-child policy (and it was repealed in October 2015). Instead, a series of family planning interventions in the lives of China's sprawling population offered, first, incentives and then, beginning in the late 1970s, disincentives, penalties, and even, in some cases, forced sterilization surgeries following births deemed to be "over-quota." Thus, under the banner of making China a "modern" nation one prosperous family at a time, the government undermined the importance of the extended family, particularly the reverence for elders, by shifting the focus to "few, long, and late" births.

Today, demographers suggest that China may have already been on a "natural" road to curbing its population problem even without these drastic family planning projects. In any event, the government policy produced a generation of "only children" who enjoyed soaring educational and professional prospects in the proliferating "modern" cities. However, because the government did not invest the same resources in the countryside as it did in the cities, the income gap between urban and rural residents remains one of the largest in the world today. Rural villagers without electricity and modern sanitation systems struggle to garner the opportunities for their children that residents of "investment capitals" such as Beijing and Shanghai enjoy, where prosperous, single-family units and elite education systems abound.

To take advantage of urban opportunities, migration to cities has skyrocketed, despite a stringent "household registration" system of internal passports, intended to restrict such movement. Families, both rich and poor, find it advantageous to split up and rely on grandparents or other relatives in seeking the best opportunities for their children. Poor migrants often leave their children behind, to be raised by their elderly parents while they pursue factory jobs in cities hundreds of miles away, returning just once a year via packed trains during the national celebration known as the Spring Festival.

For their part, prosperous families in cities rely on grandparents to cart their children to school and after-school training opportunities, while they work at strenuous jobs late into the night. Perhaps not surprisingly, traditional domestic problems of husbands' infidelity and violence against wives now combine with modern challenges to family stability, including divorce and relatively unrestrained sexuality, threatening the continuity of families across China. Yet many Chinese families tolerate disruptive separations as acceptable tradeoffs for the opportunity to have a "high-quality" child who can earn a college degree and provide security for his or her family.

In the wake of this rapid social change, social critics and scholars alike have begun to scrutinize these "necessary modern evils" and critique what they perceive as a growing level of immorality across many sectors of Chinese society. Stories abound in the media about food insecurity, scandals, and smuggling. Social distrust is high, especially in the modern cities, where residents and migrants find it impossible to have faith in the government, in corporations, or even in their neighbors.

In 2011, a toddler named YueYue was run over by a van in a parking garage, and a security camera caught on film nearly twenty strangers passing by before a trash collector scooped up the wounded little girl and attempted to find her parents and get her medical treatment. National and international outcry surfaced, questioning whether this inhumanity was typical of the new breakneck pace of China's development, and whether the social value of children, or even of human beings in general, was in jeopardy.

On social media websites, people commented that, unlike most individuals, the trash collector who picked up little YueYue had very little to lose. These conversations suggest that the promise of the Chinese dream, not unlike the American one, is not available to all, and that increasing numbers of individuals are being left behind. These unfortunates include the countless number of baby girls aborted, abandoned, and adopted since the onset of the "one-child policy," as well as the soaring number of children with deformities and disabilities in China's overcrowded child welfare institutions. Previously hidden from view, these populations have now become visible, since China opened up to international adoptions in 1995, and the majority of adoptions from China to the West since 2004 have been of "special needs" children.

Other vulnerable populations remain less visible. One is the generation of "left-behind children," sequestered in the countryside due to China's restrictive migration policies. Virtually devoid of any meaningful relationship with their parents, they are being raised by aging grandparents. These grandparents have meager pensions or savings, due to having come of age during the Cultural Revolution, and many find themselves destitute – lacking the assistance of their own children or other family members, who are themselves burdened with the increasingly expensive demands of modern life. At stake here is not merely the decay of support systems for the old and the young under modernity, but the cultural conventions of filial piety and childrearing, and the integrity of the Chinese family itself.

Many scholars decry the disintegration of "filial piety," the traditional system of socially valued reverence for elders. Others claim that this apparent disintegration is actually being reinterpreted as calculated reciprocity, wherein elderly grandparents strategically manage their resources and offer their childcare services in exchange for financial security provided by their middle-aged children. Are such exchanges of goods and services within familial relationships evidence of weakening social bonds? Or are they reminiscent of the deeply intertwined emotional, economic, and even legal cohesion that characterized extended family units in the pre-Mao era? Are young families "outsourcing" childcare to their aging relatives at a cost, or do these arrangements constitute a viable and ethical solution to modern demands?

With these social contracts comes generational friction, especially as grandparents become primary caregivers with little support from other family members. While doing fieldwork in both rural and urban settings in China, I realized that conversations regarding childrearing between daughters and mothers, as well as between daughters-in-law and mothers-in-law, reflected the complicated dynamics of these contemporary cultural shifts. However, as I noted above – and as I hope the reader will gather through the imagined childcare guide that follows – conflicts did not always break down along clear-cut lines of "traditional" versus "modern" identities. Even as young couples resisted their parents' "traditional" advice, they often valued and internalized these childrearing strategies as viable in the face of uncertainty and change. Meanwhile, grandparents did not unilaterally romanticize the past but often displayed a willingness to evaluate and accept modern medical and technological advances (see Figure 3.1).

As a young woman of childbearing age doing research on families in China, I received countless pieces of advice on childrearing and childbearing when I was living there. Through these interactions, I came to discover that, despite its argumentative nature, advice-giving was very much a "love language" in China – a microculture through which women, especially, have established, and continue to establish, their wisdom and concern for one another despite the many realms of their lives that remain beyond their control. The imagined childcare guide that follows explores how these childcare conflicts are now being received and resolved, and it hints at what the family unit in modern China can be expected to look like in the foreseeable future.

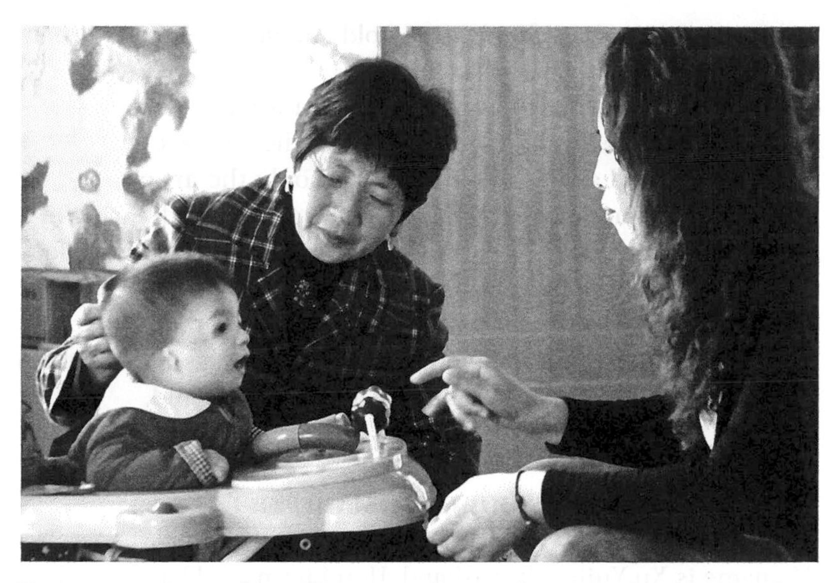

Figure 3.1 In modern China, mothers-in-law and daughters-in-law negotiate different childrearing strategies as they jointly raise the next generation.
Photograph by Jason Fouts.

FROM CULTURAL REVOLUTION TO CHILDCARE REVOLUTION: CONFLICTING ADVICE ON CHILDREARING IN CONTEMPORARY CHINA

About the Authors

This manual is constructed as a dialogue focusing on a classic struggle in Chinese family life – that between mother-in-law and daughter-in-law. For Xu Yujin and her mother-in-law, Liu Xiaoyuan, raising a child in modern China involves constant negotiation between modern psychology and medicine, traditional wisdom, and many contemporary societal challenges emanating from migration, global capitalism, and other major changes. While demographers may argue that today's "only children" and small families signal China's transition to "modernity," childrearing experiences in ordinary families suggest remaining conflict between old and new, rural and urban, modern and traditional ways of life.

These societal changes are apparent in Xu and Liu's relationship. Their candid expressions of their hopes, frustrations, and assumptions reveal not only the art of compromise, but also the multiple languages of childrearing in a context in which the social value of the child in China is in deep flux. In this dialogically constructed advice manual, a fictional daughter-in-law addresses young, pregnant women such as herself, while her fictional mother-in-law addresses older women who will soon became caretakers of a new grandchild.

XU YUJIN: A MODERN DAUGHTER-IN-LAW

My name is Xu Yujin. My husband, Hou Limin, and I are both part of what is called the "post-eighties" generation – children who came of age during the progressive reforms made by Deng Xiaoping's policies that ended the isolation of the People's Republic of China and made our nation a superpower in the modern world. Of course, in addition to encouraging the foreign trade and investment that made China grow so quickly and become so wealthy, those policies also included the so-called "one child policy" mandating that couples in urban areas could have only one child.

My husband and I are part of that first generation of "only children" raised in modern cities. I'm not completely ignorant of more traditional ways of life, though. When I was growing up, my family traveled to my mother's family home in the countryside every year during the Spring Festival, and sometimes we'd also head to my father's home village to honor the ancestors at a funeral or for the Tomb Sweeping Festival. During these long bus rides, I would stare out the window at farmers in the rice paddies and at people farming with water buffalos and their own two hands. These sights inspired pride in my family and in traditional Chinese ways of life, but I still couldn't help but think that this type of farming seemed rather backward for a country on the road to prosperity and success.

From Cultural Revolution to Childcare Revolution

For the most part, unlike the generation before me, I consider myself a modern city girl. After all, I grew up in a small but modern, two-bedroom apartment that looked out on busy highways peppered with cars, roaring buses, nearby high-rises, and electrical lines as far as the eye could see. While my parents were sent to the countryside during the Cultural Revolution and had almost no opportunity to improve themselves, I've studied day and night since I was a young child, even attending extra tutoring and training in the evening hours, since my parents couldn't help me with my homework. In fact, from a very young age, it was abundantly clear to me that I represented my parents' hope for future security, since they had no other children and virtually no savings. They had migrated to the city before I was born and had worked at menial jobs for long hours, leaving me in the care of my grandmother.

Still, our life was a lot better than that of the migrants nowadays who must leave their children behind in the countryside because of the "household registration system." Because of their grueling work schedules in factories, they can only return to the countryside to visit their children once a year.

I was the first person from our family to finish high school, and then I was also given the opportunity to attend the local teachers' college, where I earned my degree. Now I teach in a prominent elementary school in the city. Although I work long hours, the job and the pay are steady, which is an important achievement for a woman of my age and status.

I met my husband at the teachers' college. Since graduation, he's changed fields: he now works in the regional office of one of China's large cell phone companies. Ever since we married five years ago, our parents have been pressuring us to have a child. It's actually quite unusual for young couples to wait this long; usually after just a year of marriage, the first child has arrived. No one sees any need to wait, as that's the purpose of marriage, and everyone knows the fatigue of having a child after you're thirty!

But for my husband and me, because we're more modern and forward-thinking, we wanted to have our fun and freedom before becoming parents. During our first few years of marriage, we enjoyed going out to dinner, decorating our apartment, and

Figure 3.2 Contemporary Chinese children develop close relationships with their grandparents; this toddler is enjoying an outing with his grandfather.
Photograph by Evan Schneider.

meeting friends for drinks at bars. My husband and I could spend our hard-earned money on whatever we wanted.

But now, I'm pregnant! Our lives have already changed drastically: my in-laws have moved into our tiny apartment to cook and clean for us, preparing for the time when they will take care of the baby (see Figure 3.2). With the baby coming, we're starting to feel the pressure of being part of the "sandwich generation," as they call it – needing to provide not only for our own children, but also for our two sets of parents. Especially since I'm an "only daughter," my parents will have no support in old age other than what I can provide for them. While it's customary for a woman's in-laws to move in to provide childcare, don't think that my mother and father, who also live nearby, won't expect to be involved in our child's life – and to be cared for, themselves, as well.

Even before I became pregnant, my head was hurting from the advice that both my mother-in-law and my own mother were heaping on me about dietary restrictions, exercise, and many of their old-fashioned, superstitious ideas. Now, they act as though the child in my belly is theirs, not mine. Yet, I'm the one who continues to work long hours on my feet at school and suffer the responsibilities of being a wife and a dutiful daughter – not to mention back pain and morning sickness! While my husband and I appreciate the help my in-laws provide, recognizing that we could never get by without their assistance, relationships between daughters and mothers-in-law in China have never been easy. Perhaps even as almost everything seems to be changing, some things never do.

I hope the reader will find my advice for pregnant women and new moms helpful in navigating family tensions and modern pressures. I've read a lot of contemporary childrearing manuals myself, many of which provide modern, Western advice, but none of them instructs Chinese women on what is perhaps the most challenging aspect of becoming a mother: managing your mother-in-law!

LIU XIAOYUAN: A DOTING MOTHER-IN-LAW

My name is Liu Xiaoyuan. I was born in 1958 – a time of much change and struggle in China. I grew up in a small, remote village where my family had farmed rice for centuries. Our tall wooden home looked out on picturesque rice terraces where my mother and father plowed the fields behind our water buffalo. We cooked over an open flame, which stained the walls of our humble home, and I fell asleep at night to the sounds of the pigs grunting in the stable below. I was one of five siblings, but with lots of family nearby: there were always aunts, uncles, or grandparents to look after us when Mom and Dad were in the fields.

Communism came early to our area, but little changed at first, except the redistribution of lands and those who farmed them. During those years, I worked in the fields in our commune, earning "work points," singing revolutionary songs – and secretly hoping for a better life. One of the benefits of the Revolution was that we had more interaction with young people of the opposite sex, so I got to know my husband in those same fields. Instead of being married off to someone from a far-off village and feeling very sad about being sent away forever, my future husband and I developed "good feelings" for one another, and we were able to remain near both of our families when we married.

Unfortunately, neither of us had much of a chance to attend school during the Cultural Revolution, when teachers were persecuted and schooling was suspended. By the time Mao died and the Cultural Revolution ended, we were too old to go to school. We had little money, so we were lucky to migrate to the city, where we had our one and only son, Hou Limin.

At first I was discouraged by Deng Xiaoping's aggressive birth planning policies, and I wanted to have more children. But my husband pointed out that the Chinese population had grown out of control under Mao, and restricting our population was necessary if we wanted to become a prosperous, modern nation.

I now see the wisdom of Deng's progressive policies, because everything changed. No longer did you need "ration cards" to obtain meager supplies of rice or oil that you had to stretch to last the month – now, you could go to the store and pick out anything you wanted! Where dirt roads and fields used to be, the government constructed modern highways and high-rises. I hardly recognize the China of my youth, and the young people today certainly cannot appreciate the amazing changes and freedoms that came with the Revolution. My son and his wife were so lucky to be able to study, and even attend college. In my day, no one could imagine such opportunities, especially for women.

Perhaps this is why my daughter-in-law, Xu Yujin, tries to convince my husband and me that girls are just as good as boys. But of course, we hope the child she is carrying is a boy. In the city, boys may no longer be needed to work the land, but men are still responsible for caring for their parents in old age, and they're the only ones who can carry on the family line and bring honor to the ancestors. Those customs aren't so important to the young people these days, but in China, family still matters much more than love or money. Family is everything.

THE MANUAL

Liu Xiaoyuan: Fish Soup and Years of Tradition

When your daughter-in-law is pregnant for the first time, you should consider moving in with her and your son. My husband and I moved in with Yujin and Limin. Since they both work at jobs all day, we know that they barely have time to cook or clean for themselves, let alone prepare for this baby. Once the baby comes, new parents need a lot of help day and night. I may be nearly illiterate, but my daughter-in-law is so ignorant of which foods to eat during pregnancy, and which precautions to take. I shudder to think what she would do without me, especially when the baby comes. Perhaps she would not even sit for the required month after birth, and that might bring illness to her or the baby! There may be benefits of Western medicines and vitamins, but they can't replace the nourishment of pigs' feet, fish soup, and years of tradition!

Let me describe some of the ways to care for new mothers and babies that were passed on through the generations but are losing esteem with young people such as my son and daughter-in-law. As you will see, I am not completely averse to modern medicine and new ways of doing things. But I also consider Chinese tradition a rich source of history and wisdom, without which we would scarcely know how to breathe. Being a mother-in-law, especially during your daughter-in-law's pregnancy, birth, and childrearing years, is of the utmost importance, and your daughter-in-law will need to lean on you during this important and stressful time.

Xu Yujin: Something Old, Something New

I know that eating fish soup and pigs' feet soup helps your milk come in. Every girl knows that! That common wisdom has merit because there are certain vitamins in those foods that are good for you and your baby. In the West, they recognize that a regular diet often neglects nutrients that are valuable for the baby, and that's why you should take prenatal vitamins, alongside eating healthy foods, during your pregnancy. With the prenatal vitamins, you won't have to stress so much about your diet. My mother-in-law is always urging me to eat more, but I've read that gaining too much weight during the pregnancy isn't good for either the mom or the baby. There's a wealth of parenting classes and books offered in the city to pregnant women like me, and you, too, should seek to educate yourself in the new developments in science and medicine, as well as the old ways.

When you're pregnant, I know that you should not do highly strenuous exercise, like running or lots and lots of walking – but it's hard for me to manage rest, given that I'm on my feet all day teaching. You should wear loose-fitting clothing so as not to restrict the baby's movement or your own blood flow, and in order to be comfortable. These are all traditional ideas that serve a purpose. However, some traditional ideas, like not sleeping in the same bed as your husband for the three months after you get pregnant, are antiquated. Besides, what goes on in your bedroom should be private. You shouldn't have to worry about your mother-in-law or anyone else butting in! I like to think that as educated, modern women, we can choose which traditional practices and which modern ones make sense for our children-to-be. In any case, it's your baby, not your mother-in-law's!

Liu Xiaoyuan: A Modern Skeptic

First of all, it's not true that a child belongs to a couple. Rather, a child is born into a family and finds his or her merit in a web of social relationships. As the mother-in-law and soon-to-be grandmother, it's your role to prepare the best path for the unborn child. When you're retired, you'll have lots of extra time, and you can aid your son and daughter-in-law, who will likely be working long hours. You should get up before the sun rises and go to the market in order to get the freshest produce for your family. When I go to the market early in the morning, I pick out the dirtiest greens and vegetables – so I can feel confident that no one has altered them to improve their appearance. When I get home, I wash everything in salt water to scrub off any dirt or chemicals, and then I prepare fresh meals with several dishes for my husband, daughter-in-law, and son to take to work and to enjoy in the evening.

However, my daughter-in-law, Yujin, often shops in the big supermarkets where the food has been grown with pesticides, and they scrub it clean with chemicals. She also prides herself on taking prenatal vitamins that she claims give her all the additional nutrition she needs, beyond what she eats. It's not that I'm against vitamins, it's just that with fruits, vegetables, and fish – all foods that ensure a healthy fetus – you know what you're getting. How do you know those pills aren't filled with sawdust or plastics that damage the body? There have been so many scandals in China! Instead of trusting those companies or someone else's ideas, it makes sense that we women draw upon the wisdom that has been handed down through the generations – like knowing that fat babies are healthy! If your daughter-in-law eats a healthy diet, her baby will come out fat and healthy.

When the baby is born, you will be the one who sleeps with him or her and brings the baby to your daughter-in-law to nurse. Nursing is really strenuous for Chinese women: our milk often takes time to come in, and we struggle with low supply. However, it's certainly the best thing for the baby. Still, when your daughter-in-law has to go back to work, usually a month or so after the baby is born, you will likely be your grandchild's full-time caregiver and may need to rely on formula during the day. As with pills and vitamins, there have been countless scandals about tainted formula and even babies who have died from it. If you can afford it, try to buy or import formula from the West – that is the only way you can trust that it is safe.

In my day, the extended family would rally together to care for the baby, especially when the parents were out in the fields working. But in your case, it may only be you and your husband who shoulder the burden of caring for this newborn. Relatives may send red envelopes with gifts of money, or they may show up with spirits to toast the new child, but take care to make sure the baby is sheltered and not exposed to the elements or evil spirits. Little ones are fragile, and not only their health, but also that of a mother who has just given birth, must be carefully guarded. In modern China, children's lives are even more precious, because in the city, couples are allowed to have only one child. As the mother-in-law, it is your job to ensure that your grandchild is given every chance in life to succeed and bring honor and prosperity to the family.

Xu Yujin: Pressure to Bear a Healthy Baby

Despite the prevalence of ultrasound technology, because of abuses to the former one-child policy, we have to wait until the baby is born to find out if it is a boy or a girl. My husband and I are torn over whether we prefer a girl or a boy. On the one hand, boys bring much joy to the family, and a boy is what my parents and my in-laws would prefer. Boys carry on the family line, they're legally bound to care for you in old age, and they have more opportunities for advancement in our society. But things are also changing. For instance, if it's a boy, you have to save to buy a house and maybe a car for him and his future wife, and these are so expensive. With a girl, you don't need to worry about those expenses, and you can put all the money toward her education. Girls have great opportunities these days; they are achieving more than boys in education, and often they even find it easier to find jobs, especially in the cities. Finally, although boys are traditionally required to care for their parents in old age, most people believe that girls have more sentimental feelings toward their parents and are more likely to contribute more money and provide more care. This is especially the way it is now that they don't always move so far away from home and can continue those relationships with their parents after they marry.

While it is of utmost importance that your baby is born healthy, it is hard to trust in either conventional wisdom or modern medicine. During your pregnancy, many relatives and family members may try to intervene to make sure that evil spirits are kept at bay while your child is being formed in the womb. They may go to a diviner to look at the dates of your pregnancy and the due date, in order to determine whether the child is a boy or a girl. They may give you lots of advice about how to take care of yourself to ensure that the baby is born healthy.

I feel a lot of pressure and a lot of worry, given the number of babies that are born with birth defects. I don't see many of them, but I hear stories about how coal pollution and other impurities in the environment are affecting the growth of unborn babies, and how the orphanages are all full of babies with ugly deformities, struggling to survive. I shudder to think what I would do if my baby were born with a deformity or a disability. People with disabilities in China aren't treated very well and have few opportunities. Plus, my husband and I are barely making it financially as it is, and there's hardly any government help for families with disabled children. I don't know how we would raise a child like that!

It's not good to think about these things, to be stressed when you're pregnant. Although I don't necessarily believe in it, sometimes, to assuage my fears, I do stop by the local temple on my way home from work and burn some incense and pray to the gods and the ancestors. It can't hurt.

Liu Xiaoyuan: Country to City Wisdom

I gave birth to Hou Limin in the countryside where there were only traveling doctors and no hospitals. As I squatted and labored for hours for him to come into the world, I was surrounded by a few female relatives. My husband was allowed to bring me a drink of warm water, but mostly he stayed away from the women's work of birthing.

Of course, my daughter-in-law will give birth in the hospital, which is safer. They will likely schedule a C-section for her. The doctors are so busy these days, almost every birth is scheduled, and C-sections are considered less risky, and are often preferred. I always thought it was best to let labor progress on its own, but I'm glad, for the baby's sake, that if there are complications, there will be doctors around and machines to help the baby breathe. It almost seems as though the number of sick babies these days is going up and up, which doesn't make sense in a world with so much medicine and technology. Perhaps we just see people with disabilities more now, whereas in my day, families used to shroud them from scrutiny and society.

Your daughter-in-law will stay in the hospital for a few days after the baby is born, and while she's away, you will need to clean and cook. When she comes home, prepare a wealth of healing soups – thick soup made with black chicken, pigs' feet soup with peanuts, and fish soup – to help restore her nutrients and encourage her milk to come in. Make sure she avoids rich meat and other forbidden foods, and that she drinks the warm broth that is cleansing to her body, as the old blood leaves her body and the new blood refreshes her. It is essential to make time for this healing process in order that balance be restored to the body. If she eats the wrong foods, she could be subject to a fever and chills. In any event, she will be exhausted, so keep the baby while she sleeps, and bring it to her only when the baby needs to nurse.

Your daughter-in-law should honor the tradition of sitting at home or "lying in" for a month without going out and without showering, in order to find restoration for her body. She will be very weak and will need your care. She should avoid cool air, cold water, and even brushing her teeth, as cool liquids can threaten her health and recovery. You should prepare a diet of lush greens, lean meat, and chicken broth to restore her health. You don't want her to have anything too oily or greasy while her body is healing. As outside air can chill her weak body, she should remain inside resting. Her blood will gradually replenish itself through the nutrients of these healthy foods, and her strength will return to her as she remains sheltered from the dangers of the outside world that could pollute her frail body.

Keep visitors at a minimum and make sure the new mother gets plenty of rest. If she doesn't observe this tradition of "lying in," she could become sick, or sickness could come to her baby. Nowadays, many young women feel too restless to want to rest for a full month. But they forget that they will have their entire lifetimes to care for their babies.

You should begin to toilet train the baby as soon as possible, watching his or her facial expressions to determine when he or she is pooping, and making shushing sounds to encourage him or her to pee when held over the potty. A baby's genitals need to breathe, so the best ways to toilet train are the traditional ones in which a baby wears split-pants, with a cloth in between to catch the excrement if possible. Since most houses are tiled and it's totally appropriate for babies to pee over a tree or poop on newspaper beside the road, don't worry too much about accidents, as these are part of learning. Baby poop and pee aren't dirty, they're part of life, and babies will quickly learn how to care for themselves if you reinforce these traditional ways of toilet training.

Xu Yujin: Loving out Loud

Of course, I've never given birth before, and I know it's strenuous for the body, but I can't imagine I'll want to be shut up in our tiny apartment for a whole month afterwards. I understand that certain foods are most beneficial during this time, but I think the tradition of not showering for a month or not brushing your teeth is disgusting and unhygienic! My friends will certainly want to visit, and I won't want to be all greasy and smelly when they arrive! I know my mother-in-law won't approve, but the health of babies and mothers is not as fragile as it was in times of poor sanitation and medicine, and we're not living in the village. In those times, people even avoided calling a baby "cute" for fear that the gods would covet the child and whisk it away to death. But those were just superstitions meant to account for the high infant mortality rates in a premodern world. Times have changed!

For instance, especially when your baby is a newborn, you should feel free to use diapers. I've told my mother-in-law that disposable diapers will save her much heartache, at least during the night. Instead of having to wake up every few hours to take the baby to the bathroom to relieve himself, your mother-in-law can let the baby pee or poop in the diapers and simply change them in the morning. When people lived in dirt houses and didn't find excrement so filthy, it wasn't a big deal for a baby to leave poop or pee wherever, but if you live in a high-rise apartment, this traditional way of toilet training is impractical and unhygienic. Many grandparents shudder at the expense of plastic diapers. People who have lived through times of scarcity save every *mao* and will often make you feel guilty for buying anything beyond the bare basics, but times are changing!

Indeed, babies and children need much more than just the bare necessities. Although our parents understand and are concerned with the physical needs of children, they don't seem to acknowledge the psychological side of childrearing. When we were growing up, our parents dealt very harshly with us – they rarely praised us and were constantly criticizing what they considered our lax work ethic and our low level of achievements. They never verbalized their love for us, expecting it to be evident through their devotion and sacrifice on our behalf.

But for our generation, romantic love and self-expression are really important. And even though older people often cuddle and cradle babies, they also tease them by calling them "bad," "ugly," or "rotten." Your child should grow up in an environment free from these types of criticisms, which can damage a child's self-esteem. Older people claim they use those expressions to show their love for their children, but when I was growing up, I longed for my parents to express that love out loud.

Liu Xiaoyuan: The Value of Discipline

In my own childhood, I experienced a lot of hardship. When we did backbreaking work in the communes, those lessons of endurance and persistence taught me the value of "eating bitterness." Not knowing what was in store for my children, I tried to prepare them for the harshness of life by learning to stomach bitterness as well. Between my husband and me, there have always been few words, but we demonstrate our love and devotion for one another through our actions. When it comes to children, you cannot expect them to develop respect or obedience toward their parents if those parents are constantly coddling them and praising them. Instead, you should criticize your child out of love and respect so that the child grows to be humble and strong.

Even nowadays, when I argue with Hou Limin or Xu Yujin and offer my advice, I do so because I care. If I didn't care, why would I bother to speak up? Arguing is what parents and children, especially mothers-in-law and daughters-in-law, do: we were born into these roles, and so we live them out – sometimes painfully, but also dutifully. No words I could say could demonstrate greater love than my commitment to care for my son and to raise his children.

In some ways I'm torn. I always looked forward to spoiling my grandchildren, but I fear their own parents are already too spoiled. Knowing that I'm the one who's with them day and night makes me feel strongly that I need to form them much as I did with Limin – with ample discipline and critique. I may not say it ever, but of course I'm proud of the man Limin has become and the excellent woman he has married, but I'm also nervous about how we can all make it in this big city with big expenses and the allure of big money. If I fear those things for us adults, how much more must I strive to protect and train this new baby to care for and love his family?

Xu Yujin: Modern Childhood

While the older generation bemoans that their childhood was nothing but bitterness and suffering, parents in my generation have it hard, too: our childhood was lost to books and pressure to succeed, and now we "only children" are struggling to balance the needs of our aging parents and our growing children. They call this modern phenomenon "4-2-1": four grandparents, two parents, and one child. While it's unique for a child to have the attention of six adults, it's also a profound pressure for the responsibility of this child and four aging parents to be on the shoulders of just two people. As you rear your children, you'll want to monitor your parents and in-laws closely to make sure they don't spoil or discipline them in ways that you wouldn't approve of. Modern China is not the China of their youth.

You need to balance the desire your family has for your child to succeed with safeguarding his or her childhood. Childhood is fleeting and priceless. If you don't negotiate with your family, and against the pressures of the school and the market, your child will "eat bitterness" – an experience that is best avoided. While older folks believe that bitterness builds character, I want to believe that there is a middle ground wherein children can learn and grow without either being spoiled or experiencing unnecessary hardship. These are the gifts of living in modern China – a land of much competition, but also much opportunity.

A World of Babies

It seems that nearly every nation heaps its future aspirations upon its children. In China, despite all the turmoil and change, those aspirations are still heavily negotiated within the family. Sometimes the increasing conflict over childrearing looks like a sign of strife or discord amongst family members, but ultimately I think we're all struggling together, not so much against one another, to raise our children in a different and complicated world. The sacrifices and the disagreements are all made worthy in the successes of our children and the increasing prosperity of each generation. Even though we often disagree, in the good fortune of our children we rejoice together.

CHAPTER 4

A Baby to Tie You to Place

Childrearing Advice from a Palestinian Mother Living under Occupation

Bree Akesson

A BRIEF HISTORY OF PALESTINE

Known to many ancient empires, the region often termed "Palestine" that lies between the Mediterranean Sea and the Jordan River was conquered by the Romans during the first century BCE. Derived from the Greek *Palaestina*, or Land of the Philistines, the name refers to the seafaring Philistines who settled along the coastal lands north of Egypt and along the Mediterranean Sea around the twelfth century BCE. Throughout recorded history, major religious events have taken place in Palestine, and the land continues to be held sacred by Jews, Christians, and Muslims. In the modern period, the contested claim that the lands of Palestine belong unilaterally to one of these religions has contributed to a decades-long struggle for control of land in the region.

Indeed, for almost a century, Israelis and Palestinians have been at the center of one of the most bitterly contentious and protracted land-based conflicts on earth. The conflict escalated in the early 1900s when, in response to anti-Semitic policies and pogroms in eastern Europe, young Jews began migrating to

Palestine. In 1917, the British government issued the Balfour Declaration, named for the British Foreign Secretary who supported a homeland for the diasporic Jewish people in Palestine. During that time, armed struggle over control of Palestine intensified, accompanied by political maneuvering over the fate of both Israel and the Palestinian people.

The armed struggle culminated in the 1948 Arab–Israeli War, which began after the State of Israel was officially formed in 1948, and resulted in the invasion of Israel by the surrounding Arab states of Egypt, Iraq, and Syria. Due to the violence, a large number of Palestinians left, fled, or were expelled from their homes, in a process to which Palestinians refer as *al-Nakba*, meaning "the catastrophe." Since then, Israelis and Palestinians have engaged in a seemingly intractable conflict over control of land and resources.

The West Bank, the Gaza Strip, and East Jerusalem – which are collectively termed "Palestine" – were claimed by Israel in 1967, marking what some have identified as the longest military occupation in modern history. As a response to growing frustration with Israeli policies to build more settlements in Gaza and the West Bank rather than negotiate for an independent Palestinian state, Palestinians initiated two major Palestinian uprisings (*intifadas* – Arabic for "shaking off"). Starting in 1987, the first *intifada* was characterized by Palestinian-driven, non-violent, civil disobedience and boycotts against Israel, and was known by Palestinians as "the popular struggle." The first *intifada* ended in 1993 with the signing of the Oslo Accords between the Israeli government and the Palestinian Liberation Organization (PLO), which in 1994 was formally established as the Palestinian Authority (PA), and which has since been increasingly criticized by many for serving as an extension of the Israeli occupation and policing their own people through extra-judicial means. The second *intifada* (2000–05) was more devastating and was marked by higher levels of violence perpetrated by both Palestinians and the Israeli army.

The occupation of key Palestinian lands by Israel, deemed illegal by the United Nations General Assembly, has greatly contributed to ongoing violence in the region, with tens of thousands of both Israelis and Palestinians injured or dead. Israeli-imposed restrictions on Palestinian movement – enacted in the name of Israeli security – are a byproduct of the occupation, and include a separation wall, checkpoints, and a permit system, as well as the demolition of Palestinian homes.

Perhaps the greatest source of violence, and the most formidable barrier to peace in the region, comes from the group of Israeli "settlements" constructed on Palestinian land in violation of international humanitarian law according to the United Nations General Assembly and the Security Council. According to Article 49 of the Fourth Geneva Convention, which was ratified by Israel in 1951, "The Occupying Power shall not deport or transfer parts of its own civilian population into the territory it occupies." Furthermore, the Hague Regulations prohibit an occupying power from undertaking permanent changes in the occupied areas unless these changes are due to military needs, or unless they are undertaken for the benefit of the local population. Despite these international norms and the decrease in public support for "settlements" even among Israelis, the Israel government continues to sponsor the development of settlements in the West Bank (although it previously dismantled others in the Gaza Strip). Alienated from their land, and confined for years by restrictions to their movement and freedom, Palestinian families must negotiate everyday boundaries, borders, and barriers within their homeland.

THE PALESTINIAN FAMILY: CULTURE AND CUSTOMS

Family is a prominent feature of everyday life in Palestine. The *'a'ila* is the small or "nuclear" family, represented by a father, mother, and children. The *'a'ila* is complemented by the *hamula*, a large, "extended" family represented by countless uncles, aunts, cousins, and others who are more distantly related. Palestinians tend to maintain very strong ties with many in their *hamula*, even though members of a given *hamula* can number in the thousands. In many cases, clusters of related nuclear families live near each other, contributing to much daily interaction and socialization as well as security. In fact, over 90 percent of Palestinians in the southern West Bank, and 80 percent of Palestinians in Gaza, share their residences with relatives beyond those in the *'a'ila*. The atmosphere of these family-based communities is village-like, with families sharing meals if they live in the same building, and women helping each other with domestic responsibilities. However, not all family members are able to live close to one another due to various factors such as housing costs, location of schools, and place of employment, as well as the overarching occupation of the region by Israel.

Palestinians' recent political engagements with Israel have alternately challenged and strengthened family ties. Connection with one's family constitutes the one traditional structure that has survived *al-Nakba*. Whether within refugee camps far from their home villages or within the broader Palestinian diaspora, Palestinians continue to live, work, and socialize within the confines of the *hamula*.

How "family" is defined has a great impact on the way that Palestinians give meaning to the everyday occupation by Israel of what they see as their land and, as an extension, to the multiple meanings of "place." In fact, the definition of "family" determines Palestinians' levels and structures of mobility, as "family" commonly motivates what are often lengthy and difficult journeys within the West Bank. However, the subject of what actually constitutes a "family" remains a topic of debate for both Israelis and Palestinians. In its policies related to family reunification between family members inside and outside Palestine, Israel insists that the definition of "family" constitutes only *'a'ila*, whereas Palestinians have emphasized the importance of *hamula* in addition to *'a'ila* as central to Arab culture and practice. In any case, since the start of the second *intifada* in 2000, all family reunification requests have been frozen, with Israel citing security risks. The combination of the definition of "family" and the policy freeze threatens family life for Palestinians, at once severing connections geographically, socially, and emotionally. Families are unable to maintain solidarity when each unit is separated geographically and holds

Figure 4.1 This mural on the wall of the Balata refugee camp in Nablus (West Bank) reminds residents of their suffering.
Photograph by Bree Akesson.

onto different travel documents. Such a disjointed social environment has a negative effect on children when families are unable to provide for children's needs for care and support. A related consequence of the recent Israeli policy canceling "family reunification" is the fragmentation of Palestinian places, specifically the home and neighborhood community.

Palestinian families are currently experiencing the most serious threat to their existence since the 1948 *Nakba*. The ongoing Israeli occupation of the West Bank and the annexation of East Jerusalem weakens the Palestinian family by sharply reducing household income, creating widespread poverty (see Figure 4.1). With a fragmented social welfare system attributable to both the occupation and internal deficiencies within the Palestinian Authority, Palestinians often rely on the *hamula* to fill the gaps. Many men – who traditionally see themselves as the economic mainstay of the family – have felt compelled to leave behind their wives and children to find work in the oil-rich Gulf States, sending home money to support the *hamula*, but in the process further weakening the economic situation in the West Bank and East Jerusalem. In turn, the *hamula* pools its resources to provide for family needs such as medical expenses and education. However, Israeli territorial policies such as the checkpoints, separation barrier, and permit system isolate families from their extended kin and social networks, leaving them dependent on their typically insufficient household resources. In addition to these threats to daily livelihoods, families contend with physical threats to their lives posed by Israeli settlers and the Israeli military.

Conflict between Palestinians constitutes a further source of insecurity for Palestinian families and marks a breakdown in Palestinian communities. When the Palestinian organization of Hamas was elected to form a government in January 2006, there was a full-blown conflict among Palestinians, leaving 161 Palestinians dead and another 700 injured. In the following year, 353 Palestinians were killed by other Palestinians. While the level of violence has decreased, Hamas and its political rival organization, Fatah, have sometimes continued to target each other's activists, leaders, and supporters.

Some Palestinian civilians have also been targeted by Palestinian entities such as the Palestinian Authority, Fatah, or Hamas, on suspicion of collaboration with Israel. Since the beginning of the first *intifada*, dozens of Palestinian civilians have been abducted, tortured, and killed after being accused of being "collaborators." And since 2007, Hamas has executed fourteen people, including six "convicted spies," while in 2013, the Palestinian Authority condemned a member of the Palestinian security forces to death for being a "collaborator" with Israel. In some cases, human rights organizations have documented instances when Palestinians were pressured to collaborate with Israeli authorities in order to receive permits necessary to visit family, earn a livelihood, or obtain medical treatment. However, "collaboration" has been broadly defined to include directly assisting Israel, agreeing with Israel's political positions, brokering and selling land to Israeli authorities, failing to participate in strikes, and marketing banned Israeli merchandise. In some cases, "collaboration" has included acts that are deemed immoral by the Palestinian government, such as prostitution and drug dealing. Families of accused "collaborators" face extreme stigma and discrimination in their communities. Children of "collaborators" are often shunned by their *hamula* and the broader Palestinian community.

Despite these challenges, traditional customs and ceremonies, as well as physical proximity to one another, continue to bind members of the *hamula* together. Marriage is often central to a family's survival, whether in times of crisis or in more relaxed circumstances. Palestinian youth make the decision about who to marry, but it is important that members of the *'a'ila* are consulted in the decision-making process. A wedding is a major event in Palestinian society. It is rare for adult children to leave home before marriage. Usually one married son stays with his parents while the other married children live nearby. After marriage, women tend to join their husbands' families, although spouses are often members of the same *hamula*, or at least from the same village or neighborhood.

Palestinian society is young. The majority of the population (55 percent) is under twenty-four years old, and the average age is twenty-two. Families have an average of four to five children. Palestinian children tend to be raised with a keen sense of responsibility to family members. Although much of this responsibility often falls upon the oldest son, it can also fall upon a child who is more financially stable, or upon the family as a whole.

Members of a Palestinian family often feel that their "honor" is reflected in the "virtuous" behavior of its women, with "modesty" and "chastity" among the key traditional values. More recently, the notion of "honor" has expanded to include other elements: education, connection with the land, *sumud* (steadfastness), and service to the Palestinian people and nation-state. Moreover, the Israeli occupation of traditionally Palestinian territories, along with modernization and increased education levels, has changed Palestinian customs. Forced migration from historic Palestine, loss of land, and increased poverty – coupled with the more welcome change of increased education levels – have all challenged the maintenance of traditional values and customs.

The following "imagined" but ethnographically grounded childrearing guide is presented through the eyes of a modern Palestinian mother of two children. This fictional advice-giver is an amalgam of several Palestinian mothers I have met during my research with children and families living in the West Bank and East Jerusalem from 2010 to 2012.

A BABY TO TIE YOU TO PLACE: CHILDREARING ADVICE FROM A PALESTINIAN MOTHER LIVING UNDER OCCUPATION

About the Author

I am a proud Palestinian Muslim woman, very much connected to my culture, my religion, and my country. At the same time, I am also my own person: I feel comfortable challenging any norms of Palestinian society that I think are outdated and irrelevant.

Although I have lived most of my life within a large Palestinian city in the northern West Bank, I was educated in North America, where I earned master's and doctorate degrees in engineering, thanks to my husband and family, who have always supported me in my choice of education and career. Of course, although it is not always the case, there are many Palestinian men who support the education of their wives and daughters. Because of this, Palestinian women are considered to be some of the most educated women in the Middle East.

I now work as a professor of engineering at a Palestinian university. I am married and have two children: a ten-year-old boy and a one-year-old girl. If you do the math, you will notice that there were nine years between my two children; as I will explain below, this is unusual for Palestinian women, who often have as many children – especially boys – as possible.

What follows is advice – and, I would like to think, wisdom – that I will give to my daughter when she becomes a wife and mother. However, my words are not only intended for my daughter. For I hope that others – girls and boys, women and men, mothers and fathers both from within and outside our Palestinian culture – can learn something about the importance of the family, and of place, in childrearing.

In addition to my own experiences with pregnancy, childbirth, and childrearing, I draw from my family history, so that my daughter can know where she comes from and what her options are. The traditions that I speak about are practiced in my husband's and my communities. As with many Palestinian women, my experience of raising my children has drawn from a combination of my own upbringing (in a city) and from my husband's (in a village). Yet, our particular practices may not reflect all Palestinian traditions, which can be diverse and broad.

THE IMPORTANCE OF CHILDREN: CONNECTING WITH PLACE

Before becoming a mother, I wanted to have children in my life, just like any other person in the world. I believe that it is part of our nature as humans to raise children. Even before you get married, this notion of the importance of having children will surround you and push you to have them. Some women especially love children, but even for those who do not, the desire to be a mother is very important, and certainly a focus of nearly all Palestinian women's lives.

As a Palestinian woman, it is important for you to have children in order for the Palestinian community to continue to grow strong. It is also important to continue to grow your family to connect you more to our lands in Palestine, from which we have been displaced for several decades. In other words, your children will become a way for you to connect to the place of Palestine. Because your children will be not just *from* Palestine, but also *of* Palestine, you will see Palestine in their eyes. Therefore, like me, wherever you are living, you will be connected to the place of Palestine through your children.

Even throughout upswings in violence as a result of the Israeli occupation, Palestinian women these days seem to have many more babies than in earlier years. During the second *intifada*, when I was pregnant with your brother, so many women around me were also pregnant. Maybe having sex was a way to address the boredom of the long curfews! But for some, it was also a way to resist the occupation – by having more children, or to be comforted by having a family. Before I was pregnant with your brother, I never thought that I should avoid bringing a child into a world that was affected by the violence of the second *intifada*. Rather, I thought, *If I become pregnant with a son now, how can I protect him and help him to live a good life?* Of course, I worried how I would protect my children after they were born, but this fear did not prevent me from having children.

The Value of Having Many Children

Women who become wives and mothers want to gain the respect of the *hamula* – and to be respected, you must have a boy. The more boys you have in your family, the stronger your family, and the stronger the *hamula*. Many people also think that you have to have many boys to protect and defend you, especially while living under Israeli occupation of our land. Moreover, the more sons you have, the higher your family status in the community. As you know, I myself have had only two children – you and your brother – and many of my neighbors and relatives see me as unusual. But having only two children was not my choice. Rather, I have had a medical condition that has made it difficult for me to have children. So, if you are the mother of only one boy, as I am – even if you have several girls – you may not have high status within the *hamula,* or become well-established in the community.

Even though the number of sons you have especially decides women's status in our culture, it affects men's status as well. In Palestinian Bedouin communities, for example, a father of many boys sits in the middle of the tent. By contrast, a father of, say, five girls and one boy does not sit in the middle of the tent, because having only one son means he has low status within the *hamula*.

I speak from experience. Before you were born, other women could not understand why I wasn't having more children, since

I only had one boy. In fact, they used the number of children they had to balance the status of power between us. They would say, *She is well educated, but we have more children*. So, women – even those who are educated, as I am – want to have more boys, to maintain high status. I have definitely had moments where I felt a pressure to have more children. But considering the medical challenges I have had, I have come to realize how satisfied I am focusing on raising the two of you.

In my mother's generation, it was even more important for a married woman to have many children. That would ensure that her husband would not divorce her. Having many boys was even better: her husband was less likely to divorce her if he had high status in the *hamula* because of the number of sons he had. Having many boys also means that the boys will inherit the family's money and status when the grandfather or father dies. So, having many children, especially sons, means that your children will also protect you by supporting you financially.

The number of boys you have in your family also affects other family members beyond you and your husband. If a married woman has many brothers, she will be treated better by her husband's family, because they know that her brothers will protect her. If she is not treated well, maybe she will return to her brothers to protect her. So women try to have many boys because of that as well. Moreover, if, God forbid – *Naudhubillah!* – your husband is violent towards you, your grown sons will stop him. My mother had many boys, and the community thought that she and her family were strong. Nobody said anything against her because they knew her boys would protect her.

Palestinians don't worry about having too many babies, even if they are poor. A proverb explains: *For each baby, God will provide*. In other words, people believe that God will send us the material and social means by which to raise the child. My mother didn't have a lot of money, but she still had eight children, including myself. She didn't have a good relationship with my father. To protect herself, she had lots of children, because she believed that if her husband didn't treat her well or take care of her, then at least her children would treat her well and take care of her. As your own grandmother's experience shows, having lots of children, especially sons, becomes a very valuable currency that a mother can use for respect, status, and protection.

Unfortunately, there are several situations in Palestinian society that may influence a husband to take a second wife – something I hope you will never have to experience. Palestinian marriage is governed by customary, orthodox Sunni Islamic law, which explicitly permits polygamy. However, at the time of marriage, a woman is allowed to stipulate in the marriage contract that her husband shall not take another wife while married to her. If he subsequently breaks that part of the contract, she can legally seek a divorce. There are no recent statistics, but in the 1990s, I've read that about 4.5 percent of families in the West Bank practiced polygamy. Even though it's not a popular practice, and women are allowed to seek legal recourse, polygamy can be heartbreaking for a first wife, leaving her in psychological and economic distress. Polygamy is also stressful for children, who tend to become angry with their fathers and struggle to support their mothers emotionally and financially. If the first wife has many children with this husband, at least she remains the mother of his children, including any boys. Therefore, the first wife still has this status, even if her husband takes a second wife. Moreover, the husband's first son with his first wife is still considered his first son, even if he has taken another wife and has more sons with her. But we are a modern family, and I do not expect this to be an issue for you.

GETTING PREGNANT

When your grandmother was young, Palestinian women did not use any reliable means of birth control, and a woman had a child every year or two. Today, our families are smaller, since we women now use birth control methods such as the pill and calendar-based methods, so we have children every three years or so.

But marriage certainly encourages pressure to have a child. About a month after you get married, women will consistently start asking you, *Is there anything on the way?* This definitely puts you under stress from your husband's family and the *hamula*. Many Palestinian women prefer to have a baby within their first year of being married so that they don't feel that pressure. Since I have a medical condition that makes it difficult for me to have children, I was very pleased that I became pregnant within my first year of marriage and did not have to face that pressure.

If you have trouble becoming pregnant, as I did, you may want to consult a *dayat* – one of those independent midwives who learned the secrets of the trade while apprenticing with another traditional midwife. In Palestine, few women consult a *dayat* any more. In the 1990s, new policies discouraged home deliveries, and pregnant women started to visit obstetricians more than midwives. By 2004, only 3.2 percent of births in the West Bank took place at home. But the *dayat* is still respected, because she is so patient and good at what she does. And more recently, women have begun returning to consult a *dayat*. For example, two of your aunts have used a female *dayat* rather than an obstetrician – who is often male – because they feel that they get a lot more support from the *dayat*. In the hospital, a woman will give birth in a room with three or four other laboring women. So there is more comfort, privacy, and individualized attention if a woman gives birth at home.

The *dayat* can even help you get pregnant by massaging your belly to encourage conception. Sometimes, your insides might be out of order, and in massaging your belly, she may put everything back in place. When you are menstruating, the *dayat* might also place a jar with a lit candle on your belly, to warm your insides, increase blood circulation, and prepare the uterus for conception. And she may tell you and your husband to eat a spoonful of honey with raw nuts – not roasted – to help get pregnant. It's really amazing what the *dayat* can do! It worked for me when I was having trouble getting pregnant the first time. The *dayat* put her pointer finger on my belly button and felt a pulse there. Now, you may think that these techniques are not scientifically based. But I asked my doctor about them, and he told me that a *dayat*'s techniques can help promote blood circulation in the body, which is good for conception in women who are not yet pregnant.

A World of Babies

Pregnancy

I got pregnant with your brother about six months after your father and I were married. But I was already twenty-eight years old, because I was very focused on my career as an engineer. Even though she'd been married to your uncle for less time than your father and I were married, your aunt also became pregnant around the same time, when she was nineteen. She told everyone about her pregnancy right away, whereas I waited a bit longer to tell the family. That meant that our female relatives were saying, *We don't want this one* (your aunt) *to be pregnant, we want the other one* (me!) *to be pregnant*. They wanted the *old* one to be pregnant, not the *young* one, because they were afraid that I didn't have much time left! They used my age against me, which hurt me at the time. But I also understand that they were just worried that, at twenty-eight years old, I might already be too old to have children. For us Palestinians, twenty-eight is very, very late to begin to have children. But I actually *was* pregnant. It's not that I didn't want to tell them I was pregnant. It was just that my work at an engineering firm kept me very busy, so telling everyone about my pregnancy was not a priority for me. In fact, I was so concerned with my work and other daily activities that I didn't even think too much about the second *intifada* when I was pregnant with your brother. But once I told everyone in the *hamula* that I was pregnant, everything was fine. And I delivered your brother twenty days before your aunt delivered your cousin. So that gave me status within the family.

During pregnancy, your family and community will take care of you, especially in terms of what you eat, and even more so if your eating habits change, as mine did. Eating habits vary from woman to woman. For me, I was very sensitive to smell, and I couldn't eat anything that I had cooked myself. But I usually loved the food that other people cooked – especially if my mother cooked it! There are also some foods that you should avoid when you are pregnant. For example, in the early months, dates can cause you to go into labor early. On the other hand, eating dates during the last month of pregnancy is recommended to *encourage* labor.

A Baby to Tie You to Place

When you are pregnant, you may think that you're just dealing with a baby, but you're also dealing with all of the relationships within your family. When you become pregnant, I'll stay with you and your husband. That is the mother's role: to take care of her daughter when she is pregnant. Later, your mother-in-law's role will be to take care of the baby once he's born. In some cases, your mother and mother-in-law will both want to take care of you, and this can produce a power game, as both want the privilege of helping to get you food and to take care of the baby. Your mother may disapprove of advice that your mother-in-law gives, and vice versa. You may find that they're fighting, which can cause you stress. In my case, I didn't want to hurt their feelings. If my mother told me something that contradicted advice that my mother-in-law gave me, I just listened to both of them and didn't mention the contradiction. And to prevent them from competing for my attention, I told them that I wanted to do some things for myself, such as feeding, changing, and bathing the baby.

When I was pregnant with your brother, I was living with your father's family outside the big city, because there was a lot of violence in the city due to the second *intifada*. I didn't want to travel very much, because I was afraid of getting stuck at a "checkpoint" – one of those barriers manned by Israeli soldiers or border police to monitor our movements within the West Bank and the border spaces between Palestine and Israel. I'd heard numerous stories of pregnant women who were stuck at checkpoints and had to give birth there! During a four-year period during the second *intifada*, sixty-one pregnant and laboring women were refused passage through a checkpoint and had to give birth there, without any medical help; thirty-six babies died as a result.

In fact, when I was in the first trimester with your brother, I was once waiting at a checkpoint inside a taxi bus, and the Israeli soldiers started throwing tear gas. I'd heard many stories of women having a miscarriage after being exposed to tear gas, and I was very afraid that I would lose the baby from smelling the gas. My fellow passengers knew that I was pregnant, and they yelled at the soldiers to stop because they had a pregnant woman with them. Fortunately, I was okay.

There was another time toward the end of Ramadan when I was five months pregnant with your brother and wanted to visit your father. At the time, he was working in another city, and I wanted to break the fast together with him, during the Eid festival at the end of Ramadan. Your father told me not to come, but I decided to go anyway, because I missed him. I was walking alone along a mountain path that would take me to where the taxis were located when I came upon a checkpoint. The Israeli soldiers manning the checkpoint refused to let me pass. They told me that I would have to go all the way around the mountain. I told the soldiers that I was pregnant, and it was too dangerous for me and the baby to go around the mountain. Walking through the checkpoint would take me ten minutes, while walking around the mountain would take me three hours! They still refused to let me pass, and so I just sat there and told them that if anything happened to me or my baby, they would be responsible. This scared the soldiers, so they spoke to their supervisor, who came to speak with me. He said, *This time we will allow you to pass, but don't come again to this place.* It was scary for me, because I was alone and unfamiliar with the area. But I knew I had to do something to protect myself and your brother. After those two incidents, I decided it was best to limit my movements and stay in one place.

Because of the checkpoints and roadblocks from the Israeli occupation, my mother who was living in another city couldn't always travel to take care of me, as she should have done, and I missed her support and care. Your father's mother and our other female relatives cared for me and made me plenty of food, but, because my mother didn't make it, I didn't want to eat a lot of it. Instead, my mother would send me food packages through messengers, and when we spoke on the phone, she'd tell me to go buy a specific food. I always tried to do as she advised, while still respecting your father's family's advice.

Your father's family took care of me this whole time, making sure that I didn't do too much work, which they believe is especially important during the first pregnancy. Even though

A Baby to Tie You to Place

I was still going to work at the engineering firm every day, when I was at home in the morning and evening my in-laws didn't allow me to carry anything, walk around a lot, or do any hard housework. But I didn't like just sitting around, and I didn't believe that all that rest was necessary. My own mother – your grandmother – worked during all her eight pregnancies, and she was fine. In fact, my advice is: near the end of your pregnancy, you should start to walk around a lot, and do exercises where you stand up and sit down repeatedly, to help get you ready for contractions. This is much better than just sitting around doing nothing.

There are many traditions that predict if your baby will be a boy or a girl. If your belly is very round and big, they say you're having a girl. If your belly doesn't get very round, but just sticks out in front of you, you'll have a boy. Also, if the baby kicks a lot, it's a boy. If you start sleeping a lot, you're carrying a girl. If you have heartburn, you're carrying a boy. Well, even though these are common beliefs in Palestine, I don't believe them, and I don't think that the doctors believe them, either. Besides, in my experience, your brother didn't kick, but you kicked a lot – which is the opposite of what the traditions say. So, you can listen politely if your mother-in-law or other relatives claim they can predict your baby's gender, but I wouldn't put too much trust in these predictions.

Childbirth

I know that I told you not to eat dates during your pregnancy, but near the end of your pregnancy, you should actually start eating a lot of dates to help with your contractions. The role of dates in pregnancy is based on the Qur'an, which tells the story of Maryam's birth of the Prophet 'Isa. Maryam was in the painful throes of childbirth when Allah guided her towards a date tree and placed a stream at her feet. Allah told her that she should eat the freshly ripe dates and drink from the stream. As a result, she gave birth in the best possible circumstances.

Even though I went to the hospital and did not use a *dayat* when I gave birth to your brother, I want to share both traditions with you, so you'll be informed about the different experiences. When you go into labor, one or two of your female relatives will either take you to the hospital or, if you're staying at home, go to fetch the *dayat*, so it becomes an event just for women. *Insha'allah* – God willing – if I'm still living, I'll be with you. The men will be asked to leave the house if you have a home birth; and if you go to the hospital, the men will stay at home. Except for girls over the age of fourteen, the children will also be sent to stay at an aunt's house. Unfortunately, my mother wasn't with me during my first labor because of the political situation. With all the Israeli checkpoints and roadblocks due to the second *intifada*, my mother couldn't get to me when I was giving birth to your brother in the hospital. I really missed her support then!

If you decide to give birth at home, the *dayat* will come to your home and stay as long as it takes to deliver your baby. A *dayat* provides a lot of emotional support and will make you feel comfortable. Instead of using a surgical cut to facilitate the birth, as they often do in the hospital, the *dayat* massages olive oil around the opening where the baby comes out; this will stretch the cervix and make the process less painful for you. The *dayat*'s technique will allow you to take your time delivering your baby in a comfortable way and will reduce the chance of you tearing or needing an episiotomy, which can be more common if you give birth in a hospital. The use of olive oil isn't only practical, but also symbolic. Our people's connection to olive oil is strong, as olive trees represent a historical, spiritual, and economic tie to the land.

Once the baby is born, the *dayat* will cover your baby's body in heavily salted water: this will help your baby resist illnesses and fevers. Then she'll give you the thick drink we call *muhli*, made with coconut and cinnamon. This will help you deliver the placenta and get rid of any extra blood inside your body. Your female relatives will also give you chicken and lamb soup to eat, because it's very rich in protein, which helps replace the blood you lost from childbirth.

The *dayat* and your female relatives will encourage you to breastfeed as soon as possible. They'll give you milk to drink, to help your body produce milk for your baby. They may also give you a drink made from a little black seed called *kizhah*, which they'll crush, boil, and make into a drink that tastes as sweet as a dessert. *Kizhah* is very rich and has a lot of oil in it, which will also help you produce milk for the baby. However, if you're feeling sad for any reason, you shouldn't breastfeed until you are feeling better, as your sadness may transfer to your baby through your breastmilk. I know that not feeling sad is a challenge in a place like Palestine, where many people – especially mothers – struggle with depression because of the political situation. Nevertheless, when breastfeeding, you should try your best to embrace the joy of having your children, despite the challenges facing our people. And avoid having any fights with your husband while breastfeeding, because being upset in any way may be bad for your breastmilk. I've heard stories of mother's milk drying up from sadness. One of your uncles died just before his wife (your aunt) gave birth to your cousin, and she wasn't allowed to breastfeed until her sorrow passed.

Generally, the advice I heard is to breastfeed as long as the baby wants to, and we Palestinian women tend to breastfeed up to two years. Today, young women don't want to breastfeed for a long time, perhaps because it's a challenge for them to juggle work and motherhood. Your own brother stopped breastfeeding at five months, because I was struggling to work and breastfeed him at the same time. My workplace gave me a one-hour break during the day, when I'd rush to your brother's daycare center to breastfeed him. But, for some reason, this became physically difficult, so I started to give him formula. When I was breastfeeding you, my schedule was more flexible, because I was a graduate student and had a flexible schedule, and I was able to breastfeed you for twenty-two months.

Breastfeeding is a good way to ensure the health of your baby. It can also complement some herbal or other treatments. For example, if you think your baby has a pain in his belly, you should boil some local herbs of cumin or sage in water, drink the mixture, and then breastfeed the baby. I've found that these herbs are very effective in helping to ease a baby's discomfort.

The Postpartum Period: Forty Days to Protect Mother and Baby

Even in these difficult times, the birth of a baby is a particularly joyous occasion for Palestinians. Your family, friends, and neighbors will visit you and your husband to offer their love, support, and best wishes. Family members will softly recite the *athan* call to Muslim prayer into your baby's new ears. The *dayat* will ask you to tie a black-and-white checkered headscarf that we call a *kûfiya* around your belly, to help your body return to its original shape (see Figure 4.2). Since this design is a unifying symbol of Palestinian resistance to Israeli occupation, tying this cloth around your belly will also reaffirm that your baby is *of* Palestine and therefore tie you to the place of Palestine.

During the first week, bathing your baby every day is very important, and not just for the physical health of the baby, but also as a social activity for the family. All the children in the community will gather and form a circle around the basin where the baby is first bathed. The *dayat* will come for the first seven days to help you bathe the baby. Participating in the bathing process gives her a chance to take a good look at your baby, monitor your baby's progress, and answer any questions you may have about being a new mother. The *dayat* will also show you how to draw a soft line of black *kohl* around your baby's eyes every time he is bathed for the first forty days in order to protect him from germs.

If you have other children in your home, take care when bringing your new baby into your home. His older siblings may become jealous and act out. To avoid provoking them, be sure not to breastfeed in front of your other children, and try and give your other children plenty of attention. You can also call on those in your *hamula* to keep your other children busy and happy during these early weeks.

Seven days after your baby is born, the family will slaughter a lamb for a girl, or two lambs for a boy, to share with the whole family and community, in the religious ceremony we call *akeeka*, which we practice at the request of the Prophet Muhammad. After that first week, if you've used a *dayat* as I've suggested, she'll

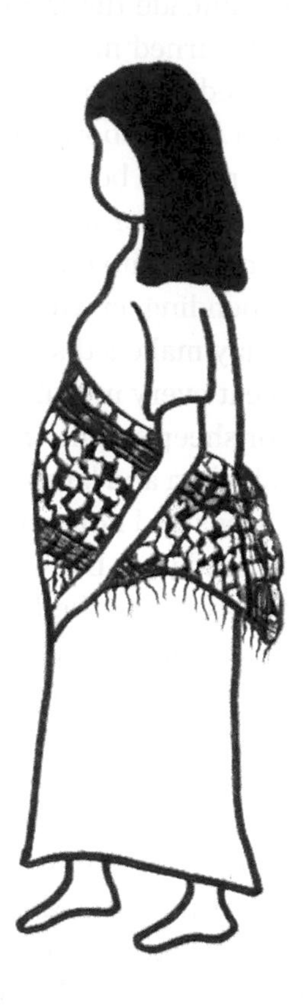

Figure 4.2 After giving birth, some Palestinian women wrap a *kûfîya* – now an internationally recognized visual symbol of the movement to achieve Palestinian statehood – around their belly. Drawing by Patti Akesson.

visit you and your baby about once a week for another month. Once the *dayat* comes less frequently, your mother-in-law will bathe your baby every other day, depending on the weather: less frequently if it's cold, more if it's hot. During this time, you should also keep warm: you shouldn't walk around the house barefoot, and you should cover yourself with many layers. When I had your brother, I didn't listen to the women's advice to stay warm and stay away from open windows. I was stubborn, because I was independent and working outside the home. I developed a bad cold during that time and learned my lesson! After I gave birth to you, I stayed warm and tried to keep to our traditions.

For forty days after your baby is born, you and your baby will not leave the house. This is to protect both the baby's health and your own. During this time, your mother-in-law will feed you extra food in the morning and evening so that you have enough nutrients to breastfeed your baby. Depending on where your husband comes from, one of your aunts may make a dish with eggs, flour, parsley, and onions, which you'll eat every morning for breakfast. You may also drink a lot of cow's or sheep's milk, the sweet *kizhah* drink made from black seeds, chicken and lamb soup, and the dense treat made of ground sesame seeds and honey that we call *halvah*. All these foods will make you and your baby stronger.

During the first forty days after the birth – which we call *arbe'en*, or "the forty" – you aren't required to pray or fast in accordance with our normal Muslim traditions. After forty days, you and your baby will participate in a private ceremony known as *hammam al-dahara.* During the ceremony, your mother and mother-in-law will bathe the baby and help you draw your own bath. When you're bathing, you'll say special prayers indicating that you're now ready to resume the Muslim practices. You'll wash different parts of your body – your face, neck, hair, arms, and feet – three times, starting with the right side and then moving to the left side. Once you complete *hammam al-dahara*, you're ready to resume your duties as wife and mother.

As the Jewish people do, we have a circumcision ceremony for boys. Doctors usually recommend that a baby boy be circumcised before forty days, to reduce the pain. But because it's difficult to secure a doctor to perform a circumcision, we usually wait until we have a few boys in the community who are ready, and we have a group ceremony. This means that the boys may be different ages when they're circumcised. For example, your brother was two months old when he was circumcised. After the procedure, the boys wear long, white gowns indicating that they've completed the ceremony. Your brother wore a gown for about a week after he was circumcised, because it was easier for his wound to heal and for him to move around while wearing the gown.

A Baby to Tie You to Place

Babyhood

As with your pregnancy and delivery, you'll never be alone in taking care of your baby. Whether you want their help or not, everyone in the family and community will help you raise your child. Because I was working in the private sector when your brother was born, I received seven weeks of maternity leave. If you work in the public sector, you'll be luckier: you'll receive three months of maternity leave. After that, working women like myself may leave our babies with the *hamula*, if we have some relatives living nearby. But if members of the *hamula* live far away, new mothers will enroll their babies in daycare centers that are near their workplaces. When my seven weeks of maternity leave were over, I enrolled your brother in daycare, because I couldn't afford to not earn a salary, and my mother wasn't nearby. Your brother attended daycare with a woman who lived on the ground floor of an apartment building near where I was working. This woman, with the help of her older daughter, was caring for about ten to fifteen other children from one year to five years old, including her own children. Every day around lunchtime, I'd leave work to visit and breastfeed your brother. Once he stopped breastfeeding at five months, I stopped visiting him at lunch, but at the end of the day I left work an hour early to pick him up and go home.

I was able to afford daycare, because our family was earning two salaries. Many poorer mothers can't afford daycare, and they tend to stay home with their children, asking neighbors or people from the *hamula* to watch their children when necessary. Today, with so many mothers working, daycare options have become more common for Palestinian families – including early childhood centers (e.g., nurseries, crèches, preschools, kindergartens, and family centers), as well as daycare for older children (day centers, after-school childcare, and child-minding).

Your baby will probably begin to teethe somewhere between three and twelve months of age. If you think your baby is suffering from itching gums while he's teething, you can give him something hard to chew on, or you can stick your fingers inside his mouth and massage his gums. Of course, since the Qur'an forbids us to drink alcohol, we would never rub alcohol on the baby's gums to ease the pain, as parents in some places do. When the first tooth finally erupts, we hold a special ceremony called *nkdah*. To celebrate *nkdah*, your female relatives will boil together some wheat, black beans, and water until they become a porridge. Then they'll send small bowls of the porridge to all the members of your *hamula* and the broader community. This is a moment for the entire Palestinian community to celebrate!

After three months, you should offer your baby all foods from the family's meals. You and your female relatives will chew the food and then give the chewed food to your baby. When I had your brother, I followed what the Internet and books had told me about waiting until the child is seven months to give him food. To this day, your brother is quite slim, which your paternal grandmother says is a result of me not following the tradition of starting to feed him from the family's table at three months. With you, I followed your grandmother's advice and chewed food for you starting at three months, and you're growing to be a strong and healthy girl.

Give your baby lots of new foods to try. Unlike what we hear about in Western societies, food allergies are uncommon in our culture. In Israel, very few children – both Jewish and Arabic – have food allergies. The only thing I'd warn you not to give your baby is fish with yogurt, which may upset his stomach.

After your baby is about nine months old, he'll start standing up on his own. Everyone from your family will help hold the baby's hand. My mother used to arrange the furniture in our house in a way that made it easier for her babies to grab, and pull themselves up to stand. Some of my friends have used a plastic walker to help their babies with walking, but I read somewhere that it isn't good for children, so I didn't use it with you or your brother.

Weaning your baby from breastmilk may be difficult. You were already in daycare when I weaned you at around twenty-two months, so I only gave you my breast in the morning and evening. But when I started to refuse to give you my breast in the morning and evenings, you'd cry and hit me! This was very tough for me, so I'd sometimes give you my breast. I knew I should be consistent, but it was so hard seeing you crying and being angry at me! All this will be much easier for you if you can send the baby away for a few days to your husband's mother. There, the baby won't get any breastmilk no matter how much he protests. This way, you won't have to hear your baby cry, which is so very difficult for a mother. I wish that I could have sent you away to your father's mother, but we were living too far from them. This made me really miss having the whole family help with taking care of the baby. If this happens to you, too, try rubbing butter on your breasts when it's time to wean: your baby won't like the taste and may not want to take your breast any more.

If you have a baby boy, on his first birthday you should hold a special first haircutting ritual. This is a widespread practice among our Palestinian communities. You should invite family and friends, who'll sing and eat a lot of food. Your son's hair will be cut by a man from the family or the community while the women will sing a song that asks the man to be careful while cutting the baby's hair. The cut hair will be weighed, and the weight of the hair will be equated with its weight in gold. The equivalent amount in money will then be distributed to the poor people in the community. This will be the baby's first contribution to the well-being of his new community.

When I was a child, this ritual used to occur at a Muslim holy site that the Jews call Joseph's Tomb and we call Qabr Yūsuf. The site is in the northern West Bank city of Nablus and is located at the eastern entrance to the valley that separates Mount Gerizim and Mount Ebal (near what is now the Balata refugee camp). Qabr Yūsuf is considered a holy place by Muslims, Jews, Samaritans, and Christians, representing the resting place of the biblical patriarch Joseph, and his two sons, Ephraim and Manasseh. Unfortunately, because it's important to so many different religions, Qabr Yūsuf has also been a site of intense conflict for centuries. Today, due to more recent violence between Israeli settlers and Palestinians, the Israeli army often prohibits Palestinian Muslims from visiting the site. Therefore we Palestinians are less likely to hold the haircutting ritual there, instead moving it to a safer location.

At around one year of age, your baby will start talking in Arabic. But, really, you should encourage this talking from an early age. For example, I would cradle both you and your brother on my lap when you were still very young infants and sing you traditional lullabies. To build a strong relationship with the baby, the baby's grandparents will also spend time with their grandchild, sharing the family's history through song. In fact, everyone in your family and the community will talk with your baby and encourage him to speak. The baby hears all the talk around him, and as a result his Arabic words will one day come flowing naturally from his lips.

Many Palestinian women will start toilet training their children when they're about fourteen or fifteen months old. These women are able to start early since they aren't working outside the home, so they have the time. As a working woman, I started toilet training your brother when he was older – about two years old. I explained to him what he had to do, and when he did it he was so excited. After that, he realized how it's done, and that was the end of that.

Once you have two or more children, your older child or children will have a responsibility to help you care for your younger child or children. As far back as I can remember, I was taking care of my younger siblings. When I was about seven years old, I remember my mother asking my nine-year-old sister and me to take our younger siblings outside to play with the other children. My mother needed us all to leave so that she could take care of household chores without distractions. But your children will also have a responsibility to help you with household tasks from an early age. Your daughters should help with the washing, cooking, and laundry. Once your sons are school age, as long as there's no threat from the Israeli army or from Israeli settlers, you can start sending them to the grocery store, or to run other errands. When your daughters are about eight or nine years old, you can also allow them to be outside the home, but only if they're in the company of their older siblings or cousins. Use your best judgment when making these decisions, as you must try to balance your children's growing sense of autonomy with the need to protect them from violence.

A Baby to Tie You to Place

Like all children, Palestinian children may learn from and model others' actions, but this can sometimes be dangerous. For example, there are times when Palestinian children (especially boys) protest and throw stones at Israeli tanks in the West Bank, and this can escalate to the point that the Israeli army responds with violence or arrests. There are also more serious situations when young people are recruited by organizations to participate in violent attacks. Of course, as a mother, I would not want you or your brother to be involved in any of these activities, but I also understand that you must make your own educated decisions about how you wish to lead your life. So I make sure that I am honest with you both about the many ways you can resist the occupation in non-violent ways, while staying tied to your Palestinian identity and developing your own sense of autonomy.

PARENTING: GUARDING AGAINST LOSS

Some Palestinians believe that having multiple children is a way to insure against the possible death of a child, especially in light of our living under Israeli occupation and threatened by daily violence. But this is not the main reason for you to have a child. When I had your brother, this reason wasn't particularly on my mind. Then, because of medical reasons, I was unable to have a child for nine more years, until I finally had you. During those years before you were born, I was sometimes scared of losing your brother, since he was my only child at the time. I thought, *What if I lose him? What will happen to me? If something happens to him, it will destroy my life*. I don't know if that is selfish. But I never thought about the implications of this kind of loss before I had him.

In this case, I think about my own grandmother – your great-grandmother – who had five sons, one of whom was your grandfather, my father. In 1982, one of her sons – my uncle – was killed by the Israeli army when he was twenty-eight. At the time, my grandmother's four other sons weren't living in Palestine: two were studying medicine in Europe and Asia, one was imprisoned in Israel, and the other had been exiled to

Jordan. For years, my grandmother felt very lonely because of your great-uncle's death. She finally moved past his death when two of my other uncles came back to Palestine to live near her in 1983. I always think about my grandmother's experience, and what would happen to me if something happened to your brother or you. So I've always been very careful to protect you both.

I imagine this is not just specific to us Palestinians. We read about how so many families in America and Europe and China have only one child these days. Those mothers must often worry, *What would happen if something were to happen to my one child?* It is really a horrible and terrifying feeling to think about losing a child. Even though I went to North America to study and I now work as a professor, my life revolves around you and your brother.

Once, before you were born, I was watching your brother play with some other children, and another boy kicked him very hard in the belly. It was really hard for me to witness, and I was scared. I became really angry at the boy's mother, because she didn't do anything to address the situation. I told her what her son had done. She understood my reaction, because at the time, he was my only child. I thought, *Oh, maybe I am overprotective, because I only have one child*. That's how the other women saw me. People may believe, *If a woman has three or four children, it will be easier for her if she loses one.* But I don't think so. Whether you have one child who dies or three, a loss is a loss. That is why I am always doing everything I can to protect you and your brother from harm, and that includes providing you with a good education – so you will choose to resist the occupation and its violence with your minds, and not with your bodies.

Final Advice for My Daughter

There's no better way to bring the *'a'ila* and the *hamula* together than to celebrate a new life. Having a baby is important and should be celebrated. But being a mother is demanding, both physically and emotionally. The involvement of your family, the *hamula*, and the community will help you with some of the challenges. The family is so important, not just to help you raise your children, but also as a means of social and financial support for you and your children. So, even though they may give you unsolicited (and perhaps annoying) advice about how best to raise your children, always treat your relatives with respect, even reverence. And try to follow the family traditions if you can.

We don't keep as many family traditions as we used to, and I feel bad that we've lost some of them. After the second *intifada*, many of these traditions were disrupted. Travel restrictions imposed by the Israeli occupation often interfere with family members' access to places, and this can prevent people from attending important ceremonies. There are also now more women working and living away from their families, further interrupting these traditions. As a result, social support systems, and traditions that go along with them, can be compromised. Some of these traditions bring so much happiness and joy to families and the community. Most importantly, the traditions are grounded in the expectation that the whole family and community will help you raise your child.

Fortunately, I'm seeing more women heading back toward the traditional ways, and I hope that you will, too. When you start having your babies, try to practice some of our family traditions. For example, after giving birth, be sure to eat well and stay warm. Of course, not all of the traditions make sense. For example, rubbing the baby with salt and putting *kohl* around his eyes might cause more harm than good. But some traditions are useful. Therefore, I ask you to use your best judgment and draw from family traditions and common sense to make decisions about how best to raise your children.

Be as patient as you can with your children, as I've tried to be with you and your brother. Enjoy your time with your children, and make sure to spend quality time with them. My mother was a very busy woman, and she became overwhelmed with her children at times. But I knew that she loved us. As a working woman myself, I try to spend as much time with you and your brother as possible, while still following my career ambitions as an engineer. Similarly, I would like for you to also spend as much time with your children as possible, while not compromising any dreams you may have for a career.

I don't know what will happen to Palestine in the future, though I hope for the best as you consider bringing children into this world. Whatever happens between Israel and Palestine, your children will change your own life at the same time that they will carry on our precious Palestinian traditions.

CHAPTER 5

Childrearing in the New Country

Advice for Immigrant Mothers in Israel

Deborah Golden

A BRIEF PORTRAIT OF ISRAELI SOCIETY

There are numerous ways to portray a country. Each way says much and omits much else. In many cases, such portrayals are contested – especially when the country at stake is not only embroiled in ongoing political conflict, but also immersed in internal struggles among different social groups regarding the fundamental character of the country and the shared identity of its citizens. Such is the case of Israel. How best to present its complexity? In this introduction, I offer a brief overview of Israeli society based on two dimensions that are commonly understood to have shaped the way the country has come to be what it is today: its wars and its waves of immigration.
In the childrearing manual that follows, we shall see how some of the basic concerns at the heart of Israeli society stemming from its military and migrant histories inform both perceptions and practices of those who care for babies and young children.

A World of Babies

A Country at War

The modern period of Jewish settlement in Palestine began in the late nineteenth century. In those early decades, settlers consisted primarily of young immigrants from Russia and eastern Europe seeking to participate in the quest for Jewish self-determination by establishing a national home in the ancestral homeland. At that time, the region of Palestine fell under Turkish rule as part of the Ottoman Empire. The indigenous Arab population, which far outnumbered Jewish settlers, was mostly Muslim, rural-based, and dependent upon agriculture for a living. Those early decades saw the setting up of the foundations of the new Jewish society in Palestine – at once administrative, economic, military, social, and cultural. Distinctive accomplishments included the revival of Hebrew as the language of everyday communication (a language that, until the mid-nineteenth century, was used as a language of prayer and religious writings), as well as the establishment of the *kibbutz* – a utopian experiment in living that consisted of cooperative, agricultural communities founded on a combination of socialist and Zionist principles.

That same period also saw the beginnings of conflict between settler Jews and indigenous Arabs, with the latter increasingly threatened by the burgeoning Jewish presence, fearing increasing encroachment, if not displacement. These fears were reinforced by the position adopted by international powers in the region, particularly Britain – which had taken charge of Palestine in 1917, following the defeat of the Ottoman Empire, and declared its support for the establishment of a "Jewish national home in Palestine" in the 1917 Balfour Declaration. The 1920s and 1930s saw an increase in violent confrontations between Arabs and Jews, as well as growing tensions between both Jewish and Arab communities and the British Mandate. The rise of Nazism during the 1930s brought about a large influx of German Jews into Palestine. The fate of the Jews in Europe during the Holocaust reinforced the determination on the part of the Jewish community in Palestine to ensure statehood. By 1947, the 600,000 Jews living in Palestine were a tightly knit, centrally organized community, with the vast majority of European birth or origin.

Childrearing in the New Country

On November 29, 1947, the United Nations General Assembly voted to partition Palestine into two states, one Jewish and the other Arab, with Jerusalem and Bethlehem designated as an international zone. The UN partition plan was accepted by the Zionist leadership but rejected by Palestinian Arabs and neighboring Arab states. Fighting between Jews and Palestinians broke out almost immediately and intensified over the ensuing months. On May 15, 1948, the British evacuated Palestine, and Zionist leaders declared the establishment of the State of Israel. Immediately following the declaration of the new state, neighboring Arab states (Egypt, Syria, Jordan, and Iraq) invaded Israel.

Up until 1948, Palestinians formed the majority population living in Palestine. During the war – called the War of Independence by Jews, and the *Nakba* (or "catastrophe") by Palestinians – over 700,000 residents were expelled or fled from areas that came under Israeli control. Those Palestinians who remained – some 150,000 – became Israeli citizens. Today, Palestinian citizens of Israel, or Israeli Arabs, number well over a million; most are Muslims, but there are small Christian and Druze communities. Together, these Palestinians constitute around 20 percent of the population of Israel, the total population of which currently stands at around 8.5 million. However, another approximately 2.6 million Palestinians live in the West Bank, including East Jerusalem; 1.6 million in Gaza; and 5.6 million in the diaspora, mainly Jordan (although these figures are somewhat variable). Hence, the first Israeli–Arab war of 1948 saw the emergence of the Palestinian refugee issue – at the kernel of the unresolved Israeli–Palestinian conflict to this day.

Agreements reached in 1949 divided the territory into three parts, each under a different political regime: Israel (which now controlled more territory than was offered in the original partition plan); East Jerusalem and the West Bank, under the control of Jordan; and the Gaza Strip, under Egyptian control. The conflict did not stop there. Further wars took place with Egypt in 1956; Egypt, Syria, and Jordan in 1967; Egypt and Syria in 1973; and Lebanon in 1982 and 2006. During the 1967 war, Israel conquered East Jerusalem, the West Bank, Gaza, and the Golan

Heights. East Jerusalem was annexed, while military rule was imposed on the West Bank and Gaza, ushering in the beginning of the military occupation of Palestinian territories and the establishment of Israeli settlements there. Peace treaties signed with Egypt (in 1979) and with Jordan (in 1994) have remained in place. A first Palestinian mass uprising (*intifada*) against the occupation of the West Bank and Gaza took place in 1987, and a second in 2000. Various negotiated agreements transferred partial control of the West Bank and Gaza to a local political entity, the Palestinian Authority. Elections held in Gaza in 2007 ushered in rule by Hamas (a political rival of the Palestinian Authority). Since then, Israel has made three military incursions into Gaza (2008–09, 2012, and 2014).

To date, no viable and long-term resolution to the Israeli–Palestinian conflict is in sight. Recurrent wars with Israel's Arab neighbors, along with the unresolved political conflict with the Palestinians, present a persistent security threat, as well as dictating the need for compulsory military service for young Israeli men and women (although orthodox Jews and Israeli Palestinians are exempt). A sense of underlying threat to Israeli Jews is reinforced by the memory of the Holocaust, with this collective memory of disaster as an integral constituent of the identity of the state and its Jewish citizens. Aside from causing the loss of life and suffering on all sides, the ongoing conflict also has ramifications for relations between Jewish and Palestinian citizens of Israel. Indeed, the cleavage between Jewish and Palestinian Israelis is considered one of the basic rifts in what has been termed a "deeply divided society." The position of the latter is rendered even more difficult by the self-designation of Israel as a Jewish state.

Israel as a Jewish and Democratic State

As stated in its Declaration of Independence, the State of Israel was to be both a Jewish and a democratic state. The new state was to be "open to the immigration of Jews and for the Ingathering of the Exiles from all countries of their dispersion," echoing the ancient biblical prophecy, "Thy children shall return to their own borders" (Jeremiah 31:16). This ethno-national dimension of the state is reflected in the formal identity of Israel as homeland of the Jewish people; in the enshrinement of this principle in the 1950 Law of Return, which grants the right of settlement and automatic citizenship to Jewish immigrants; in the use of Hebrew as dominant language (with Arabic as Israel's second official language); and in the use of symbols adapted from Jewish tradition, including the country's name, flag, emblem, and calendar. But Israel was also envisioned as a democratic state, committed to "uphold the full social and political equality of all its citizens, without distinction of race, creed or sex," as reflected in its basic laws, institutions, and political system of parliamentary democracy. Whether and to what extent the idea of Israel as both Jewish and democratic is viable, or a contradiction in terms, not only is a source of scholarly debate, but has ongoing political, legal, and social ramifications. As Chapter 4 in this volume chronicles, the Palestinian minority suffers from discrimination in the allocation of resources, and Israeli Palestinians are located toward the lower end of most measures of social, educational, and economic well-being.

The tension between the Jewish and democratic dimensions of the state not only has an impact on relations between the Jewish and Palestinian citizens but also shapes relations between state and religion, as well as between religious and non-religious Jews. A dual judicial system grants authority to Jewish, Muslim, Druze, and Christian religious courts in matters pertaining to personal status, including marriage and divorce. This dual-leveled system has implications for the continuing unequal status of women, contributing to the entrenchment of the view of women as primarily wives and mothers. Among Jews, the division between religious and secular Jews has been characterized as the second major rift in this "deeply divided society." However, it is probably more accurate to describe a continuum of religious belief and adherence to tradition among Israeli Jews, rather than a strict dichotomy. Many Israeli Jews defining themselves as secular observe certain aspects of religious tradition, particularly in relation to rites of passage. Degree of religiosity varies according to ethnic origin: while most Mizrahi and Sephardi Jews (with historical origins in the Mid-East/Asia and Iberia, respectively) tend toward the traditional or religious end of the spectrum, most Ashkenazi Jews (with historical origins in Europe) tend to define themselves as secular. In matters of both self-definition and observance, Jews from the former Soviet Union are the most secular. As will become apparent in the following manual, the perceived importance attached to adherence to Jewish tradition is a theme that arises in encounters between Israelis and newcomers.

A Country of Immigrants

The establishment of the state in 1948 saw the opening of Israel's borders to unrestricted Jewish immigration. Over the first three years of statehood, 700,000 newcomers entered the country, doubling the existing Jewish population. Although a sizeable minority of Mizrahi Jews existed in Palestine prior to 1948, most early Jewish immigrants to Palestine were of east European origin. From 1948 to 1954, nearly half the immigrants were European Jewish refugees seeking refuge in the aftermath of the Second World War. However, in the few years following the establishment of the state, the percentage of Mizrahi Jews in the population increased to 40 percent. Initial contacts between the newcomers and the veteran Ashkenazi founding settlers, who were by then entrenched in positions of power in all spheres of life, left an indelible mark on the relative social and economic positions of these two groups, and on relations between them. Indeed, the cleavage between Ashkenazi and Mizrahi Jews has been singled out as the third major rift in the "deeply divided society" that is Israel.

In addition to the social, economic, and cultural gaps between the two populations, Ashkenazi old-timers greeted the Mizrahi newcomers at best with ambivalence, if not disdain. This meant viewing the newcomers through an Orientalist prism as culturally inferior, as well as constructing an umbrella "Mizrahi" identity under which their diverse backgrounds were subsumed. Moreover, adherence to a local version of the "melting pot" ideology (called *mizug galuyot* or "blending of the exiles") meant that, in practice, the newcomers were encouraged to discard old ways. Finally, these immigrants were at once settled in recently abandoned Arab towns and villages, and dispersed to peripheral areas, in what were called "development towns." Thus, from the start, geographical, social, and political marginalization, coupled with social discrimination, meant that Mizrahi newcomers were placed at a disadvantage. The effects of these handicaps continue to reverberate through Israeli society today. Nevertheless, although economic and educational gaps between Ashkenazi and Mizrahi Jews persist into the second and third generations, rates of intermarriage are on the increase, and a burgeoning Mizrahi middle class now counters old stereotypes.

Some of the difficulties faced by Mizrahi Jews in the early years of the state were echoed in subsequent waves of immigration from Ethiopia, 17,000 of whom arrived in Israel during the 1980s, followed by a further 45,000 during the 1990s. Many of these immigrants were inadequately prepared for a modern economy, arriving with low levels of education and literacy. Furthermore, family structure – consisting of large numbers of children, single-parent families, and aging fathers – meant that economic resources were spread thin. These limited resources were further reinforced by these large families, like their Mizrahi predecessors, being settled in marginal towns and neighborhoods. This geographic marginalization was echoed at the spiritual level: the rabbinical establishment refused to recognize the newcomers as Jews, or to recognize Ethiopian religious leaders as rabbis, thus adding to these immigrants' difficulties and deep sense of humiliation.

Moreover, while Israel initially expressed welcoming intentions in "rescuing" these large numbers of Ethiopian Jews from difficult circumstances, a lack of understanding hindered effectively accommodating their unique needs. Many Ethiopian children were sent to religious boarding schools – at once separating them from their parents, and bringing about de facto segregation from mainstream Israeli society. In effect, the policy of special care, albeit well intentioned, produced stigmatization and negative stereotyping. Ethiopian Israelis, while displaying improvements in educational and economic measures, particularly among the generation born and educated in Israel, still fare relatively poorly on these indicators. They also continue to suffer from ongoing discrimination and racism, as unequivocally expressed in violent demonstrations that took place in 2015 on the streets of Jerusalem and Tel Aviv.

The 1990s saw a further huge influx of immigrants from the former Soviet Union. Within the first five years of that decade, over a million newcomers arrived, irrevocably changing its social, economic, and political fabric. The vast majority of these immigrants (especially during the first years) were Ashkenazi Jews from Russia and the Ukraine, while a minority hailed from the Asian republics of the Caucasus, Georgia, and Bukhara. On the whole, these immigrants were motivated more by "push" than by "pull" factors – notably, the crises and uncertainties engulfing the former Soviet Union after the collapse of the Communist regime, including the lack of a positive economic outlook, and an accompanying fear of an upsurge in anti-Semitism.

In contrast to state-regulated mechanisms for integrating newcomers in the 1950s, and for immigrants from Ethiopia, Jews arriving from the former Soviet Union enjoyed a policy of "direct absorption." Rather than being provided with housing or employment by the state, each family received an allowance consisting of income support and rental subsidy, free health care, and free instruction in Hebrew. In addition, newcomers were provided an interest-free bank loan for a limited time, as well as a substantial mortgage subsidy, and within a relatively short time many had become home-owners. Though relatively lacking in material wealth, the immigrants brought with them strong cultural capital, with an average level of education far above that of the local Israeli population. The newcomers included large numbers of scientists, engineers, physicians, and technical specialists. However, due to the lack of knowledge of Hebrew, lack of fit between professional standards, and structural conditions in the local economic market, many of these professionals found themselves unable to find relevant employment and were compelled to earn a living at jobs far below their qualifications. Notwithstanding this trend of downward mobility, there is a relatively high rate of employment among the immigrants. Moreover, rather than concentrating in the lower rungs of the social scale, Russian immigrants have entered different sectors in Israeli society, with many following a path of upward social mobility. On the whole, immigrants from the former Soviet Union maintain a strong social and cultural enclave, and this also serves as a basis for political mobilization. Among children and adolescents born in the former Soviet Union, most youngsters have managed to successfully navigate Israeli institutions, including the military and higher education, and they develop the skills necessary for upward mobility: Hebrew proficiency, and understanding of local social codes in various spheres of life.

However, particularly at the start of the huge influx of newcomers, relations with Israelis were strained, with the immigrants perceived as lacking knowledge of Jewish tradition and Zionist sentiment, as well as disinterest in integrating into Israeli society. Such attitudes were particularly marked among Mizrahi Jews, many of whom viewed the Russian immigrants as competitors on the employment market; in turn, the newcomers viewed Mizrahi Jews with much ambivalence themselves.

In the Israeli Declaration of Independence, as noted, Jewish settlement is portrayed as the realization of an ancient, historical imperative – an "ingathering of exiles," to the original birthplace of the Jewish people, or a homecoming. In this understanding, Jewish migration to the land of Israel is viewed in terms of moral upward movement or "ascent" (*aliyah*), and immigrants as those who ascend (*olim*). This moral component attaching to Jewish immigration to Israel informs policy and also mutual relations and expectations between native-born Israelis and newcomers in everyday exchanges. Notwithstanding Israel's ideology of welcoming Jewish immigration, in practice, as we have seen, relations between locals and newcomers have often been strained. Some of these strains and expectations come to bear in the manual that follows, as a kindergarten teacher of Moroccan descent instructs newcomer mothers, primarily from the former Soviet Union, in what she thinks they need to know and understand in order to bring up their babies and children in ways deemed properly Israeli.

Family, Women's Employment, and Early Education

Israel "represents a unique blending of a very family-oriented society with a developed, modern economy." Despite changes in the family in recent decades – including later age of marriage, decline in the average number of children, and a rising divorce rate – the family remains a central pillar of Israeli society. Relative to other industrialized countries, and notwithstanding its modern economy, Israel has high rates of marriage, high birth rates, a low divorce rate, adherence to more traditional gender roles, and a traditional cultural heritage in family lifestyle. The high birth rate is not restricted to women belonging to social groups that adhere to a traditional outlook; secular women, too, tend to have more children than do women in other economically developed countries. The predominance of the family in Israeli life reinforces the primary role of women as wives and mothers – a role accorded national significance. Indeed, the state employs various means to encourage a high birth rate. For example, Israel provides free, unlimited coverage of in-vitro fertilization (IVF) procedures for women up to age forty-five for up to two children, and high rates of women take up this option. In addition, although reduced substantially from their relatively high levels in the 1990s (a reduction that adversely affected large families, particularly among the ultra-Orthodox and Israeli Palestinians), a monthly government allowance is allocated for every child in every Israeli family with children under the age of seventeen, regardless of income. In spite of Israel's modern economy, one in five Israeli families lives below the poverty line, particularly in ultra-Orthodox and Palestinian Israeli households. Even when these populations are excluded from the analysis, Israel still has some of the highest rates of poverty in the economically developed world. In contrast to other countries, where poverty tends to disproportionately affect the elderly and single-parent families, in Israel it is young, large families that tend to be poor, leaving children most vulnerable.

The central importance accorded to family in Israeli society, while reinforcing the primacy attached to the role of wife and mother, does not preclude relatively high employment rates of women, particularly among more educated women. On the whole, rates of participation in the workforce among women remain largely unaffected during motherhood. Women in Israel are relatively well educated; nevertheless, as elsewhere, the rate of participation in the labor force is lower for women than for men, and women's wages are consistently lower than those of men. Pregnant women who have worked for one year are entitled to twenty-six weeks of maternity leave (which may be shared with the father), of which fourteen weeks are paid by the state, as well as legislated job and benefits protection during maternity leave.

Care for children from birth until three years of age falls under the responsibility of the Ministry of Economy. This includes daycare centers run by community centers, local municipalities, and non-profit groups and women's organizations. Most of these daycare facilities, which provide care for children from 7 a.m. until 4 p.m., require payment from families. However, some families are entitled to fee reductions or even free care on account of low socio-economic status, or by virtue of belonging to certain social categories, including new immigrants, single mothers, and the unemployed. Another option for childcare is private home-care settings that cater for up to five children.

From age three onwards, children's education falls under the responsibility of the Ministry of Education. Israel's education system consists of two years of preschool (for children aged three to four), one year of kindergarten (for children aged five to six), six years of primary education, and six years of secondary education. Starting with preschool, the education system is divided into four distinct school systems – secular Jewish, religious Jewish, Arab, and ultra-Orthodox, with attendance according to neighborhood in the desired stream, and little movement from one stream to another. The Ministry of

Education is responsible for school curricula, educational standards, buildings, and supervision of teaching personnel – the majority of whom have certification, most with academic degrees. Local authorities are charged with school maintenance, purchase of equipment and supplies, and the employment of non-teaching personnel. Almost all Israeli children of compulsory education age (five to sixteen years) are enrolled in school. While 90 percent of Israeli children complete secondary education, and the average rate of matriculation among students is on the increase (50 percent of seventeen-year-olds), such rates vary greatly according to the location of the school and the socio-economic profile of the population it serves. Income inequality, coupled with unequal investment in education on the part of the state and local authorities, as well as neo-liberal trends that facilitate various forms of privatization (including supplemental payments by parents to schools, and increasing numbers of private or semi-private schools), mean that the role of education as a tool of social integration and social mobility is diminishing.

Countervailing this trend, a 1984 law expanded the responsibility of the state to provide free education to include children aged three to four. Implementation of this law began in 1999 in neighborhoods of low socio-economic status. In 2012, following protests against the cost of living, which drew hundreds of thousands of Israelis onto the streets, the government decided to expand its responsibility and provide free schooling to all children within this age group. Within three years, the Ministry of Education established new preschools throughout the country and took charge of existing private ones. On the whole, numbers of children attending preschool are high and on the increase, although attendance varies in different sectors of the population, particularly between Jewish and Arab sectors. Still, other families continue to rely on their own family members (especially grandparents) to take care of the children, or they turn to private childcare. Among immigrants from the former Soviet Union, some families prefer to send their children to Russian-language preschools. These form part of a flourishing network of Russian educational settings established in the nineties by newcomers keen to preserve the Russian language among their children, as well as ensure that their children adhere to Russian educational standards.

Early childhood education in Israel has always held great importance in the context of nation-building, particularly in its role as contributing to the assimilation of immigrant children and their families. The following manual takes the form of advice put together by a (fictive) Israeli kindergarten teacher of Moroccan descent in her encounters with immigrant mothers, mainly from the former Soviet Union, as they adjust to new ways of childrearing. The teacher's voice is a personal one, with her particular social biography shaping her encounters with the newcomers; instructing newly arrived women in what she considers to be proper ways of bringing up children is at the same time teaching them how to belong to Israel.

CHILDREARING IN THE NEW COUNTRY: ADVICE FOR IMMIGRANT MOTHERS IN ISRAEL

About the Author

My name is Esther, but people usually call me "Esti." I am a teacher at a kindergarten that caters to children aged five to six in a city on the northern coast of Israel. I am fifty-six years old and have been a teacher ever since I graduated from teacher training college. That's nearly thirty years of teaching! Perhaps it's too many years doing the same work – often, I feel quite worn out. It is very demanding, and our pay is not so good. But I love the children, and I'm very experienced now. I feel that I have a lot to give them – and to their parents, too. Often, the mothers ask my advice about their babies and even their older children. In the old days, mothers dropped off their children in the morning and picked them up at lunchtime, and that was that. These days, they seem to worry more and want to know lots of details about what's going on with their children: Did they eat enough, do they have friends, should they be reading yet? Usually

I'm quite happy to talk to the mothers, though not when they call me late in the evening – which happens quite a lot! They don't seem to have any sense of boundaries, just like their children. But my own children are grown up now, and I have more time on my hands, so we chat about all sorts of things on their minds in relation to bringing up children.

My family came from Morocco in 1961, when I was one year old. We had a very hard time then – my family really struggled. Even now, things are not easy but, thank God, and with a lot of hard work, most of my brothers and sisters have managed very well – we are all educated, own our apartments, and have wonderful families (although, unfortunately, my older sister just got divorced). I've worked in the same neighborhood all my life. I used to know many of the families at the kindergarten; sometimes I've gotten to know two or three children from the same family. I'm often invited to family occasions like circumcisions and weddings, though I always decline. With nearly thirty-five children in the kindergarten, if I accepted these invitations I'd either be going out every night (and spending most of my salary on buying gifts!), or I'd have to choose which invitations to accept – something I could never do, as I wouldn't want to hurt anybody's feelings. Having said that, if, God forbid, there is a death in a family, I do try to go either to the funeral, or to the family's house during the week of mourning that we call *shiva*.

But things have changed, and many new families have moved into the neighborhood whom I don't know. Huge numbers of new immigrants came at the beginning of the 1990s – some from Ethiopia, but mainly from Russia. We call everyone from this last group "Russians," and I'm sorry to say that in the beginning, we didn't like them very much. There were too many of them; they spoke a language we couldn't make heads or tails of; they ate different foods from the rest of us; they opened up new delicatessen shops selling pork sausages (definitely not kosher!), dark bread and vodka; and they filled our ears by playing classical music in the street, in the hope that passers-by would dig into their pockets. Not only that, but we thought that they were quite snobbish and looked down at us Mizrahim. It felt like reliving the fifties, when the Ashkenazim thought we were primitive!

We were even suspicious of the immigrants' motives for coming to Israel. Many of them didn't seem to know or care very much about Jewish tradition at all, and they weren't really Zionists. Some of them didn't even look Jewish – especially those elegant, blonde women. We worried, Were the newcomers going to take our jobs? Over time, we haven't got much closer, and we more or less keep to ourselves – though we eventually got used to them and their ways. In our neighborhood, housing is relatively cheap (though nothing's really cheap in Israel, certainly not housing), so many immigrants end up in my neighborhood, and I often have children from these families in my kindergarten. At one point, over a third of the children in my kindergarten were Russians.

Over the years I've had some children from Ethiopian families, too, but not many. I must admit, I am quite relieved about that. Not that I don't like them: on the contrary, I have very warm feelings toward them. But they have their own particular problems, and there are a lot of tensions between the Russians and the Ethiopians, which I would find tough to handle.

In the beginning, I found it difficult to talk to the Russian mothers. It's not only that they struggle to speak Hebrew, but I also had the feeling that they don't understand basic things about how we do things here in Israel. Sometimes, I'm not sure that they even want to understand. This has been a real challenge for me.

Over the years, I've come up with some ideas about what's important for immigrant mothers to know and understand about bringing up young children, to help them be properly prepared for life in Israel. I thought it might be useful to write down some of these ideas, not only to help immigrant mothers in their new circumstances, but also as a resource for other caregivers and teachers in their encounters with newcomers. Although each group of immigrants – and teachers – is different, they all face similar issues. In these guidelines, I'll be advising pregnant immigrant women and young mothers, mainly those from Russia, about how to adjust to new ways of bringing up babies and educating children. So here I am, over fifty years after my own family came from Morocco, doing my bit for Israel by helping new immigrants in their new home!

But, first things first . . .

A WORD OF ADVICE ABOUT LISTENING TO ADVICE

When I was a young mother, knowing how to do things right seemed fairly straightforward. Nowadays things aren't so simple. You young mothers are bombarded with choices, possibilities, and advice from all sides: experts on television and the Internet telling you how to bring up children, shops enticing you to spend money on buying things for your babies and older children, doctors and nurses at the clinics, mothers, sisters, and friends – all telling you what you should and shouldn't be doing. And here in Israel, everyone's sure that they're an expert on everything, and no one hesitates to offer advice about, or even criticize, what you are doing. That's especially the case with babies and young children, because everyone here takes an interest. As you've probably already experienced, when you're pregnant, people you don't even know take the liberty of touching your rounded belly, as if it belongs to them, too.

All these new experiences can be overwhelming for young mothers who grew up in another country, because the ways that you grew up there can't really serve as guidelines for how to do things in this new country. You can't depend on advice from your mother or grandmother, because they often did things wrong. As a young mother here in Israel, I certainly did things differently from what my mother had done in Morocco. Not because our mothers meant any harm, but their ways were different, and they just didn't know as much about bringing up children as we do now.

In the guidelines that follow, I will add my own bit of advice to the pile – but I try to stick to what most Israelis think are the most important things when it comes to raising children. Although you should listen to what everyone has to say, my main advice to you is that, in the end, you're the mom and this is your child, so you have to decide what's best. I know that's easier said than done – especially with your first child! – but you will see that as you have more children, you'll gain confidence as a mother. Someday, you'll be giving advice to the even younger mothers around you – not to speak of your own children, as they become parents themselves, with the help of God!

THE IMPORTANCE OF FAMILY

When you're pregnant, I know that it's tempting to complain. It's hot, you're tired or nauseous, you're finding it hard to drag yourself up the stairs to your apartment at the top of the building, there's a long line at the local clinic, your husband doesn't help enough. In spite of all these irritations, you must understand that having children is the most important thing that we women can do. Family is the most important thing there is, and family means children.

How many children? My mother got married in Morocco when she was very young, and she had eight children. Today, many Orthodox Jewish families have lots of children – sometimes ten or more. That's definitely too many, especially nowadays. Life is very expensive here, and if you have so many children, how are you going to be able to make sure they have what they need? Besides, most women nowadays get pregnant late, and they also need to work, so they have less time to devote to bringing up children. In Russia, I know that families were very small – many of you, and certainly your parents, are only children, with no brothers or sisters. But that doesn't really count as a family. I think that the optimal number of children is three or maybe four, if you can afford it. I myself have three children – one girl and two boys. In the old days, the Ashkenazim used to laugh at us Mizrahi families because we had lots of children – they took that as a sign of us being primitive. But now, lots of women are having more children, even Ashkenazi women.

You may ask why family is so important. First, the happiest times are with family, like the big family gathering at Passover, or just a regular Friday night – one of the women of the family has lit the Sabbath candles, the father has made the blessing on the wine and the delicious challah bread, we're all sitting around the table laden with good food, arguing loudly about politics, or complaining about the cost of living, or discussing the latest episode of a reality show, with lots of kids running around making a racket. Sometimes we quarrel with each other – but, still, family is family, and always there for you – a shoulder to cry on or to help you out with money troubles. And family life is part of our tradition. Although some of us don't bother keeping all the religious laws, being Israeli means keeping at least the basic parts of Jewish tradition; maybe you've heard the biblical phrase, "Be fruitful and multiply." And Israel is still a very new country – just sixty-eight years old! We're still building it up. Doing your part to have several children is one way of making sure that there is a big Jewish population. Also, although this is a painful subject, it is part of the reality of our life here: our children have to go into the army, and many of our boys will do combat service. Both of my boys did. I was proud that they were serving the country but, naturally, I was worried, too. If, God forbid, something should happen to one of our children during military service, it's important that there are other children.

PREGNANCY AND GIVING BIRTH

While pregnant, you must make sure that you get proper medical care. That means regular visits to the doctor. You can go to your gynecologist at your Health Fund, or to the Mother and Child Clinic (*Tipat Halav*), which is a free service for pregnant women and babies run by the Ministry of Health. These visits are extremely important for following the development of the baby and making sure that everything is proceeding as it should. I also recommend that you get as much information as you can by reading, and by browsing the Internet. But do be careful of what you read on the Internet – it can be useful, but also very frightening, since you might read about the worst-case scenarios, which I'm not sure you really want to know about when you're pregnant. Our Ministry of Health gives very good guidelines, and their website is in many languages, including Russian, Arabic, English, French, and Spanish. I think that regular monitoring by the doctors while you're pregnant is one way of dealing with the anxiety that something might go wrong.

There are also all sorts of superstitions around pregnancy for warding off what some people call the "evil eye." For instance, many women don't spread the news that they're pregnant for the first three months of their pregnancy, just in case something goes wrong. You, too, might not want to let too many people know at this early stage, because here in Israel nobody really minds their own business, and you'll have to answer all sorts of questions if something goes wrong. Even if women prepare in advance for the baby's arrival by buying things they'll need for the new baby – crib, diapers, clothes – they may opt to leave everything at the store; if they do bring them home, they keep everything wrapped up in their boxes. These customs can't do any harm, and you need all the luck you can get when you're pregnant, so why not keep to them? When my first child was born, a neighbor came round with a tiny booklet of Psalms that she told me to put under the baby's pillow. I did as she suggested, and I must admit that I've kept the booklet ever since. It certainly didn't hurt: that baby boy is now about to become a father himself!

To prepare for your birth, I recommend that you go to birth education classes. These are short courses of three to five meetings and are usually given at the maternity ward of your local hospital for a fairly token fee, or through the Health Fund; or you can go to a private class, if you have the money. The classes are meant for husbands too, to give them a better understanding of what the woman is going through and teach them what to do at the birth. When I gave birth, my mother and sister were with me. Now, it's more common for husbands to be there, as well. I'm not sure that's a good idea – sometimes they're very nervous themselves, and then the wife has to worry about him, rather than attending to having the baby.

If everything goes as planned, you'll usually spend no more than two nights in the maternity ward. In some hospitals, you can choose to have the baby with you all the time, but in many hospitals you're encouraged to put the baby together with the other babies overnight, so that you can get some good rest. I think that's the right thing to do – you're going to need all your strength over the next while. Most men don't take much leave time from their jobs and are back to work a day or two after you get home from the hospital. You're going to need all the help you can get! If you live quite far from your mother, it might be wise to go and stay with her during the first month after your baby is born, or perhaps she can come and stay with you.

LOOKING AFTER YOUR BABY

It's best to breastfeed your babies if you can. Mother's milk is the healthiest start for children, and it also gives you an opportunity to have special time with your baby. In the old days, my mother continued breastfeeding her baby until she was ready to get pregnant again: she would stop nursing her baby and start feeding him homemade food. Nowadays, even though you probably intend to breastfeed, sometimes things don't work out – for instance, you aren't producing enough milk and the baby isn't gaining weight, or the baby has tummy pains, or your breasts become sore, or you're just too tired. You can get some guidance on that from the Mother and Child Clinic. Don't worry: there are lots of good formula milks on the market nowadays. In fact, many women start using formula quite early on, even at the hospital. If you're working, at best you'll only get a few months of maternity leave, and you'll probably move to using formula when you return to work, although, if you have the energy, you can pump your own milk into a bottle for your mother or mother-in-law to use.

Where should your baby sleep? It's probably wise to put the baby to sleep on his back. But wherever the baby sleeps, I recommend that for the first few weeks, you set up the baby's crib in your bedroom so that you're close by if the baby needs you during the night. It's up to you, but I think babies have to learn to be independent quite soon, so it shouldn't be too long before your baby is moved into his own bedroom. You can probably trust your maternal instinct to know when your baby needs you – most mothers sleep very lightly and wake up at every sound their baby makes. Apart from that, most Israelis live in apartments, and they are small enough that a parent may hear the baby's breathing, and certainly crying, in the next room. But if you're worried, nowadays you can buy a gadget so that you can hear your baby crying, or that will set off an alarm if the baby stops breathing, God forbid.

You must try and make sure that your baby has a good night's sleep. At the beginning, it's quite difficult to control things: babies have their own rhythms, and you just have to go along with that as best as you can. When the baby's a little older, it's a good idea to set up certain routine ways of getting him to sleep. You should do the same things every night at the same time, and in the same order: have a bath, put on pyjamas, brush teeth, then read a story – this is also really important for getting your child off to a good start in reading. Then give her a kiss and a hug, and say good night. That way, going to bed turns into a sort of ritual that makes it easier for everybody. But there are experts for everything these days, and if things don't settle down, you can always get some advice from a child psychologist.

It's very important to take the baby for regular checkups, free of charge, at the Mother and Child Clinic. During the first year, there are about eight checkups, which include measuring your baby's height, weight, head circumference, and reflexes. The nurse who does the checks marks all the results out on a graph so that you can know straightaway how your child is doing. Although children develop at their own pace, it's important to know as early as possible if there's a problem that needs attention. At these checkups, your baby will also be given various inoculations. Although there's some talk about vaccines not being good for children, especially among young New Age parents, I don't put much stock by their worries. I put my faith in the doctors' recommendations, as well as my own common sense. Children pick up so many things at preschool – lice and even tapeworms. These are annoying but can be easily taken care of, and even prevented, if parents would just be more vigilant about hygiene. Why risk more serious illnesses that can put your child at real risk?

NAMING

What names do I suggest for your children? In the Jewish community in Morocco where my family came from, many of us were given Biblical names, like mine. That was lucky, because at that time many other immigrants who came to Israel from elsewhere were told that they had to change their names to Hebrew ones, and we didn't have to change ours. But times are changing. There's less pressure on you newcomers to change your names, and many of you seem keen to keep your old names. Even so, I recommend that you choose Hebrew names for your children. I think it's a sign that you really want to belong here. Also, some names, especially the Ethiopian names, are hard for Israelis to pronounce and might make it difficult for the children to fit in. Sometimes Ashkenazim name people after a deceased relative as a sign of respect; we Mizrahim don't do that, although we do sometimes name our children after living relatives. Anyway, there are lots of names to choose from. Names go in and out of fashion. Nowadays, it's quite fashionable to call children by names that connect them to nature, like Maayan, for instance, which means a natural spring and is a popular girl's name. But Biblical names like Daniel or Tamar seem to stand the test of time, even among secular Jews.

CIRCUMCISION

If you have a son, you must immediately make arrangements for the circumcision to be held on the eighth day of his life (unless for health reasons it has to be postponed). This can be quite stressful – you've just given birth to a baby, and chances are that you're feeling tired and overwrought. It's natural to be a little nervous about the circumcision itself. After all, it's not very pleasant, and even though the *mohel* who does the procedure will give your baby a few drops of wine, your baby may cry. But you really have no choice in the matter. Even if you're secular, there are certain basic rituals that we do the Jewish way, and circumcision is one of them.

Still, there are certain details you can choose. For instance, you can choose if you prefer someone who is a ritual circumciser we call a *mohel*, or a doctor who's also a certified *mohel*. And you can choose to have the circumcision done in a hospital, or at the local synagogue, or even at home. You can also choose whether you want a small gathering at home, or a big event in a hired hall. The ceremony is the occasion on which your son will officially receive his name. In fact, some people say that you shouldn't tell anybody his name until the circumcision, just to keep away the evil eye. When my first son was born, we hadn't told anybody his name, and when the *mohel* read it out at the local synagogue where we held the circumcision ritual, everybody clapped. That was a nice moment and made me almost forget how bad I felt when he cried.

During the baby's first week, don't forget to choose a godfather for him – the person we call a *sandak*. This can be one of the baby's grandfathers or uncles, or even a close friend of yours or your husband's (see Figure 5.1). It's a great honor to be the baby's

Figure 5.1 This photograph commemorates a Jewish circumcision ceremony in Israel. The grandfather is serving as the baby's *sandak* (godfather).
Photograph by Deborah Golden.

sandak. During the circumcision, his job is to hold the baby; afterwards, although he doesn't have many formal obligations, he should take an interest in the boy as he's growing up, and help him along if need be.

If you have a baby girl, there's no ritual. But these days, many families want to celebrate the arrival of girls as well as boys, so it's quite common to have a party or a large family gathering for girls too, without any religious component. Of course, it's nice and important to get friends and family together, but I think we Israelis tend to go over the top in having lavish occasions. Sometimes I think the money could be better spent.

THE CALENDAR: RITUALS AND HOLIDAYS

The circumcision is the first of many rituals and ceremonies that your children will be attending, so you might as well get used to it. First of all, there's the weekly Sabbath. You should always make sure that the family gets together for a Friday night meal. Try and remember to light candles, too, and say the blessing, but even if you don't say the blessing, the candles create a nice atmosphere.

Beyond the weekly Sabbath, the entire year is full of festive days – and, unfortunately, also Memorial Days. Here is the list of holidays we celebrate: New Year, Yom Kippur, Sukkot, Channukah, Tu'beshvat, Purim, Passover, Independence Day, Lag Ba'omer, Shavuot, and Tisha be'av. And here is the list of Memorial Days: Holocaust Remembrance Day, National Memorial Day for Fallen Soldiers and Victims of Terror; and, since 1995, when the prime minister was assassinated, we've had Rabin Memorial Day. Don't forget that Sukkot, Passover, and Shavuot last for an entire week, and all the other days start the evening before, so they actually extend over two days. If you add all these together, you may get the feeling that we have more ceremonial days than routine days! As a teacher, all these holidays make us feel that we never have enough time to teach the basic curriculum. As a mother, even if you're not religious or keep the tradition, you do need to know the basics so that you can prepare your children for each occasion and answer their questions, and they will know what's going on.

You need to be especially prepared for the Memorial Days. These are quite difficult to explain to young children. What are you supposed to say? Even if you want, you can't really shield your children from these days. Young children are very sensitive: on all the Memorial Days, they hear adults talk, see pictures on television, and hear the two-minute siren when everyone stands up straight, looking serious and sad. It's complicated to find a way of explaining things to children in a way that they will understand, but without frightening them. Often, I feel it's better to try and avoid talk of war and political conflict with young children.

But not everyone holds that opinion. Recently, our Ministry of Education introduced a mandatory curriculum for Jewish kindergartners that focuses on the study of the Holocaust. We kindergarten teachers are supposed to teach this unit on the three days surrounding Holocaust Remembrance Day, especially to prepare the children for the siren – which is turned on at exactly 10 a.m., when the kindergarten day is in full swing. Of course, our children must learn about what happened to the Jews under Hitler, but I am undecided about whether or not it's a good idea to teach this to such young children. When the new curriculum was announced, there were lots of arguments and discussions among teachers and parents, as well as articles in the press. We'll see what happens this coming year. In the meantime, there's been a change of government and a new Minister of Education. Often, the new ones do away with much of what their predecessor had put in place.

Even if that happens with this new curriculum, when your children are much older and in eleventh grade, they will most likely go on a school trip to the concentration camps in Poland. Apart from history lessons, that is one of the ways that the schools here try to ensure that our children will never forget what happened to the Jews in the Holocaust. And when they graduate from school, they will have to go into the army. War is part of our life here, and so are terrorist attacks. It's very difficult to know what to say to the children at times of war, or when there are terrorist attacks. Not only because of the fear but also because here we are trying our best to teach children how to solve their quarrels with each other in a non-violent, constructive way, and yet we adults are not setting a very good example for them.

Every generation of parents hopes that, by the time their children are old enough to become soldiers, there will be peace. But so far, that hasn't happened. You are new here, but this is a small country, and almost every family has someone dear to them who was killed or injured in one of our wars, or in a terror attack. Sooner or later, children will become a part of this reality. You have no choice but to prepare your children for the life that lies ahead.

But you must also remember that when they're still very little, you do need to protect them from the harsh realities. Keeping that delicate balance is where your job as a mother comes in. You have to filter things for them. They experience the world through you, so the way that you respond when there is an air raid siren or a bomb attack is very important. It's difficult not to get upset, but for your children's sake it's important to stay calm and give them the feeling that they are safe, even if it's a bit of a pretense – because you're probably scared, too. When your children are still young, I advise you not to go into too many details about what's going on, and why, since they probably won't really understand. It's better just to talk to them about how they're feeling – they're scared or sad. If they can't express their feelings in words, you can ask them to draw or paint a picture.

But let's try and leave all that aside for the moment. I'm getting ahead of things. Thankfully, there's a little time at the beginning, when babies are still too young to understand what's going on around them. That is a time to be cherished.

EARLY EDUCATION

There's nothing as important as giving children a good start in life, and part of that is making sure that they get a good education, right from when they're really young. The big question is what age you should put your child into childcare, and what sort of arrangement will provide the best possible care for your baby or child. Here in Israel, mothers send their babies and children to childcare when they're quite young. That's partly because of the short period of paid maternity leave. If you're going back to work after three months of maternity leave and your mother or mother-in-law can't help on a regular basis, then you need to find a suitable place to send your child as soon as possible. There are many possibilities. Some women's organizations run professional daycare centers, but they can be quite big and impersonal. You might prefer to send your baby or child to be looked after by a woman in her home. She may not be a professional, but usually the group of kids is small, and it's a home-y atmosphere. In the end, you have to choose. I think it comes down to a mixture of liking the atmosphere of the place and the woman in charge, and whether she manages to create a home-like feeling for the children. Spend some time there, check it out, ask friends for recommendations. Does the woman in charge hug and kiss the children? Does she know how to set boundaries so that they don't get too out of hand? Does she make fresh, homemade food? Of course, cost and convenience are also important factors, including hours available, and proximity to where you live.

When your child turns three, you can send him or her to a preschool run by the local municipality, or you can go private (see Figure 5.2). When it comes to choosing a preschool, of course the teacher must be warm and affectionate toward the children, but you must take additional factors into consideration. There's more and more pressure on preschool and kindergarten – from parents and from the Ministry of Education – to make sure that children will be ready for actual school. In fact, we teachers feel more and more pressure, from parents and from the Ministry of Education, to get children ready for reading and writing. Unfortunately, this trend is at the expense of important things like play.

But it's not a good idea to leave everything to us teachers. As a mother, you must get involved with your children's education. Keep your eye on what's happening in your children's classrooms. Of course, you want the best for your children, and

Figure 5.2 These preschool children are celebrating the end of the Israeli school year. The Hebrew letters they are holding up collectively spell out the phrase "Goodbye . . . Preschool, Good Luck."
Photograph by Limor Weissbard.

you understand that a good education is vital for them to get on in the world. I know that many new immigrant parents can't really help their children with some school tasks. When I was growing up, my mother and father couldn't help me very much. My father could read some Hebrew, but only the prayer book. My mother couldn't read or write in any language. Still, she understood the importance of education and did her best for us. We didn't have money for private lessons, so my mother agreed to clean a woman's house in exchange for English lessons for me. When you first arrive, you might not know Hebrew well enough, and you might not know what to teach the children. For instance, if you had no background in Jewish tradition back in Russia, how can we expect you to pass on religious traditions to your children?

Apart from your lack of knowledge in basic subjects, you may be having quite a hard time making ends meet. Perhaps you're out at work all day, maybe even working two shifts a day. If that's the case, you simply won't have the time or the energy to attend to your children's needs. Still, even if it's difficult, it's very important that you spend as much time as you can talking and reading to your children, and even playing with them. Don't spend your hard-earned money on fancy clothes for your babies and older kids; instead, spend it on educational toys and games, even though they're very expensive.

I know that because of these difficulties you may prefer keeping your young children at home to be looked after by their grandmother; or you may consider sending your children to a Russian-speaking preschool. I understand how important it is to you that your children keep up their mother tongue. I also understand that where you were brought up, people were stricter with their children, and you may think that children here in Israel aren't disciplined enough, and that they waste too much time playing and don't do enough proper learning. But during my teacher training, I learned that play is the best way for youngsters to explore and learn. Also, how else are the children going to learn Israeli children's stories and nursery rhymes? And how will they learn about Jewish festivals? For instance, at kindergarten, every Friday we light the Sabbath candles and prepare special challah bread, so that each child can take home some bread that he or she has made. Those traditions are really important.

Besides, it's through playing together that children learn how to get on with each other, how to be friends, how to resolve conflicts. That's very important! On the one hand, children here must learn to be assertive – to stand up for themselves and speak their minds. If they're too soft and well-spoken, other kids will see them as weak and will take advantage of them. Life is difficult here, and children must learn to be tough. On the other hand, they have to learn to be part of a group, and the sooner the better. They can't do that if they're at home with Grandma; and since Israel is their home, it makes sense to get used to playing with Israeli kids. In short, I think it's very important to send your children to a regular Israeli preschool. They need to learn to belong from the start. Besides, that's also the best way for you to learn how to belong in your new country – through your children!

CHAPTER 6

Luring Your Child into this Life of Troubled Times

A Beng Path for Infant Care in Post-Civil War Côte d'Ivoire

Alma Gottlieb

WHO ARE THE BENG?

The Beng are one of the smallest and least known of about sixty ethnic groups in the West African nation of Côte d'Ivoire, or Ivory Coast. With a population of approximately 17,000, they live in some twenty villages located in an ecological border zone between the rainforest to the south and savanna to the north.

The Beng are surrounded by neighbors who speak different languages from theirs (especially Baule, Ando, and Jimini). Their language is one of the group of Southern Mande languages that are spoken far to the west and southwest. Most of their neighbors consider the Beng as the indigenous population in the region. However, their early history is complex and somewhat mysterious. Linguistic evidence suggests the current nation of Mali as a starting point from which the group split off and began a long series of migrations over 2,000 years ago.

The Beng have no memory of the Atlantic slave trade that devastated the continent. Perhaps whenever they felt the threat of slave traders passing nearby, their ancestors managed to elude them by fleeing deep into the forest. As farmers living in relatively small villages in or near the rainforest, they certainly knew the forest well, making regular use of its animal and plant resources. They also engaged in long-distance trade in kola nuts, pottery, bark cloth, and other local products, largely with villagers and long-distance Muslim traders from the north; they often used cowry shells as currency in these transactions.

Their first memories of contact with Europeans are quite recent, commencing with the French occupation of the Beng region in the early 1890s. As pacifists, the Beng prayed to their ancestors and the Earth for deliverance from the colonizing force, but they offered no military or political resistance to the French invaders – unlike other nearby groups that actively resisted colonization. Using violence, the French colonizers compelled Beng farmers to build roads and also to devote time to planting new crops (especially coffee, cocoa, and new varieties of rice and cotton) that the Beng were required to sell back to the French to gain cash, which they were then compelled to give back to the French colonizing force as "taxes"; these forcibly extracted revenues helped support the French colonial empire in West Africa for several decades.

The nation of Côte d'Ivoire gained independence from France in 1960. A wealthy Baule plantation owner, Félix Houphouët-Boigny, became the nation's first president and held that position until his death in 1993. Beng villagers overwhelmingly supported Houphouët throughout his long reign, even though his final years were marked by increasing national debt, corruption, poverty, urban crime, and repression – accompanied by mounting criticism by educated citizens. Scholars began noting signs of upcoming trouble early on, as the president racked up mounting state debt for boondoggle personal projects such as an enormous, air-conditioned, but mostly empty Catholic cathedral in his home village. However, the nation had produced impressive statistics for the global financial sector, and the myth of an "Ivorian miracle" cast a long shadow that obscured the increasing likelihood of economic catastrophe.

When Houphouët died in 1993, he left behind neither clear succession structures nor a clearly appointed heir. The resulting power vacuum allowed bitter political rivalries to foment. The

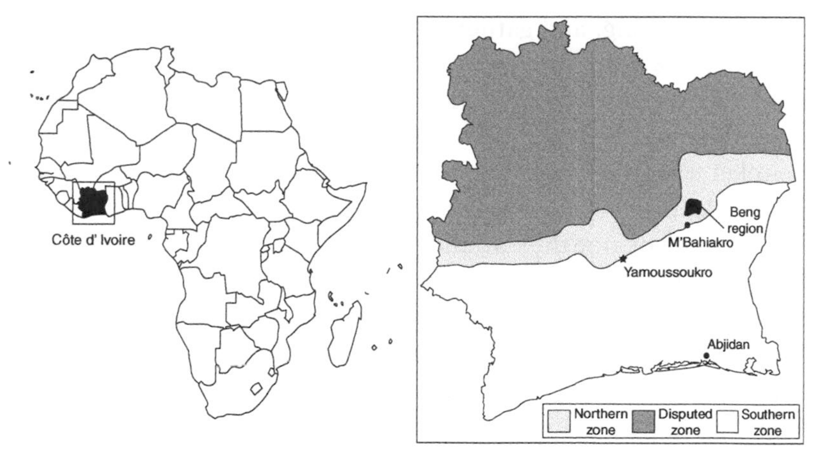

Figure 6.1 In Côte d'Ivoire, the location of their villages – on the border between rainforest to the south and savanna to the north – placed the Beng community in harm's way during the nation's civil war, which pitted north against south.
Map by Billy W. Fore.

country sank into increasingly violent conflict, vigilante justice, and, eventually, intermittent civil war. Beyond a variety of economic and political challenges, the conflict drew from underlying tensions created by the colonial French regime, which had favored development in the (nominally) Christian southern region of fertile rainforest over the (largely) Muslim northern region of more arid savanna. Located along the boundary of the northern and southern regions, Bengland unexpectedly became the site of protracted conflict (see Figure 6.1). Rebels destroyed many houses and farms. As pacifists, the Beng did not become actively involved in the fighting. Instead, many villagers fled the region for the relative safety of nearby towns and cities, while others took refuge in the forest. Now that the war is over, many Beng have made their way back to the villages, where they are endeavoring to rebuild the homes, and lives, they were forced to flee.

Although the nation's conflicts over the past two decades had devastating effects on the Beng, life in the villages had always been challenging in many ways. Then and now, everyone works hard for meager material rewards, practicing a mixed economy of farming, hunting, and gathering. Men typically work in the fields from about 8 a.m. until 5 p.m., sometimes followed by some light village-based work in the evenings. Women typically work even longer hours because of their full-time work on the farms coupled with their near-exclusive responsibility for cooking, house cleaning, water hauling, wood chopping, and childcare.

Whether or not they attend primary school, children are trained in local farming techniques. Even toddlers of two to three years of age are expected to help in agricultural tasks to the best of their abilities. In precolonial times, some men (and a smaller number of women) also hunted game in the forest. However, the growth of a cash economy, with its labor-intensive farming techniques, has reduced the time available for hunting, and the price of bullets and trapping line is too high for many would-be hunters. As a result, the amount of animal protein eaten has declined in recent years. Women, men, and children continue to collect edible wild plants (especially berries and leaves), as well as a variety of small forest creatures such as snails.

Despite extensive Western rhetoric about promoting "development" in the "Third World," as with many other peasant populations of Africa the Beng became progressively impoverished under both the French colonial regime and the postcolonial governments. In the 1990s, some Beng families had reverted to a virtual subsistence economy. Following the ending of national conflict, government rebuilding of infrastructure has been slow, and democratic structure remains fragile. The weakness of the state makes the nation vulnerable to a range of troubling effects, from toxic waste dumping by irresponsible multinational corporations to problematic moral codes of youth. Religious and ethnic xenophobia have been stoked since Houphouët's death, exacerbated by Othering processes (especially directed toward Muslim immigrants from the nation's northern neighbor of Burkina Faso) that became institutionalized during the period of political conflict. This stigmatization of the nation's Muslim residents is leaving it vulnerable to religious extremism and human rights abuses.

As elsewhere, the declining economy and weak infrastructure have profound implications for children's lives. Some Beng parents cannot afford childhood inoculations, and the relatively new health post in the Beng region is often closed for lack of personnel, and bereft of medicines when it is open. Many parents who would like to send their children to school cannot afford the expenses for uniforms and school supplies that the nominally free school system requires. The nearest junior high school remains outside the Beng region, requiring uprooting of children from their families to attend, and the nearest high school is even farther, requiring creative strategies to find appropriate housing.

Beng villages are grouped into two internal political divisions, each of which is ruled by a king-and-queen pair (who are considered to be sister and brother). A local court system has an appeals structure built into it; only rarely do people resort to the highest level of appeal – the national government.

The schools are modeled on the French educational system, with all instruction conducted in the country's official language of French. Although elementary school is compulsory for six years, many Beng parents do not comply with this law, in part because of distrust of anything related to the French colonial regime and its aftermath. Until the 1970s, some parents who were forced to send their children to school even prayed to local spirits that their sons and daughters fail their exams so they could leave school.

Currently, more young people are rejecting the conservatism of their elders, and more young parents are complying with national law and sending their children to elementary school for at least a few years. Still, the failure and dropout rates of Beng students, even at the elementary school level, has been quite high. For example, in 1993 in one Beng village's elementary school, eleven out of thirty-nine first grade students failed, and only thirteen out of thirty-six students in the last grade passed an eligibility test to attend junior high school. As of this writing, only one Beng person has achieved a doctoral degree (in political science).

Beng families are usually large. In the villages, birth control efforts are generally limited to a taboo on sex until a baby can walk independently. Although there are many variations, extended families typically consist of a husband and wife (or wives), all their unmarried daughters, all their sons, and their married sons' wives and children. Until the 1960s, extended families generally lived together under the thatched roof of a single large, round house. In the 1960s, the government, citing risk of fire, bulldozed these houses and required smaller, square houses with tin roofs for all new buildings meant for sleeping. Nevertheless, extended families still manage to live near one another, with family subgroups often inhabiting small buildings surrounding an open courtyard.

A double system of clans crosscuts the family structure, with each individual belonging simultaneously to two clans – one whose membership is traced exclusively in the female line (matriclans) and another whose membership is traced exclusively in the male line (patriclans). At marriage, neither men nor women change their membership in either of these clans. Until recently, virtually all first marriages of young women were arranged by their families, according to a complex system determined by birth order. This system is still actively maintained, although some women have begun rebelling against it.

Until the 1960s, most Beng devoutly practiced an indigenous religion. In the past few decades, more people have become attracted to Islam, and some have endorsed Christianity (both Catholicism and Protestantism). A mosque now exists in one village, and most other villages have at least a significant minority of Muslim Beng (as well as immigrant Muslims of other ethnic groups, especially Julas). However, like many West Africans, most Beng who have endorsed one of the "world" religions continue to practice at least some components of their traditional religion; only a few have completely converted.

The indigenous religion requires people to offer regular prayers and sacrifices to the sky/god (*eci*), ancestors, a variety of bush spirits, and other spirits affiliated directly with the Earth. Indigenous religious practitioners are primarily of two sorts – diviners and Earth priests. Diviners, who may be either male or female, use a variety of techniques to communicate with invisible spirits of the bush and of ancestors; they then interpret the spirits' communications to their clients. One of the commonest reasons for villagers to consult diviners is to discover the cause and/or cure for a child's illnesses. Mothers of sick children frequently consult a secular herbalist first; if the child's symptoms remain after she has carried out the herbalist's orders, the mother then consults a diviner.

Often, the divination indicates that a sacrifice to the Earth is necessary. In this case, the client then consults an Earth priest. These priests, who are almost always male, worship the Earth spirits once every six days (according to the traditional six-day Beng calendar). They offer prayers, as well as sacrifices of palm wine, kola nuts, eggs, and domestic animals, on behalf of people who seek protection against witchcraft, relief from afflictions deemed to have a spiritual cause, or atonement for past sins. They also offer sacrifices on behalf of those who want to give thanks for wishes granted or good fortune experienced.

A divination may reveal that a given illness is being caused by ancestors who feel neglected by their living descendants, who may not be making the desired offerings. As elsewhere in Africa, Beng ancestors are incorporated into daily life. Most adult men and some adult women pray and make offerings (especially palm wine) to their ancestors regularly. For example, before drinking palm wine, beer, or commercial wine, people always spill a few drops onto the ground for their ancestors. Male and female heads of clans also make regular offerings to the clan's ancestors on behalf of the entire clan.

Once people die, their souls, or *nining*, are said to become *wru*, or spirits, that travel to *wrugbe*, the land of the dead. As ancestral spirits, the *wru* lead full lives parallel to the daily lives of those on earth. Eventually the ancestors are reincarnated into this life. All newborns are seen as having just emerged from *wrugbe*; sometimes their ancestral identities are revealed early in childhood.

The "manual" that follows is based on typical Beng village infant care practices. Some Beng mothers now living in towns and cities in Côte d'Ivoire try to replicate these practices in an urban setting. Other Beng women living in town return to their village when they are pregnant, or soon after delivering. Still others have begun to modify or even abandon the infant care practices of their grandmothers in favor of those deemed "modern."

Like people in any society, individual Beng villagers offer a variety of perspectives on childrearing. The manual that follows highlights two perspectives that are particularly important: that of grandmothers, who offer pragmatic/secular advice based on their years of childrearing and its exhausting labor demands; and that of diviners, who offer herbal cures as well as what might be called "pastoral counseling," based on their communication with the invisible spirits that populate Beng consciousness. The grandmother's voice is a composite of dozens of Beng grandmothers I have known, while the diviner's voice is a composite of three Beng diviners I have known. However, the distinction between the two voices I present below is not absolute. Diviners may themselves be grandmothers or mothers and offer pragmatic advice on occasion as well. Moreover, like all Beng adults, grandmothers are acutely aware of the spiritual aspects of infancy, even if they do not articulate the subtleties of this awareness as regularly and clearly as diviners do. It is a matter of emphasis rather than of knowledge. Indeed, for Beng villagers, the religious and the mundane are not easily distinguished. The infant care practices that follow illustrate that general principle.

LURING YOUR CHILD INTO THIS LIFE OF TROUBLED TIMES: A BENG PATH FOR INFANT CARE IN POST-CIVIL WAR CÔTE D'IVOIRE

About the Authors

A GRANDMOTHER

I've lived a long time. My white hair shows I've seen more than two days, and my children have had children; my grandson's wife is pregnant with my first great-grandchild. I've taken a belly nine times, nursed and bathed nine babies, painted nine babies' faces, carried nine babies on my back, made jewelry for nine babies, and kept nine babies from walking too early – and that doesn't include all the grandchildren, nieces, nephews, and neighbors' babies I have also cared for. Only two of my little ones died during their first year; the other seven have survived.

Not all elders become wise – some merely become more foolish as they grow older. May our sky/god, *eci*, let me have learned something I can show you before I join the ancestors. Since I never attended school, I don't know paper; I've told what I know to one of my granddaughters who has gone to school, and she's written down my words. Through her, I'll show you how to raise your child.

A MALE DIVINER

Everyone needs diviners. Most villages have at least one; even animals have the porcupine who wags its tail to answer their questions. We diviners reveal the other world to people of this world.

When I was born, our sky/god, *eci*, gave me the gift of speaking with the spirits. At three, I was already reading cowry shells – the spirits spoke to me through them. Even now, I am still young. My wife and I have only two children – but people often walk from faraway villages to ask me to show them who or what has harmed them, and what they must do to cure their illnesses.

I went to school, but as for books, the rainwater didn't seep into my house – I didn't learn much because I had to leave after three years to help my father in the fields. So I've told my words to a schoolboy who's written them down. May *eci* let him know well the ways of paper.

SHOWING YOU THE BENG WAY

Since two of us are talking, we may sometimes show you different things to do. If you follow one of our recommendations and it doesn't help, try the suggestion that the other one offers. Better yet, do everything we both show you, and you won't go wrong.

In our villages, girls and women usually take care of babies, so we've addressed this manual to you. Still, we know that some boys and men like caring for babies. There's no shame in this – you, too, can learn much from these pages.

If you are a Beng woman and were raised in a Beng village, you don't need this paper, for all your mothers – your own mother and her sisters, and indeed all the village's women – will be your teachers. But because of the war, many young Beng women nowadays were born or raised in the city, while their parents were fleeing the rebels occupying our villages. After growing up in towns and cities, some Beng youth have found someone to marry who is not Beng. If you are such a woman who is, perhaps, Baule or Jula and has married a Beng man, this manual will be especially useful to you. You will learn how your Beng husband's sisters are raising their children, and what your Beng mother-in-law will expect you to do in raising her grandchild.

A more difficult subject to speak about concerns the rebels who occupied our villages. We know that some of them raped our women. Since we do not do anything to prevent becoming pregnant, some of our women took a belly from these men. If you are a Beng woman, perhaps this happened to one of your older sisters or cousins. She may have told you how traumatic her path to motherhood has been, and this may scare you. But remember, those dark days are over. Even if your family has forced you to marry a boy you didn't choose, you will grow closer to your husband as you become parents together, and the love you both feel for the child you lure to this world will help you develop new love for one another.

Wherever you live, and whoever the father of your child, it's important to preserve our ways. After all, if your husband is Beng, you'll want to please him and his family. If you're Beng, you'll join our ancestors in *wrugbe* when you die; after staying there some time, you'll be reborn – perhaps into one of the villages. Besides, you know well how few Beng there are. If our children don't carry on our customs, our ways will vanish.

Luring Your Child into this Life of Troubled Times

TAKING A BELLY

A Grandmother's Words

If yours was an arranged marriage, you already know that your first duty is to "take a belly" as soon as possible. At your wedding, people undoubtedly blessed you, "May *eci* make it right!" You probably realized that this meant you should have many children. If you married your husband in a love match, you probably won't feel in quite such a rush to take a belly just to please your families, but you will probably want a child soon for your own reasons. If a few moons go by and you don't see signs of pregnancy, it may be because you're too hot. Try drinking some "raw medicine." Pound together some leaves, add some crumbly white clay to it, and drink the mixture cold. You can ask a healer to recommend good plants for this purpose.

Once you become pregnant, you must observe many precautions. You should keep your breasts covered when you walk around the village. If they're exposed, a jealous woman might bewitch you and make your childbirth difficult. And your hair must remain on your head – if you were to shave it off, as we do in mourning, you'd die during childbirth.

As your belly swells, the skin becomes tight. If you can afford it, buy some shea butter in the market (or make it from kernels of the shea tree's fruits), and rub it on your belly to keep the skin nicely stretched. Don't wear tight shirts, or your baby won't breathe properly.

Be careful not to eat *fufu* made with plaintains, or your baby will get too fat. Avoid eating meat from the bushbuck antelope with striped lines, or your baby will have striped or patchy skin. Don't eat purée of boiled yams or leftover foods; if you do, your labor will be difficult, and you'll defecate during childbirth – a great embarrassment! Don't drink palm wine during the first few months, or your pregnancy will be totally ruined.

While you're pregnant, you should give yourself special enemas every day. If you make an enema using the slippery and shiny leaves of the *vowló* vine, your placenta will become slippery, too, and will slide out quickly after the birth. If you don't know this plant, ask your mother or mother-in-law to show it to you in the forest; if you're living in a city, ask a village relative to send it to you.

If you're living in the village, you must bear in mind another risk. Never eat food while walking along the paths to your fields. Should you forget this, a forest snake may eat the crumbs that fall on the path and will develop a longing for human food. To continue feasting on our delicacies, the snake will switch places with the fetus inside you, and you'll give birth to a snake-child. At first the baby may appear human, but as the diviner will explain, its true character will one day be exposed. May *eci* let you escape from this misfortune! If you're living in town, you won't need to worry about this danger.

Whether in town or country, be careful to stay far away from corpses of people and of dogs – both kinds are dangerous to the baby inside you. If you touched such a corpse, your baby would be born with the disease "Dog" or "Corpse." Just in case you might touch a corpse by mistake, bathe regularly with a decoction of leaves from the *wéé* plant – this should protect against the disease catching your fetus. (Even after birth, your baby will remain vulnerable. If you bring your little one to a funeral, make sure to stay far from the corpse, or it might entice your baby back to *wrugbe*.) Still, if another pregnant woman dies from witchcraft while you're pregnant, you must join in her funeral. The funeral dance in which you must participate would be held outside in the courtyard of the woman who died, but it's really a secret women's dance. The women who dance wear nothing but the old-style bark cloth underwear, and no men or boys may watch.

But enough of such sad affairs. May *eci* grant that you never hear any rotten news! Let us turn to another subject.

After you've taken a belly, your actions will determine your baby's character. You must try very hard to be good so your child will have a good character, too. If you steal something while you are pregnant, your child will develop the long arm of a thief; if you bewitch someone, your baby will become a witch. Don't set hunting traps – pregnancy is a time to nurture life, not take it. Try not to offend others. If someone is so angry that they invoke the Earth to curse you, your pregnancy is in jeopardy. You must immediately sacrifice an animal to the Earth to apologize; otherwise you'll have grave difficulties during the delivery – truly!

Once you take a belly, you shouldn't return to an old boyfriend or take a new lover. If you do, you may suffer a miscarriage, and your lover would suffer for the next seven years. For his part, your husband must observe certain precautions. He should stop hunting, especially at night when it's difficult to see well, because he might kill a female animal that is pregnant. If that should happen, both you and the baby inside your belly would die! Even though people and animals are separated into the two worlds of village and forest, they remain connected; occasionally, they can even switch places. What happens to forest animals can affect what happens to you and the baby inside your belly.

You can continue to have sex with your husband throughout your pregnancy. Any position is fine as long as it's comfortable. Toward the end of your pregnancy, side-by-side will probably be the only position possible. If you prefer not to make love, your husband shouldn't insist. Of course, your husband may be off working in a city, or on one of those cocoa plantations down south, and the pleasures of his company may not even be an option for you.

If you and your husband argue and he threatens divorce, your family should tell him that whether it's good for him or it ruins him, he should remain with you until after the child is born – otherwise you'd have a very difficult time during childbirth. For that matter, if you die during the birth, it's your husband who must offer sacrifices – and if he's divorced you, who would present the offerings?

Giving birth is dangerous. In the old days, our ancestors had strong medicines to protect us against witchcraft, and we old people say it was rare for a woman to die while trying to give birth. Nowadays, even though they say it's the time of modernity, there are more witches who may threaten your pregnancy. If you're living in a village or small town and are afraid that someone may bewitch you during your delivery, earn or borrow some money so that before your eighth month you can take a bus to Bouaké or Abidjan to give birth in a doctor's room. May *eci* grant that you reach there safely! It'll be difficult for the witches to find you so far away.

A Diviner's Words

If you're having trouble taking a belly, consult a diviner. If the seer throws cowry shells on a mat, one may land on top of another – a sign that you'll become pregnant and will carry the baby on your back, just as one cowry shell is carrying another on its back. Two shells landing apart from the rest means you'll become pregnant with twins. If the two cowries apart from the rest are stuck to one another, it signifies that there must be twins living in your family who've disrupted your menstrual cycle. All twins are witches, so you must offer the twins a sacrifice to ask their forgiveness. If they accept it, you'll become pregnant.

Once you take a belly, before the seventh month of your pregnancy make sure that your husband sacrifices an egg to the Earth of your village. After receiving the sacrifice, the Earth will protect you and your baby through the rest of the pregnancy, and the delivery.

WHEN YOUR BELLY STARTS TO HURT

A Grandmother's Words

When your belly starts to hurt, your baby wants to be born. May *eci* let it be good for you! Since we still don't have a maternity clinic in any of our villages, you'll probably give birth in your hut just like your mothers and grandmothers did before you. Tell someone in your compound your belly's hurting, and some women in your husband's or your family will come to help. Sit on the floor with your legs outstretched, and one of your companions – preferably someone who's strong and not too old – will support you as you lean back. For your first birth, it's normal for you to be afraid; trust the older women in the room to tell you what to do.

Luring Your Child into this Life of Troubled Times

Once the baby has been born, one of the women will cut the umbilical cord with a razor blade. Try to find a new one to use, as the nurses tell us that an old razor can cause the "serious disease" I will tell you about soon. Still, if a witch is determined to kill your child, she will do all she can to find other means.

Once the placenta's out, someone will announce the news around the village. At least one person from every household will soon be at your door. If you live in a large village, the line of well-wishers may be long! One by one, they'll bless you and ask, "What have you given me?" You can just reply, "A girl" or "A boy," and they'll thank you. That way, everyone in the village will feel that they're part of your baby's life, and your newborn will feel welcome to the village.

A Diviner's Words

If you're having trouble giving birth, may *eci* get you out of it! We diviners know some good herbal remedies. For instance, you should deliver soon after someone rubs the leaves of two particular plants between the palms of her hands and squeezes some of the water onto your head and some into your mouth, and then rubs the rest onto your belly.

If you're still having trouble after such treatments, one of your or your husband's relatives should consult a diviner. We may diagnose that either you or a member of your mother's clan has sinned against the Earth. In this case, we'll instruct someone in your family to make an offering, usually a chicken, to the Earth right away, to apologize. Then the birth should proceed without problem. Or, we may hear from the spirits that the baby inside you isn't joining this world because no one's calling the baby by the right name – the name the baby wants. One woman I know was having a very difficult childbirth. The diviner said that spirits had named the baby Mo Jaa, and she was waiting to hear her name before coming out. When the women in the room called, "Mo Jaa, come out quickly!" the baby was born right away.

BEFORE THE UMBILICAL CORD STUMP FALLS OFF

A Grandmother's Words

Soon after the birth, if the breast water that will sustain your baby over the next year hasn't yet poured out, ask female elders of your village for leaves to lay on your breasts to make the water come in. If your breasts are also swollen, witchcraft is the cause. Some healers know other leaves you can heat and apply to your breasts, to reduce the swelling.

Meanwhile, start doing *kami* right away. When the baby cries, before offering your breast, get a cupful of cool water from your large ceramic water jar. Cradle the baby in your arms, tilt the head back a little, and give a small palmful of the water. If your little one refuses the water, go ahead and force it down the throat. You must teach your baby to like the taste of water. That way, when you can't be together – say, you're chopping trees for firewood, or collecting water from the well – someone else can satisfy your hungry child with plain water until you return with breastwater. You know how much work we women have to do, and we can't always take our babies along. If you don't train your baby to do *kami*, your life will be difficult!

A Diviner's Words

Right after the birth, the baby needs a very thorough bath. In the old days, the female head of your mother's clan would have washed your baby in a large wooden bowl; nowadays your mother might bathe the baby in an enamel basin sold in the market. Remember that your new child has just been living in *wrugbe* with our ancestors, so your mother must wash off as much of *wrugbe* as possible. For the first bath, she should use home-made black soap – the kind we use for washing corpses. This makes sense, since newborns and the newly dead are both moving from one world to the next. (In future baths, you can use the white soap sold in the market.)

Following the first bath, your mother will wash out your baby's mouth with lemon juice; she may also attach a whole lemon to a cotton cord and tie this around your infant's tiny wrist as a bracelet. These, too, will help chase away death and protect your baby from witches. The lemon is a powerful tree, helping us move from one world to the other and keeping us from the other world when it is not yet our time to go. (At a funeral, people also wear lemon bracelets to protect against witchcraft and death, and they wash corpses with leaves from the lemon tree.)

Your mother will bathe your baby four times a day until the umbilical cord stump falls off, which usually happens by the third or fourth day. To dry out the stump quickly, one of your mothers or grandmothers will dab a tiny bit of an herbal mixture on the dangling cord every few minutes all day long and even through the night. This is a tiresome task, but it's too important to neglect! Until the umbilical cord stump falls off, your newborn hasn't yet begun to become a person. The tiny creature is still living completely as a *wru* in the other world. If your newborn stops breathing during those first few days, we won't hold a funeral; having never left *wrugbe* at all, the baby hasn't really died.

WHEN THE UMBILICAL CORD STUMP FALLS OFF

A Grandmother's Words

The day that your baby's umbilical stump falls off, you and some female relatives will gather in your dark bedroom and give the baby the first enema. For your first child, your mother will teach you how to crush the leaves of the *kprawkpraw* plant together with a single chili pepper and some warm water, and then put the mixture inside a bulb-shaped gourd that we women grow for this purpose. With the little one lying across your knees, and a basin below, insert the gourd into your baby's bottom hole. You will hear some loud screams, for it's like breaking the hymen the first time a girl has sex. You remember how that hurt, don't you? Still, you'll feel proud that you're starting to introduce your baby into this life, since we give ourselves enemas regularly all our lives. Indeed, from now until the baby walks, you *must* administer such an enema every morning and every night (though you can use a rubber bulb syringe sold in the market, rather than the old-fashioned gourd). Usually the baby will shit into the basin as soon as you've removed the gourd.

A few hours after the first enema, your mother (or another older woman) will make the baby a simple necklace from savanna grass or the bark of a pineapple tree. After she puts the necklace around the baby, your mother may bless it by saying, "May *eci* let it never rip." Your baby will wear this necklace night and day. Only after this cord is attached can your little one begin to wear jewelry with beads, shells, and other ornaments. If your baby is a girl, a female elder can pierce her tiny ears that very day, leaving a black cotton thread in the hole until it sets and your baby can then have real earrings.

A Diviner's Words

The day that a baby's umbilical cord stump falls off is important, truly! It shows that your newborn has begun to leave *wrugbe*. As soon as the stump has dropped off, rub *nunu pléplé* leaves onto the spot. Along with lemon trees, the leaves from this plant are used at funerals, where they chase away the smell – and contagion – of death. On your baby's belly button, the leaves will help your baby leave the death of *wrugbe* behind. Still, you should know that this is a long, slow process that takes your child a few years to complete. One day you'll know that your older children have left *wrugbe* forever when they tell you or your husband about a dream they had, saying that it was only a dream. But that may not happen until your child is older, maybe even six or seven years old.

Until then, your baby will miss certain things from the other life. You should consult a diviner as soon as possible to find out what these are! Our fees aren't high – rarely more than fifty CFAs. This is far less than the price of a bus that you will pay going to the city clinic if your baby gets very sick because you did not consult a diviner!

We diviners have several methods. Some swirl milky-white water in a bowl; others dance. Me, I throw cowry shells on a bark cloth mat. Once I water my cowries, the spirits of the bush and the ancestors are drawn to the shells. Since your baby was just living in the other life, your little one can speak to these spirits, which also inhabit *wrugbe*. As I throw the cowries onto my mat, the spirits arrange the shells to speak for your baby, and I read their secrets from the patterns.

Usually we tell you to give a cowry to your baby as a first gift. This is because long, long ago the cowry was money for our ancestors; it's still money in the other life, so the spirits of our ancestors all like them. Remember, your newborn was just living among the ancestors a few days ago, and a shell will remind your baby of that life in *wrugbe*. You can string the shell onto cotton thread that the baby can wear as a bracelet.

YOUR BABY'S NAME

A Grandmother's Words

No matter what your child is named, the baby's grandparents may want to be present for the naming. In the old days we named our babies for spirits in the rivers, hills, and other places. Nowadays, few parents do this. Depending on the day the baby was born, most parents just use the day names we've borrowed from our Baule neighbors. For example, if your daughter is born on a Tuesday, her name will be Ajua (for a boy, Kouadio). Keep in mind that our day ends at sundown, so if your baby is born after dusk, you must use the name of the day beginning that evening. If your daughter (or son) is born the same weekday that an older sister (or brother) was born, add *kro*, or "little," to the baby's day name, and *kala*, or "big," to your older child's name. That way, they won't both come when you call!

Each of the day names has a somewhat secret name – a "name underneath" – that goes with it. You'll find good occasion to use this name with your child – for instance, if you're angry at your child for being naughty, or if you want to calm down your child from being upset. But remember that even though the baby's "name underneath" is shared with all the other people who have that day name, we try to keep these names hidden. Only say it aloud to your child in your own compound, or it won't remain concealed for long! I won't divulge the names here – find out your baby's own "name underneath" from an older relative.

In addition to the day names, if you have twins, a girl will also be named Kolu or Klingo; a boy, Sã or Zi. If you have three daughters or three sons in a row, the third will be named Nguessan; if your next child is another daughter (or another son), the name will be Ndri. If you have the misfortune to have two babies die one right after another, the third child born after those two will be called Wamyã (for a boy) or Sunu (for a girl). With all these names, wherever your children go in our world, people will know something about them.

In addition to our Black people's names, some parents choose to give French names to their children. In truth, I don't know what these White people's names mean or where they come from, so I can't say more about them. The teachers seem to prefer calling our children by these names in school. I suppose these names' time has come.

A Diviner's Words

If your baby is born the very same day that a grandparent dies, the little one should be named after that grandparent. Or your baby may be given the same name as a grandparent who is already in *wrugbe*. In both cases, your baby is a replacement of his or her grandparent, and many people will call the child Grandma or Grandpa.

Nowadays our naming system is not good. Many of our parents just assign day names without imagining who the baby was in *wrugbe*. This is not realistic! Everyone had another identity in the other life, and many babies prefer us to acknowledge that. Other babies are gifts of spirits and should be named after them, or the spirits will become angry. As I'll explain, if you have chosen the wrong name, your baby may become very sick.

PROTECTING YOUR BABY AGAINST SICKNESS

A Grandmother's Words

As a mother, it's your responsibility to keep your baby healthy and find appropriate medicines for sicknesses. Should you neglect this, your husband may criticize you. If you're still living in your parents' house, your husband may hold a private family trial requesting that you return to his home so he can make sure you are giving the baby proper treatments.

We have many ways to protect our babies from falling ill. An important one is a long bathing routine. Once the umbilical cord has fallen off, you *must* bathe your baby twice a day – every day – until the child walks. Otherwise, the little one will come down with the very serious disease we call Dirt, which causes a bad Dirt Cough. This disease doesn't come from the ordinary dirt that sticks to the skin when your baby lies or crawls on the ground; no, it comes from another form of dirt that we can't see but that's much more dangerous. This is the dirt that comes from being held – or even touched briefly – by a man or woman who hasn't bathed in the morning after having had sex the night before. All grown people know that we must *always* bathe every morning so that if we had sex the night before, we won't bring the sickness of Dirt to babies we might touch that day. Shame on the person who forgets! Even after your baby is no longer vulnerable to this kind of dirt, keep the child accustomed to bathing twice every day so that, as an adult, your son or daughter will never forget to bathe the morning after having sex.

The next most important way to keep your baby healthy is to put many strands of jewelry onto the little one. Perhaps you have thought that all the necklaces, bracelets, and anklets that our babies wear are just to make them look beautiful. Some of our men think this! In truth, only a few of the necklaces and waist bands are meant just to embellish our babies; most are to protect them from diseases. I'll tell you about some items of jewelry, but keep in mind that we have too many types for me to list them all here.

Your mothers and grandmothers may give you some beads and shells, and you can also buy beads in the market – though

Figure 6.2 This Beng baby is wearing colonial-era French coins on his necklace to remind him of the afterlife he is said to miss. Photograph by Alma Gottlieb.

some are hard to find, and expensive. Still, your baby should wear as many strands as possible – the more jewelry, the better protected against disease (see Figure 6.2). For example, you can guard against Dirt by keeping a Dirt Cord on your baby, made with some of your own hair, or from pineapple tree bark and some beads and knots. Don't worry that your baby might strangle from the necklaces – remember that the cords protect your baby so they can't possibly cause harm.

Another danger to your baby's health is Full Moon. If a baby is caught by the bright light of a full moon, the little one's stomach will become quite round and swollen – like the full moon. At another time of the month, the disease Bird can catch your little one if a rotten bird (such as an owl or a vulture) flies overhead on the night of a new moon. This is even more serious – your child's neck may break and bend backwards, the body become cold, the elbows stiff, and the eyes white.

You may wonder why the new moon and the full moon – the beginning and end of the moon's cycle – are dangerous to babies. Perhaps it's because babies occupy the beginning and end of our own cycle – the beginning of their stay in this life, and the end of their stay in *wrugbe*. Fortunately, a waist band can protect your baby against both Bird (from the new moon) and Full Moon. Make it by tying together a black cord (like the black of a new moon night) and a white cord (like the light of a full moon).

Danger is also associated with daily cycles. One form of fever that can kill your baby quickly is caused by touching dew, which is too powerful for babies. Dew, of course, appears at the beginning and end of the day (before dawn and after dusk) – a bit like babies themselves, who also occupy the beginning and end of our life's cycle. If you put a cotton Dew Cord around your little one's knees or ankles, and maybe running up the shins, the child will be well protected from dew touching a leg on the way to the fields in early morning or late evening.

All the jewelry I've described must be as clean as your baby's body. Every morning and evening, after you wash your baby's skin, carefully clean each strand with soap, then squeeze the moisture out with a towel. By this time your baby might be very hungry from not having nursed for a while and may start to cry or pull on your breast. But don't rush washing the jewelry – it must be done properly! As you scrub the jewelry, inspect each strand – if it's frayed, repair it right away, otherwise the beads may fall off and your baby, no longer protected, could fall sick. One of your mothers can show you how to retie the complicated knots.

You can also protect your baby by painting brightly colored medicines onto the face and head. Many babies have an orange dot on their fontanel, which is the end point of a "head road" that runs down to the throat. If the path becomes blocked, the throat will close, the baby won't be able to nurse or eat well, and the little one may develop a fever or cough. Keep your baby's head road open by painting an orange dot on the fontanel during every morning and evening bath. Make the orange paint by chewing a red kola nut, then spitting out your saliva – which will be bright orange – onto your finger. (The kola is a powerful fruit – in the old days it was trading kola nuts that gave us our wealth.) Keep applying this orange kola water twice every day until your child starts to walk. At this time, the head road will close up and your little one will no longer be at risk.

In addition to these ways we have for keeping our babies healthy, White people have some useful customs, too. If you're lucky enough to find the health post open when you go to the one in our village, you might get some good White people's medicines or advice if the nurse is on duty. In addition, every so often, vans of nurses show up in our villages to inject us with medicines. My schoolgirl granddaughter tells me that if a woman gets one of those shots, any baby in her belly will be protected against the "difficult disease" that the White people call "tetanus." But, truly, it takes a lot of courage to line up with your children for the shots. The nurses shout orders in French, and who can understand them? Besides, you have to pay for the needle, and if you don't have a medical record notebook, you'll need to buy one from the nurses. You'd better start saving now!

A Diviner's Words

There's another thing you can do to keep your baby healthy. If your husband offered an egg to the Earth while you were pregnant, this has created a debt. Soon after the baby is born, you or your husband should offer another sacrifice to the Earth. This time, it must be a chicken – as thanks for having protected the baby while still inside your belly. With this second sacrifice, the Earth will continue to watch over your baby.

WHEN YOUR BABY GETS CAUGHT BY SICKNESS

A Grandmother's Words

May *eci* let your baby be healthy! Alas, our babies fall sick quite often. The nurses say it's because of our water and all the insects around us. But we know that a witch will find ways to cause someone harm no matter how clean the water or how few the insects.

If your baby falls sick, go see a healer. Our healers know many health-giving plants that can cure illnesses. Even the poorest among us can pay a healer. Of course, if the healer is a relative, you won't have to pay anything.

If your baby's body is hot, one of your mothers can tell you about plants that can bring down the fever. After bathing your baby, lay some leaves on the embers of your hearth fire to wilt them. After a few moments, rub them between your hands to squeeze out their water, then pat the leaf water over your baby's warm body.

If a carrier of the contagious disease Dirt touches your baby, soap will never wash it off. Instead, try bathing your baby with leaves from the *vowlo* liana, which are quite slippery – maybe the disease will slide off the baby. The disease itself is so powerful that you should bathe your baby five or six times a day with the leaf wash. Collect a fresh bunch of leaves in the forest for each bath. While your baby is sick with Dirt, this disease will keep you very busy! Try to find someone to weed or sow your fields, chop wood, and haul water for you, so your work isn't neglected.

Another dangerous sickness you can treat with medicinal plants is Corpse. Leaves that touched death can cure your baby if the little one has touched a dead body. If your baby son is caught by Corpse, go to any woman or girl's grave and take some leaves of any plant growing on top. If your baby daughter is sick, have your husband do the same with the grave of any man or boy. Then make a leaf wash to cure your baby.

Some time during the first two to three weeks, your newborn may start crying very loudly. If the screams continue and become sharper, the little one's tiny arms and legs get stiff, the back arches, and the baby seems truly miserable, this may be the "difficult disease" – the one White people call "tetanus." Unfortunately, there is little hope. If you're rich, you can take your baby to the hospital, but the medicines you'll have to buy may cost more money than you've ever seen. You'll probably need to borrow money from a lot of relatives for the medicines. If the health center they built in one of our villages isn't open, or there's no nurse there, you'll need to borrow more money for a bus trip to town for yourself and one of your mothers, or your husband. Then, the doctor will tell you to stay nearby for a few days to make sure the baby is better before returning home, so you'll have to buy a lot of expensive food in the market. You may also be humiliated by a nurse showing off by speaking French, even if you clearly don't understand a word. If he makes fun of village remedies like the jewelry protecting your baby, ignore it and ask for his medicines. The worst part is that after you endure humiliation and spend maybe a year's earnings, the doctor will tell you that, at best, only half the babies he treats with his medicines survive the "difficult disease." *Aiie*, perhaps, after all, it's better for you to save your money to feed and clothe the rest of your family.

Aside from all I've said so far, there may be days when your baby will cry for no obvious reason. It may be that she's not sleeping enough. You know that babies like to fall asleep on someone's back. If you have some work to do in your faraway fields way deep in the forest (or in another section of town, if you live in a city), tie your baby onto your back with your *pagne* cloth and start walking – your baby will sleep well on your back as you walk.

If, despite all your efforts, your baby keeps crying, it's time to consult a diviner.

A Diviner's Words

Remember, babies have just come from the land of the dead, where they were someone else. The younger your baby, the more the little one is still living and thinking with our ancestors, especially the baby's *wrugbe* parents. If *eci* agrees, your baby will leave *wrugbe* behind some day. But this won't happen right away, for babies still hear the language of the other world, and it calls to them. Your little one may miss *wrugbe* and be eager to return. Falling sick or crying is a way to tell you something the baby is missing, or who the baby was in *wrugbe* – but like most adults, you probably can't understand. When you consult a diviner, your baby will speak to the spirits of the bush and of *wrugbe*; the spirits will then speak to the diviner, who will interpret their words for you.

The diviner may hear from the spirits that the little one is unhappy with the name you've chosen and prefers another one – perhaps the name the baby had while in *wrugbe*, or the name of the spirit who gave you your baby. Offer gifts to these spirits every so often to keep them happy, or they'll make your baby sick again. For instance, if your baby was given to you by the *Anie* spirits that live in one of our sacred pools of water, put some fresh water into a calabash every so often as an offering to those spirits, and call your baby Anie.

In addition to being misnamed, your sick or crying baby may be trying to tell you about some things from *wrugbe* that are missed. Young babies especially miss cowry shells, old French coins, and silver jewelry – the treasures they had while in *wrugbe*. We might recommend a single shell or coin on a necklace, or lots of cowries strung together on a bracelet. In giving your baby this jewelry, you'll show that you respect your child's memories and desires. As soon as you provide the jewelry and begin using the name the child wants, your little one should stop crying and return to good health. That will show you that we diviners speak the truth!

Another way your child may fall sick is if you, your husband, or someone in your families has violated one of the Earth's taboos and hasn't yet offered a sacrifice as an apology. This is very serious. The Earth may remind you of your debt by making your baby sick. The diviner will tell you what to offer the Earth to apologize. Buy the egg, chicken, or palm wine right away so that you don't delay your child's recovery. Remember, once they fall sick, babies can die quickly.

IF YOUR BABY DIES

A Grandmother's Words

I know it's very sad to think about, but in our world it's likely that you'll bury at least one of your children, perhaps more. Twin babies are especially vulnerable. For example, if a visitor thoughtlessly remarks that one twin is larger than the other, the smaller twin may feel insulted and decide to return to *wrugbe*. If your baby dies, the body will be buried in a muddy patch behind your home. I'm sure you and your husband will be too upset to attend the burial.

If this is your first child to die, there will be a special *fewa* funeral. Before being buried, your baby's body will be laid out on many layers of special cloths. You and your husband must stay for three or four days in a newly built house without coming out at all, except to go to the bathroom. While you're in the house, two or three ritual specialists will sit with you. These women have paid dearly for their knowledge: to gain the secret information they now possess about how to do a *fewa* funeral, they each had to bewitch a pregnant or laboring woman in their family, whose soul they sold to the ritual specialists who taught them! You should respect them, for power is on them. The oldest among them will sleep in the same room with you and your husband, and for two or three nights you and your husband must have sex in front of her. If the baby died just a short time after being born, sex will be very uncomfortable for you, but you have no choice.

After this, the old woman will take you and your husband into the forest. There, she'll shave the hair on your heads and bodies, wash you with special medicines, and put mourning jewelry on you both. Many other things will happen that I can't reveal. People who haven't gone through *fewa* themselves can't approach you during these rituals, or their own children – current or future – will be at risk!

Nowadays, some people, especially Christians and Muslims, don't want to bother with this ritual. They say it's too difficult and humiliating. Shame on them!

Luring Your Child into this Life of Troubled Times

A Diviner's Words

There are many reasons that babies die. One is that the mother hasn't consulted a diviner to discover who the baby was in *wrugbe*, or what the baby misses from there. Such babies are so sad that they decide to return to the other world. Another reason is that you're mistreating your baby. If you don't nurse your baby enough or seek good medicines when the baby is sick, your child's *wrugbe* parents will call their suffering one back. Still another reason is that the Earth may be punishing you. For example, you know that when you first married, you were supposed to ritually confess the names of any lovers you had before your husband; if you covered up a name or two, the Earth may kill your baby unless you offer the proper sacrifice. Consult a diviner right away to find out what you should offer the Earth.

If you're unlucky enough to have two babies in a row die, one of them may take pity on you and return during your next belly as a *Sunu* (if the baby's a girl) or *Wamya* (if a boy). *Sunus* and *Wamyas* are pleased if their mother pats mud over their body every so often, to remind them of the muddy patch in which they were buried after dying in their previous life.

If your child dies, it may comfort you to remember that the younger the baby, the more the little one was still living in *wrugbe*. If the umbilical cord hasn't fallen off yet, the babe hadn't even begun to leave the land of the ancestors, and the village chief won't announce a funeral. If the umbilical cord *has* fallen off, you must wait until the chief announces the funeral to the village before you start to cry.

GOING BACK TO WORK

A Grandmother's Words

For the first two or three months after the birth, you can relax while your mother and other relatives pamper you. Your major job is to nurse and bathe your new one. I always tell mothers to stay a full three months at home, but nowadays women often rush back to their farms after only two months. Start slowly – at first, only one or two half-days a week in your fields, then three or four half-days. If you start back working full-time too early, you won't recover properly from the delivery.

All this will be much easier if you find yourself a *leng kuli* – a baby carrier to care for your baby when you're busy. This is especially important if you have other young children. Your *leng kuli* can carry your child when you walk to the fields balancing a heavy load of crops, farm tools, cooking pots, or firewood on your head. While you're working, she can take care of the baby in the fields, and you'll only need to stop working every so often to nurse.

Try asking an older daughter, a younger sister, or a niece to be your *leng kuli*. If you can't find a relative, look around the village or neighborhood. To interest someone, make sure the baby looks beautiful! After the morning bath, apply your baby's face paints carefully: draw the green medicine lines across the little forehead and down your baby's nose as straight as possible; and chew a kola nut well before spitting out the juice, to make sure it's a bright orange for the dot over your baby's soft spot. In addition to the medicine jewelry that your mother's given you or that the diviner's prescribed, add a few other items for beauty – a belt of shiny green beads, an anklet of bells. Rub shea butter all over your baby's skin after the bath. The skin will glow, showing off your baby's beads, shells, and bright face paints to great advantage. If your baby is irresistibly beautiful, someone will be eager to carry her for a few hours; if you're lucky, she might offer to be a regular *leng kuli*.

Even a seven- or eight-year-old can be a good baby carrier. Make sure you show her how to tie the baby onto her back firmly with your *pagne* cloth. Of course, if she's young, she won't be able to carry the baby for too long, but at least your little one will get a lot of short naps. If your *leng kuli* does a good job, after a few months you could buy her a pair of earrings at the market. At the end of a year, buy her a dress if you have the money. Then she'll be happy to continue as your *leng kuli* for another year.

AS YOUR BABY DEVELOPS

A Grandmother's Words

It's important to watch for signs that your baby is developing properly. Several steps are especially significant.

Teething

Babies shouldn't be born with teeth! If your baby *is* born with a tooth, this is a bad omen: the baby is in a rush to leave *wrugbe* and trade places with an elder in this life. In the old days, we asked a female elder to drown such a newborn.

When your baby starts to cut the first tooth, pray that it comes through as a lower tooth. If your baby cuts an upper tooth first, this is also a bad omen. In the old days we would drown such a baby as well, or else someone in the baby's family would die.

Nowadays, we don't kill such babies, for we know we could go to jail if the gendarmes heard about it. We just worry and look to see who in the family will die.

Walking

When your baby starts to crawl, you'll be proud, for this is the beginning of learning how to walk. But you must discourage the baby from walking until a full year in this life. (The diviner may explain why this is so important.) You might need to keep the child strapped to someone's back as much as possible, and your husband may have to spank the baby for trying to walk too early. If your child is still determined to walk before the first birthday, string a *lagba* bead onto a cord and tie it around the baby's waist. With this powerful belt, your baby should just sit still.

Nowadays, some young parents don't listen to their elders and they allow their babies to walk early. Some even look for medicines to *encourage* early walking! Perhaps they're trying to be modern. I hope you don't listen to these people.

On the other hand, if your baby is over a year old but has not yet started walking, you should make every effort to find proper medicines to encourage those first steps. After all, having sex is absolutely forbidden for you until your baby can walk properly!

This restraint is important to protect your child. If you become pregnant before your baby learns to walk, the new one in your belly will steal breastwater from your baby. The baby will never learn to walk properly, and eventually the poor child will die. If you have a co-wife, it won't be so difficult for your husband to wait until your baby walks before having sex with you. I am sorry to say this, but if you have no co-wives, it would be better for your husband to visit one of the Ghanaian sex workers who bake "women's bread" in our villages than to bother you.

Your Listening and Talking Baby

You'll probably talk to your baby from the first day of life in this world. When your baby cries, as you offer a breast, you'll look into the little one's eyes and say, "Shush! What's the matter? I'm sorry!" or other such phrases. Doubtless you've seen many mothers talk like this from their babies' first days in this world.

When your baby's a little older, it's important to teach the words for all the relatives. Your baby won't be able to say our elaborate greetings properly until learning this, since we always address each other as Uncle, Big Sister, Little Mama, and so on when we greet anyone. And you know how important it is to say *hello* to almost everyone in the village every morning and evening, to show that we're all part of the community.

After learning to greet politely, the next thing your baby must learn is how to tease certain relatives by tossing dirty names at them. Anyone your little one calls Grandma and Grandpa – not just your parents and your husband's parents, but all their sisters and brothers as well – will tease your baby son by calling him jokingly, "Shit prick!" "Red prick!" "Raw shit scrotum!" or your daughter, "Shit cunt!" "Black cunt!" "Tiny cunt!" Your child will soon learn that this is all in good fun, and you should teach the little one to engage in the repartee by laughingly shouting back dirty insults. There's nothing cuter than a one-and-a-half year old shrieking out with delight, "You red balls!" to her doddering grandfather or "You black asshole!" to his old grandmother. Later, when you become much stricter with your children, it will be a comfort to them to have such a relaxed and teasing relationship with their grandparents. They may even seek refuge with them if you chastise or punish them too severely one day.

A Diviner's Words

Some children's character comes from who they were in their last life. For instance, Wamyãs and Sunus are sad a lot. Having died as a baby in a previous life, they can foretell a death. If a Wamyã or Sunu appears sorrowful, gets angry easily, or even hits people for no reason, don't be too harsh, or the child may decide to return to *wrugbe*. Remember, the bad behavior you're seeing is simply a sign that your son or daughter is distressed from secretly knowing that someone will soon leave this life for *wrugbe*.

Walking

Grandmother has already warned you that your baby must not walk before the end of the first year. Now I will explain why. As you know, babies are reincarnations of our ancestors. With souls crossing back and forth every day between this world and *wrugbe*, babies and elders are closely connected. They both have only a fragile hold on this life, and it's easy for one to replace the other. An infant who walks before a year walks on the spirit of one of his or her grandparents, and that elder will soon pass to the other world.

As Grandmother mentioned, you must also make sure that your baby doesn't start to walk too late. If your child doesn't begin to take some steps soon after a year, it may be because you and your husband started having sex before the baby began to walk. Forbidden sex can cause a very serious condition that we call "split leg," which can prevent a child from ever walking. If this could be your child's problem, you'd better consult a diviner who can prescribe the right remedies, or your child will soon depart this world.

On the other hand, if your baby is slow not just in walking, but in other ways as well – perhaps not talking on time – it may be that you committed a serious violation while pregnant. If you ate food while walking along the path to your fields in the forest, your child may actually be a snake. If so, there's no treatment; the child will never be human. If you can afford it, consult a specialist who can offer what appears to be medicine, but is really snake food, to your child in a secret ritual in the forest. If your child ignores the food, it probably means that your son or daughter is actually human, and there's some other reason accounting for developing so slowly. But if the medicine seems delicious, your baby will eat the food and immediately start turning back into a snake and slither off into the forest. If you're lucky, the creature won't return the next time you take a belly, and you'll give birth to a person. If you suspect your baby may be a snake, you should do this ritual as soon as possible. The longer you wait, the more the ritual specialist will charge, and the harder it is for the medicine to take effect – in the end, you may be left with a snake-child. The creature will never have a family, for who would marry a snake?

Your Listening and Talking Baby

In *wrugbe*, unlike life in this world, different groups of people live together and understand each other's languages. When a *wru* is reborn into this life, the baby remembers all the languages that were spoken in *wrugbe*. For this reason, your baby will grasp everything that you – or anyone speaking any language – says. As your baby starts to leave the afterlife and join this world, the memory of all those languages will start to fade. Eventually your child will understand only the languages that he or she hears in this life.

Until then, your baby understands everything anyone says, so talking may help lure your little one into this life. If you look your baby in the eyes and speak softly, your child will probably babble something back. Doubtless you and everyone else around will delight in such sounds. You should teach your baby to talk real words by speaking *for* him or her. For example, if someone asks the baby, "How are you?" you can hold up the child and answer, "I'm fine." After a few months of this, your little one will be able to join in conversations.

At the same time, you should train your baby not to interrupt adults' speech, since children must respect their elders. If your baby is interrupting your conversation with another adult, even with adorable noises, you must say firmly, "Stop talking!"

On the other hand, if your very young infant utters a real word or two in Beng or any other language we know, this would be a very bad omen. While babies understand all languages, they *speak* only the language of *wrugbe*. Speaking a language of this world would be a sign that your little baby has already left *wrugbe* completely to enter this world far too early. This is bad – a grandparent will soon die.

TOILET TRAINING

A Grandmother's Words

You and your mothers began to toilet train your baby the day the umbilical cord fell off, and I assume you've continued to give your baby an enema twice a day, every day, since then. By the time the little one is a few months old, you shouldn't have to worry about pooping during the day at all, as long as your baby stays healthy. This is good – then you can give your baby to a *leng kuli* without worry that the baby carrier's clothes will be soiled as she carries the baby, for that would be a great shame on you! Later, when your son or daughter is walking, you can show your child the places we have in the forest for shitting. When you teach your child about wiping with a dried corn cob, emphasize how important it is to use the left hand, *never* the right.

As for urine, it really doesn't matter where a little baby pees. If someone's lap gets wet, they'll just hold up their clothes to let the urine drip off. Once your baby can walk well, show the little one to pee anywhere on the village outskirts.

WHEN TO HAVE ANOTHER BABY

A Grandmother's Words

You may be considering how many children to have, but *eci* is the one who decides this. We old women do have secret methods to keep from getting pregnant, but ordinarily they aren't for young women with only a few children, so I won't divulge them here.

However, if you have one difficult pregnancy or childbirth after another, a witch may be trying to kill you. Perhaps she's sworn a pact to bewitch a pregnant woman in the clan, as an entrance fee into one of the women's secret ritual associations. Until she kills another pregnant or laboring woman in your mother's clan, your own pregnancies won't be safe. In this case, do anything you can to prevent becoming pregnant again for a while. You can even try to find out about the new methods available in the cities.

AS YOUR CHILD GROWS UP

A Grandmother's Words

As your baby grows, teach the child that being young means having no authority over anyone except those who are even younger. Remember that in our language, one word for "child" really means "little slave." As soon as the little one can walk confidently, don't hesitate to send your child on errands in your village or neighborhood. Even two-year-olds should be able to find their way to Grandma's and Little Mama's houses and back again.

You can accomplish many important things by sending your toddler on an errand – say, to tell your sister you'll carry her baby tomorrow, or to give a dish of palm nut sauce to your mother. Your child will get to know many people early on. This is very important, since our lives are always filled with people. It will especially help the little one learn who's who in the family. For instance, when you tell your child to bring a dish to one of your husband's younger brothers or male cousins, refer to him just as Little Father, but provide hints – the Little Father who lives next to so-and-so, or who has light skin, or who's short. In this way, the baby should soon understand which of the many Little Fathers in the family you mean.

From doing errands, your child will also become familiar with the neighborhood; by three at the latest, your little one should be able to navigate anywhere in the village (or your *quartier*, if you live in a city). Then, your child will feel confident to join in the groups of children who play together, roaming far and wide around the village or neighborhood when they aren't working for their parents. And of course you'll gain a helper – a great boon, considering how much work we women have to do!

A FINAL WORD ABOUT GOOD MOTHERS AND BAD MOTHERS

A Grandmother's Words

Being a good mother isn't something that comes naturally to every woman. Almost all of us will bear children, but that doesn't mean we must be the ones to raise them. If you show tendencies toward being a bad mother, consider giving your children to others who are more fit for the job. Perhaps your sister is an especially good mother – give her one or more of your sons or daughters to raise with her own. Your and your sister's children are sisters and brothers anyway, not cousins, so this isn't a matter of adoption. If you turn out to be bad at mothering but don't acknowledge it, your relatives and neighbors will let you know. If you beat your children too much, one of your husband's relatives is bound to take the children. Even a frail but loving grandmother is better for children than a vigorous but mean-spirited mother.

Still, being a good mother isn't really difficult or complicated. Of course, you have to make enough money to buy what's necessary for your children. You'll need plenty of soap to bathe them twice a day, and if you buy cooking oil, salt, and occasionally a fish or a piece of meat, your children will appreciate your tasty sauces. Other than that, if you're kind, it's enough. Even a madwoman in one of our villages is a good mother, because she manages to feed and bathe her children. If she can raise her children well, you probably can too.

A Diviner's Words

Bad mothers don't consider that their babies have *nining* – souls that come from another life. These mothers don't consult a diviner to discover the lives that their babies were leading in *wrugbe*. As I've been telling you all along, when your baby emerges from your belly, the little one is leaving behind a life lived elsewhere with another set of parents – in a place that's invisible to you, but that your baby can describe to the spirits, who can then describe it to us diviners. One of your main responsibilities is to figure out who your baby is and what your baby misses from *wrugbe*. This is so important, I can't remind you enough times! If you consult a diviner regularly about your growing child, you'll be a good mother.

Everything I've told you, I've learned from the spirits. Have I lied?

CHAPTER 7

From Mogadishu to Minneapolis

Raising Somali Children in an Age of Displacement

Sirad Shirdon

SOMALIS IN THE UNITED STATES

The East African nation of Somalia was born in 1960, following the unification of the British and Italian Somaliland administrations. In its early years, Somalia had two civilian administrations, spearheaded by Presidents Aden Abdullah Osman and Abdirashid Ali Sharmarke. In 1969, Muhammad Siad Barre seized power through a bloodless coup, following the assassination of Sharmarke by one of his bodyguards. Although he was often portrayed as a dictator, Barre's reign speaks to the contradictions of post-colonial African regimes during the Cold War era. In his early years, President Barre instituted economic and educational reforms that had a positive effect on the country.

Two key advances were in the area of literacy and education. In 1972, following the introduction of a written script for Somali, the government initiated a country-wide campaign to improve the literacy skills of the general population. As a result, 400,000 Somalis in the urban centers were reportedly educated in the new Somali literacy. Moreover, Barre's government announced that 1.2 million Somalis were reached with the rural literacy campaign, which the government claimed improved literacy by 70 percent (a number that may, however, have been inflated). As a result of a sizeable increase in the number of classrooms and teachers during the early years of Barre's regime, primary school enrollments increased from 40,000 in 1970 to nearly 300,000 in 1979. Women's participation in education also increased dramatically: Somali girls made up 20 percent of primary school students in 1970, but nearly 40 percent by 1979. The percentage of women teachers also increased from 10 percent in 1969 to about 30 percent in 1979.

Barre came in with a socialist agenda for the nation, aligning the country with the USSR. Similar to other developing nations of the time, Somalia was used as a pawn in the Cold War struggle. The beginning of the end for the Somali nation came during the 1977–78 war with Ethiopia, which had the goal of reclaiming the Ogaden, a predominantly Somali region in eastern Ethiopia. Barre went into the war with promised support from the USSR. Realizing the potential role of Ethiopia in expanding its influence in Africa, the USSR switched sides to support Ethiopia, resulting in Somalia's defeat.

Following the end of this war, the central government of Somalia became increasingly autocratic. Although Barre had come in on a platform of staunch nationalism (*Soomaalinimo*), a government once inclusive of all clans became increasingly dominated by the president's clan. Not surprisingly, this move raised ire among members of other clans, and the Somali government was toppled in January 1991. Fleeing the ensuing turmoil, Somalis dispersed throughout the world. Families with financial means were able to flee early, seeking asylum in countries as diverse as the US, Canada, Pakistan, Saudi Arabia, the United Arab Emirates, and the United Kingdom. Less fortunate Somalis either stayed in the country or fled to refugee camps in neighboring countries, including Kenya, Ethiopia, and Yemen. Due to its drawn-out history of internal political, military, and social turbulence, Somalia remains the third largest refugee-producing nation, with 1.2 million refugees worldwide, behind only Syria and Afghanistan. Most Somali refugees who arrive in Western countries do so after spending time in refugee camps in Kenya.

From Mogadishu to Minneapolis

Today, Somali refugees in Kenya number 413,170, with most residing in the Dadaab refugee camp. An arid and hot town tucked away in Kenya's predominantly Somali-populated northeast, Dadaab is an unforgiving place often described as an open-air prison, where Somali refugees reside in tents. Due to the number of Somalis in the camps, local schools can only accommodate about half of the school-age population. Refugees subsist on meager food rations. Furthermore, due to an encampment policy, they are unable to leave the camps – defying international law, which stipulates freedom of movement for refugees.

The camps are overcrowded and underserved. Fleeing the many hardships, families often seek improved livelihoods in Kenya's major cities. This movement of refugees was tolerated until 2011, when a series of domestic terrorist attacks occurred that were blamed on the Somali militant group al-Shabaab. In 2011, the Kenyan government instituted an unprecedented crackdown (Operation *Usalama* Watch) on Somali refugees, resulting in harassment, detentions, imprisonment, and deportations. Although designed to cleanse Kenya and Nairobi's Eastleigh neighborhood of terrorist elements, this "operation" had the unfortunate consequence of criminalizing all Somalis in Kenya, as "Somali refugees-cum-suspects" in the Kenyan imagination. These actions have led to heightened urgency among Somali refugees to seek repatriation to third countries. However, only a small minority of refugees are ever successfully resettled in a third country. Moreover, for refugee families who are selected for resettlement, the process is a long and arduous one that, unfortunately, often divides families. A sizeable portion of refugees are resettled in the United States.

Somalis originally began arriving on US shores in the 1920s, as seamen settling along the Eastern seaboard. Following their nation's independence in 1960 and through the 1980s, many Somalis migrated to the United States seeking work and education. These early Somali immigrants settled predominantly in Washington, DC, Virginia, and New York. Migration to the US increased in the late 1980s, bolstered by increasing numbers of Somalis fleeing political turmoil and the outbreak of war with the country's northern region, Somaliland. (For a variety of reasons, population estimates of Somalis in the United States remain both rare and inaccurate.) Following a series of transitional governments, the first postwar federal government in Somalia was established in 2012.

For many Americans, Somalia represents the quintessential failed state of our time. The nation's long civil war has led to the portrayal of Somalia in international media as a land of war, famine, terrorism, and piracy. These narratives have been reinforced by recent Hollywood movies, including *Captain Phillips* and *Black Hawk Down*. Somalis living in the diaspora have suffered from these images, which are incomplete, misleading, and inaccurate. In diasporic communities, Somalis are too often associated with poverty, over-reliance on welfare, criminality, and, more generally, an opposition to integration into their adopted home countries.

In the US, the unlikely town of Lewiston, Maine serves as the major flashpoint in the discourse surrounding Somali integration. In the late 1990s and early 2000s, Somali refugees began resettling in substantial numbers in Maine – the state with the highest proportion of White people in the US. The town of Lewiston, where many of the immigrants settled, was then a dying mill town with a high unemployment rate. Local Lewiston residents became increasingly concerned that the Somali newcomers were taking the few jobs left and exerting pressure on the city's social service system. As a consequence, in 2002 Lewiston's mayor penned a letter requesting that Somalis stop encouraging their friends and families to come to Lewiston, as the city lacked the resources to cope with more refugees. Mayors in Manchester, New Hampshire and Springfield, Massachusetts followed suit, filing requests with the US Department of State in 2011 and 2014 respectively, to cease expanding refugee resettlement programs in their cities. Ironically, Somali refugees have since been credited with reviving Lewiston – increasing per capita income and decreasing crime rates in the city.

But it is Minnesota that houses the largest Somali population in the US. It has been suggested that the Somali presence in that state has given rise to a racialized xenophobia, insofar as Black

Somalis have become the face of Islam in Minnesota. In the current battle around immigrant integration and assimilation in America, the primary marker of Somali difference has been women's headscarves, a sometimes contentious image in post 9/11 America. In 2013, a male police officer in St. Paul, Minnesota was reprimanded after he dressed up as a Somali woman with a headscarf for Halloween.

More broadly, discourse around US immigration in the last few decades has become increasingly characterized by xenophobia, spurred by the presence of millions of undocumented migrants, especially from Mexico and Latin America. In the context of relatively high levels of unemployment, fears have increased that refugees and immigrants from nations such as Somalia are taking jobs from native-born citizens. Many American citizens are asking why the nation is accepting such individuals. To exacerbate matters, Somalia has in recent years become a target in the US "war on terror," due to the presence of al-Shabaab, a Somalia-based terrorist organization that has wreaked havoc on the country for the last several years.

Currently, the majority of Somalis in the US reside in Minnesota, which is attractive to them for a combination of reasons: a relatively large existing community of refugees from Somalia and a variety of other nations, including Cambodia and Sudan; a well-developed social service industry; generous state aid programs; and the availability of unskilled jobs. Despite enormous challenges, including racism, xenophobia, Islamophobia, and anti-immigrant sentiment, Somali families have managed to make successful lives for their families in their adopted homeland. Indeed, in spite of the common stereotype that unskilled refugees are a drain on the economy, Somali refugees and immigrants have contributed positively to the economies of the cities they inhabit. For example, Minneapolis is home to over 550 Somali-owned and run businesses ranging from shops that specialize in Somali products to home health care agencies, restaurants, transportation companies, and even charter schools. As has occurred in Lewiston and other cities in which Somalis have settled, previously neglected neighborhoods in Minneapolis have been positively transformed by the presence of Somali businesses. Moreover, a large percentage of Somali business owners are women, who often own shops in Somali malls, selling Somali clothing and goods.

However, the few publications about the culture of the Somali diaspora in the United States tend to have a *deficit* orientation, focusing on all that Somalis lack. Existing literature tends to be dominated by reports on educational and health disparities, clans, racism, female genital cutting, and terrorism. While serious issues indeed affect the Somali diaspora, Somalis object that mass media rarely offer a realistic, more balanced portrayal of the community.

Although Somali culture in the diaspora is in flux, oral culture remains a foundational pillar of Somali society. For centuries, poetry (*gabay*) was elevated as a means of cultural expression, with both Somalis and non-Somalis marveling at the stunning memory and recitation skills of Somalia's famous orators. Earlier generations of Somalis used poetry to express everything from love, resource sharing among clans, and family ties to broader Islamic values. Poets such as Hawa Jibril, Hadraawi, Gaariye, and Careys Ciise were held in very high regard, with Somali adults and children memorizing and passing down the poems across generations. Proverbs are also an important part of Somali orality, used to impart values and lessons to children and adults alike.

The literacy skills of the Somali diaspora are variable, largely dependent on the refugees' point of origin and prior schooling. Somalis from major cities such as Mogadishu typically attended formal schools and were literate in Somali, as well as in a colonial language (Italian, French, or English) and Arabic (for the purposes of learning the Qur'an). In contrast, given the lack of formal schooling among Somalis in the rural areas, pastoralist Somalis were often only literate in Arabic, given their attendance in Qur'anic school (*dugsi*). Whatever their geographic location in Somalia, all Somalis took part in *dugsi*, a form of schooling found throughout the Muslim world. Attendance in *dugsi* is considered crucial to the formation of a Somali child's Islamic identity. The diaspora has brought *dugsi* to the US, where Somali children have become adept at traversing various schooling orientations (secular and religious) and literacy traditions (English, Arabic, and Somali orality).

Similar to other African and African-diasporic communities, the Somali diaspora in the US is best described as communal and family oriented. Somali culture prioritizes social bonds, social interconnectedness among people, and mutual responsibility, while placing great value on child obedience and parental authority. This emphasis often places Somali culture at odds with the more individualistic, competitive US culture. In Somali society, adults are responsible for shaping the behavioral characteristics that facilitate children's development and learning. Older children play an important role in not only mentoring younger children, but also filtering knowledge from adults.

In short, Somali families experience an extreme gap between their daily lives and the images that other Americans hold of those lives. In the "manual" that follows, the imagined author addresses this challenge, directing her remarks to fellow young Somali women, whom she addresses as *Abaayo* – Sister.

FROM MOGADISHU TO MINNEAPOLIS: RAISING SOMALI CHILDREN IN AN AGE OF DISPLACEMENT

About the Author

My name is Halima. I am a young Somali woman now living in America following an early life filled with turmoil and struggle. I was ten years old in 1991 when a civil war ravaged my native country of Somalia. Prior to the war, I lived in the country's capital of Mogadishu, a city that local residents lovingly refer to as *Xamar* – the White Pearl of the Indian Ocean. I attended elementary school at *Hawo Tako*, named for the prominent twentieth-century female Somali nationalist. The *Xamar* of my childhood was idyllic, although you would not know it from modern-day images. Then, it was a cosmopolitan coastal city, overlooking the Red Sea and filled with beautiful, whitewashed buildings. Today, *Xamar* is a city that bears the scars of war; once-iconic buildings now bear the hallmarks of shelling and bullets. Yet, with the return of peace in 2012, *Xamar* has become a hub of construction with new buildings being erected regularly.

In Mogadishu, my family and I led a comfortable, middle-class life. My father was a civil servant for the government, and my mother was a schoolteacher. The *Xamar* of my youth was filled with people from many backgrounds, including Arabs, Italians, Ethiopians, and Americans. For their higher education, many Somalis were sent abroad to countries such as Egypt, Italy, Russia, and the United States, from which they would return speaking several languages.

Following the outbreak of war in 1991, my parents, my two sisters, my brother and I fled to a refugee camp in neighboring Kenya. The government of Kenya generously provided us with tents in a refugee camp in the coastal city of Mombasa. Given the shortage of schools in the camp, my sisters, my brother, and I soon stopped going to school. We stayed in that refugee camp until 1994, when the Kenyan government ordered all coastal refugee camps closed. That year, my family was moved to the Dadaab refugee camp in northeastern Kenya.

At the time, my parents never anticipated that we would spend the next fourteen years there. Although my sisters and I had hoped to go to school, as we would have done in Mombasa, the camp schools had no space for us due to the large numbers of Somalis in the camps. Only about half of the school-age population was able to attend school.

Back when I was in Dadaab, many Somali refugees harbored dreams of being able to gain a visa to relocate to the United States. Our word, *buufiis,* expresses a Somali's intense preoccupation with resettlement. In the camp, my sisters, my brother, and I came of age listening to tales of our relatives in far-off places with exotic names like Minnesota and Ohio. We were nervous when we heard about the extreme cold of the winter there, but we yearned to be reunited with some of our family members who were there, and to be able to earn a livelihood, following decades of having to rely on relatives sending us remittances from their earnings abroad.

From Mogadishu to Minneapolis

One of the highlights of my time in Dadaab was meeting the man who would eventually become my husband. Ali was a few years my senior and worked as an interpreter with one of the local non-government organizations. He was able to finish high school in the camp schools, where he learned English and Swahili. With his English skills, he was easily able to secure a job as an interpreter in the camp – a huge blessing for him, given the rampant unemployment that plagues refugees in Dadaab.

As with so many other Somali refugees, we had family members in the US. Most recently, an aunt and uncle of mine were resettled by the United Nations High Commissioner for Refugees in Tennessee, but from what they told us, there was no Somali community in Tennessee, and there was no mosque, which was very important to my aunt and uncle. From other family members living in Minneapolis, they had heard that Minnesota had a culture that was relatively accepting of refugees and had a growing Somali community, so they made their way up north. Yet, upon arrival in Minneapolis, Uncle Nur and Aunt Istaar were taken aback by Minnesota's cold. Like other refugees, they initially sought assistance from the refugee resettlement agencies, which helped my uncle obtain employment in a meat-packing company in rural Minnesota, while my aunt became a stay-at-home mother.

They painted a glowing portrait of life in America, in stark contrast to the desperate conditions in which we lived in Kenya. Anything would be better than that, we thought. My aunt and uncle would constantly reassure us that everyone had jobs in America, and was well off.

These stories fueled our desire to move to the US. The only negative thing we heard about America was that Somali-American youth were becoming Westernized – losing their culture, their religion, and their language, even to the extent that, at times, they had difficulty communicating with their parents.

In 2008, we received the news we had been awaiting for so many years: my mother, brother, husband, and I would be relocated to the US. Sadly, my father and two sisters were not selected for relocation, for reasons that remain mysterious to us.

A World of Babies

Prior to departing from the refugee camps in Kenya, we received the typical crash course on American culture. Then we left for South Dakota in August of 2008; later, we joined our family in Minnesota. The crash course we had received in Kenya in no way prepared us for life in America! We quickly came to the realization that the America of our dreams does not exist. Immigrants to this country generally believe the familiar adage that "America is the land of opportunity." For me, America is a place of contradictions, as it has been for many Somalis.

In some ways, America has exceeded some of our wildest expectations – especially for the level of personal security, the educational opportunities, and the jobs. At the same time, our integration process has been made difficult by major problems like discrimination against non-English speakers, poverty, racism, and Islamophobia – with all of this added to the continuing effects of the traumas that we experienced as a result of our nation's long civil war. But for me, the most challenging aspect of life in America has been to learn how to be a good mother to my child in this new country. How do we go about raising moral children who are practicing Muslims and hold strongly to their traditional culture in a nation where the dominant culture is so different?

I have written this childcare guide for future Somali sisters who will resettle in the United States. I pray that, God willing, with this childcare guide, my sisters will have less difficulty than I have had being a good mother in this new land.

RAISING SOMALI CHILDREN IN AMERICA

Getting to Know the Americans

Americans are good-hearted people, but you and they will not initially understand each other. At the beginning, there were some things that I found quite amusing. For example, Americans treat their animals differently from how we do. Back in Somalia and Kenya, we either feared animals or were annoyed by their presence. In the *Xamar* of my childhood, the streets were filled with stray cats that we enjoyed chasing. Imagine my shock when I saw American women with small dogs in their purses! Many Americans will often hug, cuddle, and even kiss their "pets." That's crazy – *yaab*!

Worse than these little cultural differences, we also have many mutual suspicions. In my early months in this country, I was distrustful of Americans. I had heard many stories of White people attending our mosques who would try to get information from congregation members about events back in Somalia. Some of our men were even put in jail for suspicion of being associated with militant groups in Somalia – the very groups that had destroyed our beloved country and caused us to flee our homeland! Why Americans would think that any of us would want to be associated with those terrible groups was beyond me.

I also distrusted White people because I heard that a lot of them dislike Muslims. I had heard stories of Somali women being teased for wearing headscarves and being told to go back to Africa. *Abaayo*, the good news is: I have come to understand that not all Americans are like this. They simply do not know about us and our culture, and it is our responsibility to teach them that Islam is a peaceful religion, built upon the principles of love, peace, and humanity. Human beings are naturally scared of what they do not know, and in the case of Americans, they are constantly being bombarded with images of atrocities committed in our name. As Muslims in a largely Christian country, it is important that we lead not only through our words, but also our actions. God willing, together we can show them that Muslims are loving individuals whose primary purpose is to better humanity.

Pregnancy

Traditionally, we Somalis engaged in a lot of fanfare around pregnancy, because we consider children to be among Allah's biggest blessings. Back home, the women in our families would assist pregnant women with daily tasks such as cleaning the house and taking care of any older children. Being pregnant in the United States proved very different and quite challenging for me. My first pregnancy coincided with my second year in

America, and I struggled a lot, especially since only my mother, husband, and brother had also been selected for resettlement in America, leaving behind my father and two sisters. While my mother was a big help, it was tough being pregnant while trying to get used to living in a new country. I hope you will have an easier time than I did.

When you resettle in America, *Abaayo*, try to do so in places where you have many female family members if it is at all possible. It will be a big help! We Somalis thrive when we are around our family and community members, and this is especially important when you are in a new environment. If you do not have any family locally, the mosque is a great place to meet fellow Somali women who will be a great support. Another source of terrific social support has been the religious tele-conferences we women have. Initially, these tele-conferences were developed as a way for Somali women to learn the Qur'an and the religion in the comfort of their homes. The teacher would either be another learned Somali woman, or an *imam* at one of the local mosques. Since that time, the lectures have evolved to include topics like eating healthy foods, healthcare, and even makeup and fashion! In these tele-conferences, I was able to connect with women who became a great support during my pregnancy, including a few who lived in Minneapolis. Some of the Minneapolis-based women would visit me from time to time, while others would call to check up on me.

Abaayo, the women here see their doctors a lot, which is different from what most of us are used to. Back home in Somalia, women rarely had preventive and prenatal care – we sought a doctor's assistance only if we felt sick. Here, the doctors always encourage us to take prenatal vitamins for our child's development in the womb. Some of our women mistakenly believe that vitamins are of no benefit, and that they serve only to fatten both the child and the mother. Others believe that vitamins are medicine, and do not understand the use of taking medications if one is not ill. It is so important that you find a good doctor who can explain these things to you in a way that you can understand – and that does not insult our culture. Once you find such a doctor, make sure to keep your appointments with her regularly!

Still, some of the advice provided by the doctor will make you scratch your head. For example, in the US, some women use what they call *birthing balls* during labor. These are huge balls that women in labor sit and bounce on. The nurses say the balls help the baby to move down the birth canal. The first time I saw a woman on one of these balls, I thought that she was engaged in some sort of a game! *Yaab*! But since it has been explained to me, I promote its use with local Somali women. *Abaayo*, this strange thing really will help your baby come down, as I have witnessed for many of my sisters! It might look very silly, but in the long run it will make things easier during your labor. The strategy did not work for me, given complications with my delivery, which I will discuss later – but I still encourage this practice.

It is especially important that we seek out anything to make our labor and delivery easier, given that many of us have undergone the female circumcision we call *gudniin*.

In fact, many doctors here believe that we are likely to experience complications during childbirth due to our *gudniin*, and we are often automatically classified as having high-risk pregnancies. As you know, nearly all Somali refugee women have been circumcised; of those women, 80 percent have experienced infibulation, which is the most severe type. Back home, you probably heard of some women suffering or even dying in childbirth because of complications due to *gudniin*. Here, they have scary-sounding names for all the suffering we already know about: long labor, cesarean delivery, internal bleeding, and more. *Abaayo*, this is why it is crucial that you are followed closely by a doctor throughout your pregnancy. It is also important that you find a doctor who understands how to work with women who have been infibulated. Otherwise, *Abaayo*, the doctor's ignorance of your surgery may lead to even more complications during childbirth. Many of our sisters feel shame and fear that health providers will criticize them when they see the *gudniin*. This is why I stress the importance of finding a doctor who has worked with women with *gudniin* before. The best way to find good doctors is to ask around in the community. Somali women who have had children here will be able to recommend someone.

Also, *Abaayo*, because Americans do not understand our culture, people in the clinics do not know that for us women it is important to have a female doctor. So let the staff know that you need a female OB/GYN. This country has different traditions, and if you do not tell them, they may assume that it is okay to have a male doctor deliver your child! Still, if no female doctor is available, it is okay to have a male doctor.

Furthermore, if your English is not yet strong, you may be assigned a male translator by the hospital or clinic, because they do not realize that Somali women are more comfortable disclosing intimate details in the presence of women. If you'll need a translator while you're in labor, ask your doctor ahead of time to request a female translator. Praise be to Allah, *Abaayo*, here in America there is a lot of respect for patients' religious needs in hospital, and they will usually work to make sure that you are accommodated.

Another difference that works in our favor is that, in contrast to Somalia, where patients typically do not ask questions of doctors, in America asking questions of a doctor is actually encouraged! I wish I had realized that I could have asked my doctors questions about such things ahead of time. Most Somali expectant mothers feel misinformed and misunderstood during doctors' visits. Our sisters wish doctors would spend more time learning their preferences. As a result of this miscommunication, doctors are not able to make the religious and cultural accommodations that we Somali women would like during childbirth. That is why I am urging you to learn from my mistakes: ask the doctor questions and inform her of your wishes. This way, you will, God Willing, have a good experience giving birth.

Another problem we sometimes have comes from rumors. If a woman believes that a mistake was made during her prenatal care, she will tell another sister, and this will spread quickly. Soon, many women believe this story and avoid prenatal care with this particular doctor, or even avoid the entire hospital. This keeps many of us from getting some important information. One rumor in particular is very strange: there is a widespread belief in our community that hospitals in Germany are superior to those in the rest of the Western world! None of us knows the origin of this belief, but I imagine it probably originated with the stories of one Somali man or woman who had good experiences in a German hospital. When listening to such stories of our sisters, we must resist the temptation to assume that we will share their experiences.

Childbirth

My son, Yasir, was delivered by a procedure the doctors call a *Caesarean section* – which the nurses shorten to *C-section*. Weeks before the delivery, my doctor informed me that there would be a high chance that I would deliver via C-section, due to my infibulation. I did some research on C-sections and was alarmed at what I found. Somali women in the US are more likely to have a C-section than are other mothers, and this is often because of something the doctors called "failed induction of labor" and "fetal distress." I learned that with "induction," the doctor essentially tries to force the baby out if he or she does not arrive within a certain amount of time. Oh, Allah! Why can't doctors in America be more patient, instead of rushing to procedures like these? Our Somali tradition is to have a vaginal birth, as our mothers and grandmothers did. Unlike Somalis, Americans do not understand that everything in life happens according to what we call *Qadr* – destiny ordained by God.

In my case, I did not understand why my doctor considered a C-section necessary. Why do Americans insist on making something as simple as childbirth so complicated? I wondered why these American doctors wanted to cut me open when most women in Somalia manage to deliver naturally back home. In Somalia, it was very rare to have children delivered with this procedure, which doctors reserve only in case of a severe medical emergency. But in this country, it is quite normal.

In my case, I was in labor for twenty-four hours, and Yasir was not descending. Most of the women in my life, including my mother, warned me that a C-section would put my health and my future fertility at risk. *Abaayo*, I was terrified of a C-section, and desperate to deliver naturally. While I was in labor, my family read the Qur'an in the waiting room. My family also made a lot of supplication and prayers for me: *Oh Allah, make Halima's delivery and labor easy for her!* The only thing I could muster the strength to say was, *AstagfiruAllah* – Oh, Allah, please forgive me. As Muslims, you know we believe that an individual with a heart purified from sins will be granted their prayers, so we are encouraged to say *AstagfiruAllah* as a means of purification. But it was God's will that I would have a C-section, and I accepted this.

When possible, ask your doctor for a midwife. Many recently arrived sisters from Somalia have informed me that their midwife made what was otherwise a stressful event much easier. Midwives are there to assist you with the birth of your child, and we Somalis are already used to them, as we used their services back home. Although they are rarely allowed to deliver a child at home as they were back in Somalia, here in America they can still be very useful in the hospital. They will coach you throughout your pregnancy, be there with you for the delivery, and help you in the days following the birth of your child.

For my sisters who want to have a vaginal delivery after having been infibulated, it is important to first undergo deinfibulation, to reverse the infibulation by cutting the stitches that close most of your vaginal opening. This procedure will prevent tearing during delivery by creating a larger passageway in the vaginal opening, which the infibulation would otherwise render tight and lacking in elasticity. This would increase the chance of the baby getting stuck in the birth canal, requiring an emergency C-section. You will need to make sure that you discuss this with your doctor ahead of time. Make sure that she knows how to do the procedure, and is willing to do it!

The First Forty Days

I must warn you that Americans do not have the same post-delivery practices that we do. For us, the woman always rests and is pampered for a full forty days during what we call the *afarten-beh* period. In America, the woman typically remains in the hospital for only two days following the delivery. That is too short a time! And you know what is worse? Some women here return to work after only a few days! Praise be to Allah, this is not enough time for a woman's body to recover. But in America, things happen so fast, and everything seems to revolve around work. Many new mothers must return to work immediately.

The weeks following my delivery of Yasir were quite challenging. Because of my C-section, I was in pain, and it was difficult to move around. I'm sure I would have been unable to bear this period had it not been for the constant reminder by my mother that my pain served as expiation for my sins. You know that we Muslims believe that any injury, even the prick from a rose thorn, will relieve us of our sins. When my post-partum pain would hit, I would say *Al'Hamduli Allah* – Praise be to Allah! – and begin reciting supplications and passages from the Qur'an. Along with this, my mother would say *Laa bas tahooran insha'Allah* – No need to worry, it will be a means of purification, God Willing – an Arabic phrase that the Prophet, peace and blessings be upon him, taught us to say. Beyond this spiritual practice, my mother would also remind me to eat some honey with black seeds (*Nigella sativa*).

On top of everything, I was expected to care for Yasir almost by myself. Back home in Somalia, during the *afarten-beh* period, I would have been surrounded by many female relatives who would cook me soups, porridge, and special teas. They would also help us care for our newborn for forty days. Although this was not the norm among many urbanites in Mogadishu, at the end of her seclusion period the new mother would have a small celebration.

Here in America, it was just my mother and me taking care of the baby. My husband worked long hours as a taxi driver, so we would only see him at night. My brother lived nearby, but he had a family of his own to care for. Upon moving to America, most of our men are employed in jobs like truck driving, driving taxis, and working in factories – jobs that take them away from their families. Most well-paying jobs in America are tied to degrees and qualifications, and unfortunately many of our men come to the

US with a very basic education. While many aspire to go to college and university prior to moving to the US, upon arrival many have to prioritize work to provide for their families. This makes life difficult for us women, especially those of us with many children, as we spend most of our days alone, caring for the children.

Naming

We Muslims always hold a naming celebration on the seventh day of a child's life. In Somalia, we call the ceremony *wanqal*. On this happy occasion, we sacrifice an animal, to thank Allah; typically, we sacrifice one ram for a girl, and two rams for a boy. The slaughtered ram is used to feed the guests at the party. In traditional Somali culture, an *imam* would either select the child's name from a list of Muslim names, or consent to the father announcing the child's name. Families in cities celebrated *wanqal* for all children, but, due to financial constraints, families in rural communities had to select only some of their children to have the naming ceremony – typically selecting only boys.

In the diaspora, parents have continued this tradition. Families typically have a ram slaughtered at a local farm or request that a butcher at a *halal* meat shop do it. The meat is then distributed to the poor, neighbors, relatives, and friends. Back home, this practice was done on the seventh day, but the timeline of families in the diaspora is variable. Some families do it on the seventh day, while others postpone the *wanqal* until months after the child's birth. Whenever you choose to do it, Minnesota has many *halal* meat shops that can assist you in doing *wanqal* for your children.

Given that our culture is patrilineal, it is tradition for Somali boys and girls to trace their family membership through their father's lineage. As a result, along with their first names, male and female children also carry their father's and grandfather's names. For example, my son's full name is Yasir Ahmad Ali. This means, Yasir, son of Ahmad (his father), grandson of Ali (his grandfather). In our community, Yasir would be referred to as Yasir Ahmad. However, this can be confusing to Americans who might assume that Ahmad is Yasir's grandfather. For that reason, I would advise you to use only two names for your child: their given first name, and the name of their grandfather. In all of his official documents, my son is now referred to simply as Yasir Ali. This is closer to the American naming system, and has made life much easier.

Another issue with naming relates to women's last names following marriage. Unlike the Western practice of a woman taking her husband's last name, Somali women (like all Muslims) keep their last name. Some Americans are confused when they notice that a Somali mother's last name is different from that of her child. As Muslim women, we view this as empowering! In marrying into our husband's family, we do not lose our identity and connection to our own family. It is odd that Western women – who often take the last name of their husbands – claim that we Muslim women are oppressed. Oh, the irony!

As you know, our names do not stop with us. The power of oral culture in Somali tradition shines through in our cultural practice of reciting the names of the men in our lineage – the practice we call *abtiris*. Children who excel at this can trace their lineage back several generations. Naming enables people to know who you are: other Somalis can typically trace your family, the region you are from, or your clan through your name. Unfortunately, we are starting to lose this practice in the diaspora, where some children can only name their ancestors back as far as their grandfather. Our children are quickly losing their cultural identities in this new land, and it's very important that we continue to promote our Somali heritage with our children. I encourage you, as a new Somali mother, to speak to your child in your mother tongue and promote the use of Somali in your home. Teach your child his or her *abtiris*. Tell your child Somali folktales and stories like *Safarada Cigaal Shidaad* (The Travels of Igal Shidad) and *Qayb Libaax* (The Lion's Share). When you are putting your child to sleep, sing them to sleep with Somali lullabies like *Hoowaya Hoowaya* (Calm Down, My Child). Educate your child about Somalia, and your early memories there. Show them pictures of your homeland. By creating a sense of cultural pride in your child early, your child will be able to navigate Western society with a strong, Somali cultural identity that they will never lose.

Feeding

Another important issue to consider when raising your child in the West is the difference in feeding. In Somalia, most children are nourished with just breastmilk for the first two years of life. In our *Xamar* days, infant formula was available, but very few women used it. These days, many Somali diaspora mothers think that formula is best. I believe that our sisters think this will help them be modern and fit into city life. Many believe that breastfeeding is primitive and unacceptable in an advanced country like America. If only our beautiful Somali women understood that, nowadays, American doctors are promoting breastfeeding because of the superior nutritional value the child receives from breastmilk. They even have a saying for it: "Breast is best!"

Many busy American mothers who work outside the home will pump their breastmilk to ensure that the child is breastfed. While some of our Somali sisters are uncomfortable with pumping, it is a great option for busy mothers. *Abaayo*, it is important that we breastfeed our children, if we are able to. Breastfeeding for two years is optimal, and this is indeed consistent with the Qur'an: "Mothers may breastfeed their children two complete years for whoever wishes to complete the nursing [period]." While exclusive breastfeeding has its challenges – including family and time demands, social pressures to supplement breastmilk with bottle feeding, cultural restraints on breastfeeding in public, and lack of information on proper breastfeeding practice – this is how we should be feeding our children, given the benefits. If you are worried about your milk supply, I encourage you to engage in traditional practices that promote lactation, including drinking fenugreek tea, Somali tea and milk, and lots of water.

Another result of immigration is that many Somali women have become overweight from eating typical Americans foods, which are low in nutritional value but high in calories. Some research has indicated that being overweight before pregnancy can make it difficult to become a successful breastfeeder.

Somali women in the diaspora have mixed opinions regarding the benefits of colostrum. Many believe that it's healthy for the baby's stomach – to clean out anything left over from when the child was still in your womb – while others believe it will negatively affect the child's digestive system and even the mother's health. In the US, the nurses now promote colostrum for its nutritional benefits. My advice would be to believe the nurses and provide your children with colostrum.

In this country, another thing you have to pay attention to is the ingredients in food products. *Abaayo*, it is not like Somalia, where we could assume that there were no ingredients in our food that the Qur'an would forbid us to eat – those we call *haraam*. In America, you have to read all labels! If you can't read English yet, or you're not sure what the names of all the ingredients on a long label mean, ask the store clerk for help.

As a newcomer, it's understandable that you may not know that ingredients like *lard*, *rennet*, *bacon*, *gelatin*, *pepsin*, and *vanilla extract* all come from or contain pigs or alcohol. Going to the supermarket can turn laborious when we have to spend time reading all of the labels. But it's better than buying what we think is just a can of beans that turns out to contain pork.

I've found it helpful to research this issue on the Internet and write down a list of all *haraam* ingredients that may be hiding in the foods that I might ordinarily buy. When I go to the grocery store, I carry this list with me, to ensure that whatever I am buying is acceptable – what we call *halal*. If you don't have access to the Internet at home, you can go to a local library and ask for assistance. People at the local mosque could also give you helpful advice in learning *halal* versus *haraam* ingredients and foods, and can direct you to *halal* grocers in your neighborhood. Thankfully, here in Minneapolis, many of our community members have opened their own supermarkets, and we also have numerous *halal* butcher shops, which makes getting *halal* meats easy. Maintaining our *halal* diet in the West is a very important part of holding firm to our Muslim identity.

Dental Hygiene

Talking about foods leads us to consider dental hygiene, which is an intrinsic part of our Somali culture and Islamic faith. Back in Somalia, we used a toothstick to clean our mouths throughout the day, especially before our daily prayers: the toothstick cleanses the mouth and pleases the Lord. Because of our close attention to our dental hygiene along with a healthy diet, we rarely heard about cavities: children and adults alike had strong, healthy teeth. *Abaayo*, since our community has migrated to the US, too many of us have adopted the unhealthy eating habits of Americans. Instead of our traditional foods like cornmeal and beans, we eat unhealthy foods that are high in sugar. For those of us who live in poor communities here in America – which most of us still do – we cannot afford to buy nutritious foods. The stores in our community carry mostly unhealthy foods, and few fresh foods. Nowadays, the newspapers even call our communities "food deserts"! Many of our adults are consuming these unhealthy foods and feeding them to our children, who are eating much more sugar than they would eat back home in Somalia. As a result, among children and adults alike, we see weight gain and something previously unknown to our community called *obesity*. As mothers, we feel guilty telling our children "No" when they plead with us to eat the candy, cake, and other sweets that they see their American friends and schoolmates eat. Since this is a new diet for us, our mothers do not know that it brings more risks. For example, it is not uncommon in our communities to see young children with many cavities and even missing teeth. As mothers, if we are going to allow our children to eat sugary foods, then we must be vigilant in ensuring that a thorough teeth cleaning follows.

Speech, Communication with Children, and Developmental Disabilities

Back in Somalia, mothers provided the basic needs for their young children: shelter, food, and security. We did not speak *with* our children, but rather *to* our children – mostly, to give them directions and teach them our traditional values. Given that mothers did not speak with their children, the way they do here in America, Somali mothers are probably not as sensitive to speech delays as other mothers are. When the child was ready, they would begin to communicate with their extended family, and this is how children learned language and social skills.

But, *Abaayo*, in this country, I have observed something that I find strange. The women of this country speak with their infants! When the child makes some meaningless sounds, the mother responds as if the child could understand her. I used to laugh when I would see these women talking to babies who cannot respond: Why are these women wasting their time?

But back in Somalia, our neighborhood was filled with members of our extended family. Our children never had a shortage of communication partners. Somali children developed language and communication skills through interactions with older siblings and extended family members – as opposed to interactions with parents, which is the case in the US. Here, we are often so isolated from each other, often living in high-rise buildings, with no other family members around (see Figure 7.1).

In my case, I only had my mother, brother, and husband. So, like the White mothers, I started to talk with my Yasir when he was a baby. I would sing to him, tell him Somali stories, and talk to him about my upbringing in Somalia. And I felt like our connection grew stronger. I also noticed that Yasir had a higher vocabulary than other Somali children his age. I must admit, I was extremely lonely during this period. I took solace and comfort from the Somali women in the tele-conferences. Some of the women were older, and coached me on how to be a good mother. Though my husband spent long days at work, he constantly called and text-messaged me to make sure I was okay, which was a great support. And of course, I took comfort knowing that Allah was there. Even on the days when my mother was unavailable to assist me, I was comforted knowing that my Lord was there for me. As I have expressed before, if you are unable to be around family, then your religion, a supportive husband, and the Somali women in your community will be of great help to you. Talking to Yasir and having conversations with them appeared to pay off, as my son developed a rich vocabulary early.

Figure 7.1 Minneapolis is the site of the largest Somali community in the US. Nevertheless, in this high-rise apartment building, whose occupants are mostly Somali families, new Somali mothers feel far more isolated than they would have back in Somalia, where open-air courtyards encouraged continual social interaction among large family networks that are lacking in the Somali diaspora.
Photograph by Sirad Shirdon.

Yet, increasingly I was noticing that many of the children in our community were talking late. Given my concerns, I consulted a second cousin of mine, who happens to be a speech language pathologist.

In our traditional culture, it was not a big deal if a child did not begin speaking by the age of five years. Among Somalis, as long as a child can make his or her wants and needs known through gestures, the language question does not concern us. But here, I have learned that Americans consider this age to be quite late for children to begin talking. Here, a child is considered a "late talker" if their understanding of language is strong, but they are not speaking by thirty months. "Late talking" can result in a number of challenges for a child's development, including being unable to communicate basic wants and needs, and being shy around other children, which may impede social skills and cause delays in literacy and kindergarten readiness. Although some parents will automatically seek the assistance of a speech pathologist, more often doctors will first identify a child as a "late talker" and then refer the child to a speech pathologist for further assessment and possible intervention. My Somali mother friends and relatives tell me that they do not consider late talking to be a problem until the child reaches school age. In fact, if a Somali mother in the US diaspora is notified that her child is talking late, other mothers are likely to relate stories of other children they know who were late talkers and "turned out fine" – whether in Somalia or in the diaspora. Due to the dominance of Somali oral culture, the stories and experience of fellow community members often carry more weight than the opinion of a medical professional.

Yet, this issue of "late talking" should be highly alarming for parents in our community, given that communication problems may be a red flag for autism. *Abaayo*, autism is a neurodevelopmental disorder that our children are increasingly being diagnosed with. The figures on autism are worrying: In 2010, one in thirty-two Somali children in the Minneapolis Public Schools between the ages of seven and nine were found to be enrolled in an autism language program, which was double the amount of non-Somali, minority students diagnosed with autism. This has been a big trial for our community.

Autism is not a disorder with which many of us were familiar back home. Many in our community here think that it is connected to vaccinations, as a result of stories they hear.

For example, a Somali immigrant mother will take her child for the eighteen-month measles-mumps-rubella vaccination. Following the shot, she reports that her child's language and motor skills have regressed. In a few years, that child is diagnosed with autism, and that mother will share her story and caution other Somali mothers against vaccination. This is how stories spread in our community. Doctors in the US say there is no truth to the rumor that vaccinations cause autism, but no one is really sure what causes it – not even scientists. Some children may be born with a predisposition to this condition, or there may be something in the environment that triggers it.

Whenever I see children who are three or four years old and are not talking, I encourage their parents to take them to their pediatrician, who can refer them to a speech pathologist; these trained professionals can often help children who are behind in talking. I know you may worry about the expense. Indeed, the US is not like countries such as Canada or the UK, where everyone has access to free medical services. In this country, until the recent introduction of the affordable health care system they call "Obamacare," unless a child had a specific diagnosis like autism many Somali parents could not afford to take the late-talking child to a speech pathologist. Even now, we have challenges getting Somalis signed up for health care in Minnesota, because language barriers have left many unaware of the federal program that could be so helpful. I encourage you to sign yourself and your family up as soon as you can. God willing, this new program will greatly assist with your family's medical needs.

Only Allah knows what is causing autism in so many of our children. As Muslims, we must accept this as a trial from Allah that we must bear with patience and faith. At the same time, it is important that we invest a lot of effort into our children when they are young, to give them a good chance to be successful later in life. This way, our children will succeed in this complicated nation where the challenges of a successful life as an adult are so different from what they were back in Somalia.

Language and Literacy

One of the biggest challenges that we Somali immigrants face in the United States is that our children are losing our beloved and rich Somali language. Many of our youth even have difficulty speaking with their parents or grandparents. Traditionally, Somali mothers spoke in Somali at home. During a Somali child's early years, parents typically talk *to* children – mostly issuing directives and teaching values – rather than *with* children, as is common in the West.

Increasingly, however, Somali mothers fear that speaking Somali in the home will delay their children from learning English. In Minnesota, many mothers are now speaking a pidgin Somali-English to their children, hoping that this will speed up their learning of English. (This sort of misconception is found throughout many other immigrant communities.) Contrary to popular belief, children need a strong foundation in their first language in order to rapidly acquire a second language. So, in fact, it is important that our children have strong Somali language skills prior to beginning school. In any case, many of our children learn plenty of English prior to starting school, anyway – through television, their peers, and daycare.

You will also find that everyone in the US, including your doctor, will stress the importance of reading books to your child. While this was a custom in some households in *Xamar* and other urban centers of Somalia, those of us from rural communities did not do this. I would encourage you, *Abaayo*, to begin using books with your child early, even from birth. If you cannot read English, that is okay. There are wordless picture books that you can use to create stories in Somali. These days, we even have bilingual Somali–English books for some of our most popular folktales, which you can use to teach your child our culture. There are also many books about Muslim children available that you can use to begin teaching your child about our basic religious beliefs and values.

Another tradition that is very important to our people is teaching our children the Qur'an. While it was standard practice back home for children to attend *dugsi* prior to beginning formal schooling, in the US our children typically attend *dugsi* only on the weekends. Here in the US they begin attending *dugsi* as early as three years of age. The *dugsis* are typically located in the apartments of their Somali teachers, which makes things easy for us mothers.

Mothers here also play a strong role in teaching their children our Sacred Book. From birth, Somali mothers expose their children to the Qur'an in the home by playing an audio recording of it in the home. This way, children grow up hearing the Qur'an, which will make them positively inclined towards Islam as they grow older. In my case, in place of lullabies at bedtime, I would sometimes recite for Yasir some of the shorter chapters of the Qur'an.

I hope that, when he is older, Yasir's memory of his early exposure to the Qur'an will inspire him to engage in the traditional practice of *subcis,* in which family members sit in a circle and take turns reciting the Qur'an from memory.

Gender, Parental Relationship, and Obedience

In our traditional Somali culture, we raise our girls and boys quite differently. In nomadic culture, boys would be trained for their future as the economic providers for their families, and our girls for their future as good wives and mothers. More generally, we encouraged our girls to stay at home and busy themselves with domestic affairs, while we encouraged our boys to be adventurous and brave, and to explore the world outside the family. Even back in cosmopolitan *Xamar*, as a young girl, I was expected not only to excel at school but to also take care of the house. Because the boys in my family did not have as many responsibilities as I did in the home, they were freer to spend time with their friends.

The importance of the traditional domestic roles of women in Somali society should not be understated. In fact, the role of Somali women disrupts common beliefs about values within a patriarchal family structure. Somali men consider women the backbone of our culture and family. In Somali tradition, a man prospers only if his wife is actively involved in all family affairs and is a source of moral encouragement for him. We have a saying: "Women make one man surpass another man."

Naturally, our community has brought this traditional model of childrearing with us to the West. For girls, the pressure to excel in school and assist with domestic duties has generally paid off. Our young Somali women have thrived in higher education and have found success in professions as diverse as medicine, academia, engineering, and business.

It has been a different story for our young Somali males. The civil war in Somalia and the resulting resettlement process had a number of negative effects on the Somali family structure. Many men were either left behind during the resettlement process, or became victims of the civil war. Both these scenarios combined to result in many Somali women left to exclusively care for their families.

The subsequent high level of stress suffered by many families led to an increased rate of divorce. As a consequence, many Somali young men were left without strong male figures, and with mothers who believed that their ultimate demonstration of love for their sons would be to fall back on traditional rearing practices for their boys. One of the many consequences for our Somali male youth is that they are not excelling in school as much as our girls are.

America is a tough place to grow up for a refugee child, and it's important that we invest more of our efforts into our Somali boys. We should also make sure that they help out with the household affairs. Trust me, if you teach all of your children (regardless of gender) to assist with the household, it will not only make things easier for you, but also help them grow up to be hard-working, disciplined, and independent individuals.

An unfortunate consequence of the differences in acculturation between Somali parents and their children is that some Somali children have begun to play the system against their parents. As you know, some of us (like many other immigrant groups in the US) use an authoritarian method of discipline – hitting – to ensure that our children are well behaved. Somalis who practice authoritarian discipline believe this will impart obedience, respect, interconnectedness, and cooperation. In our tradition, corporal punishment is practiced by both mother and father when children misbehave (regardless of gender). While some Somali families continue to practice corporal punishment, most parents in the US stopped using this form of discipline decades ago. As a result, these parenting practices often place Somalis on a collision course with American society, which tends to view such practices as abusive. Even spanking has become a contentious issue in the US, with some opponents likening it to child abuse! As a result, well-meaning social services professionals may witness this behavior and misinterpret it as abuse. Sadly, this has resulted in an increasing number of our children being removed from their family homes and being placed in the care of the Minnesota Department of Family Services.

Parenting has been a great challenge for our diasporic community. Our Somali children, who should adopt our cultural values, are now engaging in previously unimaginable behaviors. Many parents feel that our youth no longer respect their parents, or see us as authority figures. Some parents feel they have no choice but to send their children back home to Somalia, or to other countries in East Africa. The underlying belief is that if children go astray, then the environment is the culprit. If you take the child out of the Western environment, they will become well-behaved children once again. There is even a term for it: *dhaqan celis* – cultural rehabilitation.

Many of our Somali male youth today lack a male role model and consequently seek those role models in the streets. Our youth are increasingly becoming marginalized, due to something we had no experience with back home – racism. In America, young Black men have a very challenging time, due to a variety of issues including living in poverty, increased police brutality against them, and high rates of imprisonment. *Abaayo*, it seems the police in this country regularly target male Black youth and men. There's also a phenomenon called "Driving while Black." Police will stop Black youth or men if they are driving a nice car – assuming the car may have been stolen! My husband, Ali, has been stopped a few times by Minneapolis police for this reason. Each time, police will stop him and ask for his registration. Once he is able to prove the car belongs to him, they let him go. *Abaayo*, these incidents create friction between the police and the Somali community. Many of us fear and are distrustful of the police. It is hard, *Abaayo*, to have faith that the police will treat us fairly.

These issues have been exacerbated by the Islamophobia that exists in our society. *Abaayo*, it is a scary time to be a Muslim in this country. In 2015, three young Muslim university students were killed in their apartment, in North Carolina. Why? For being Muslim. *Abaayo*, I will be honest: some days, it's hard to leave my apartment. It feels like we are under siege due to our Black and Islamic identities.

It is truly tragic that we fled war in our homeland, only to encounter it in a different form in our adopted homeland. One way we can counteract this phenomenon of our male youth going astray is to encourage our husbands to be strong fathers. It is vitally important for our future generations that our men take an active role in raising capable, strong, and independent Somali men to carry us forward into the future. The men in our community lost their sense of selves in the resettlement process, and this has had implications for their survival in this new land. We Somali women have an important role to play in rebuilding the self-esteem and confidence of our men.

Given the challenges, I do not believe the process of sending our children away to other countries for *dhaqan celis* is a realistic solution. Parenting in the West is incredibly difficult, but, rather than run away from it, we should confront it. My dear sister, I would caution you to avoid physical punishment and instead use other forms of discipline, as there can be serious consequences for exercising our traditional discipline practices. If you are having challenges rearing your children, and do not enjoy the social support of your family, the local mosques offer an excellent alternative. Mosques have become immensely important community centers and refuges. A child who is strongly connected to the mosque will maintain his or her cultural values and will not stray into bad behavior.

The Role of Somali Men

Abaayo, we must be patient with our men while encouraging them to assist us in this new, difficult life. Our men have suffered following the civil war; many went from being economic providers for the family in Somalia to being unemployed in the United States. As a result, they have struggled with adaptation to America even more than we women have. Perhaps to deal with the trauma of displacement and the loss of their work identity, many of our men take solace in chatting about politics with their friends. It is not uncommon to find them in coffee shops for hours, talking about politics back home.

Traditionally, Somali men view women as the caregivers of children, so they see nothing wrong with leaving us alone with our children all day. Although I support this practice for families back in Somalia, life here is very different. In America, a family cannot survive without assistance from the man. From your early days of becoming a mother, I would strongly encourage you to request help from your husband. American women actually speak about "training" their husbands, which I think is a helpful way to think about it. In a loving manner, we have to encourage our husbands to assist us with domestic affairs. In fact, this is part of our Islamic tradition. The Prophet, peace and blessings be upon him, used to assist his wives with house duties, including washing his own clothes, serving his own food, sewing his own clothes, and assisting with other domestic tasks. A shared understanding of the struggles involved in raising a child in America will make your life a lot easier, *Abaayo*. We all have a role to play in talking with the men in our life about the importance of them sharing with women the challenging task of building a strong family unit in the US – a unit that can help us become successfully integrated into a society that holds so many different values and practices from ours.

PARENTING: AMERICAN STYLE

When I first had Yasir, I found myself overwhelmed with the parenting industry in the US. It seems that there are millions of books and programs, each touting itself as the best way to parent!

This was indeed strange; our grandmothers and their grandmothers have been parenting successfully for many generations, often with meager means.

In America, it seems that people have an obsession with perfect parenting. I encourage you to stick to our traditions and not become obsessed with all of the many parent-advice books out there. There is even something called "attachment parenting." This program advises prolonged breastfeeding to ensure the development of a strong bond between a mother and her child. I was shocked when I noticed a photo of a mother breastfeeding a four-year old child on the cover of *Time* magazine! *Yaab*.

My simple advice when it comes to parenting: the best example for you to follow remains doing whatever you can in this new land to follow what we traditionally practice in our Islamic, Somali society.

CHAPTER 8

Quechua or Spanish? Farm or School?

New Paths for Andean Children in Post-Civil War Peru

Kate Feinberg Robins

INTRODUCTION

During the 1980s–90s, internal armed conflict devastated communities throughout the mountainous, south-central area of Peru's Ayacucho region. Based on fourteen months of ethnographic fieldwork (2008–11) with children and their families in a small district capital of southern Ayacucho, this chapter addresses rapid cultural, linguistic, and political ruptures over the past three generations in a post-conflict, semi-urban town. Rather than contribute to their families through full-time labor on the farm, as their predecessors would have done, contemporary children are now expected to contribute through their academic studies, and eventually their professional work.

While this new generation of children takes advantage of unprecedented opportunities for formal education in the Spanish language, they simultaneously become increasingly estranged from their grandparents, most of whom are monolingual Quechua speakers with little or no formal schooling. By contrast, young parents are bilingual in Quechua and Spanish, having learned Quechua at home, and Spanish through forced immersion at school. Many of these parents, whose education ranges from elementary to college level, have chosen to speak to their children solely in Spanish, in an effort to spare them the pain and struggle that they themselves experienced in Spanish-only schooling. As a result, children who are Spanish-dominant are being raised by bilingual parents and Quechua-dominant grandparents who struggle to find a balance between preparing them for full participation in an increasingly modernized and interconnected world, and providing them with a strong cultural foundation through which to make sense of, and harness, the benefits of that world. Focusing on "respect" as the concept that guides childrearing in the Peruvian Andes, the "manual" that follows this introduction explores the ways that this key concept is continually shifting and adapting to a drastically changing world.

Ayacucho, Peru

The small town that now lies on a dirt highway four hours from the nearest small city used to be a prominent resting place on the Inca Trail – a 26-mile-long path highly popular with tourists visiting the ancient city of Machu Picchu. As proud residents are quick to inform both their visitors and their children, in the time of the Inca Empire, this small town in southern Ayacucho was once virtually the center of the world. Its residents, they say, included engineers plotting out complex networks of transportation, agronomists designing the latest technologies for crop production, and business people negotiating trade among the mountainous, coastal, and rainforest regions of the empire.

Later, the residents of the once-Incan town became known as *mestizo*, or mixed, as male Spanish colonists formed unions – usually by force – with indigenous women, producing a new generation of racially and culturally mixed children. Modern-day residents recall with pride their own Felipe Guamán Poma de Ayala, a *mestizo* chronicler from a nearby town whose captioned drawings that were sent to King Philip III of Spain around 1613 serve as historians' primary source of information about everyday Andean life in colonial times. They also speak proudly of *mestizo* novelist and anthropologist José María Arguedas, whose numerous works document popular folklore, traditions, and social relations of southern Ayacucho in the mid-1900s.

In the fifteenth and early sixteenth centuries, the Incan kings expanded their empire from the capital city of Cusco to neighboring regions, conquering indigenous peoples all over the Andes – sometimes by eliciting peaceful acquiescence, sometimes by use of force. Just 300 miles from the center of power, southern Ayacucho was a strategic location for the rapidly expanding empire.

In 1532, the Spanish explorer Francisco Pizarro conquered the Inca Empire, bringing Spaniards to what is now Peru, along with their language (Spanish), religion (Catholicism), and economic ambitions (seeking gold). With utter disregard for Incan authorities and human dignity, the Spaniards conquered the mountains one village at a time in the name of the Spanish crown and the Catholic Church, shedding blood as they went. Although they learned Quechua, the language of the Inca, the conquerors stomped out the local cultures and the many indigenous languages that had thrived under Incan rule.

Priests forced the indigenous people to convert to Catholicism by building churches on top of their sacred sites, assigning patron saints to replace sacred mountains as new guardians of Andean towns, and aligning local agricultural festivals with Catholic holidays. Nearly fifty years later, Viceroy Toledo gathered the descendants of these people from their scattered farms and forced them into houses surrounding the church, where they could be monitored and managed by colonial inspectors.

As the Spanish colony made the transition to an independent republic in the early nineteenth century, colonial "subjects" became "citizens." Ironically, the indigenous residents of the mountainous areas became identified as obstacles to progress, seen as holding back the nation with their "Indian-ness."

In 1823, Peru's first Constitution asserted the right and obligation of all citizens, even "in the smallest places," to be educated in religious, moral, and civic matters. The Catholic Church – and, later, evangelical Christians – took the lead in spreading the written word to the farthest corners of Peru's mountains and rainforests. The once-proud Incans were now referred to as *campesinos* – peasants who cultivate the land and grow food for the nation.

By the 1960s, Quechua people were still speaking their native language, but their ethnic identity was no longer celebrated on national Indian Day (now renamed Campesino Day). Gradually, more and more Andean families sent their children to school, convinced that the only way for their families to get ahead was for teachers to force the language and tools of the powerful upon the children.

In 1980, the Shining Path, a Maoist guerilla movement, arose in Ayacucho's capital city, claiming to speak for the masses, and vowing to bring equality to the countryside. The Shining Path made its way through the mountains, eliminating enemies and forcing young men to join its ranks. They scorned religious and cultural traditions as impediments to class solidarity, ransacking churches and targeting civilians who refused to disavow their indigenous languages and cultures. Arriving on foot, they quickly overtook towns that had no telephones, no radios, no roads, and had received no warning about the recent spread of this movement. Countless families fled, leaving everything behind to travel nearly 400 miles on foot to Lima. Others sent their sons away for high school, in an attempt to escape forced recruitment by the Shining Path.

In late 1982, President Belaúnde sent military forces to combat the Shining Path "subversives" in northern Ayacucho. Over the next two decades, as the guerilla movement continued to spread, Presidents García Pérez (1985–90) and Fujimori (1990–2000) intensified counter-subversive efforts, indiscriminately targeting suspected insurgents, and enabling Peruvian soldiers to act on the tacitly accepted devaluing of the lives of Quechua-speaking civilians. An estimated 69,000 people were killed or simply disappeared during the conflict, with rural Ayacuchans representing over a third of this number.

In the "time of the terrorists," as survivors refer to this period, countless women were raped, and countless families lost fathers and husbands. Young women raising children today lament that their husbands, who grew up without fathers, do not know how to be fathers themselves.

Together with counter-insurgency forces, the state funded roads, electricity, and phone lines. As the violence subsided, police and government officials flooded into highland towns, quickly establishing a notable state presence in the everyday lives of residents. Two decades later, in town squares all over Ayacucho, schoolchildren can be found raising the Peruvian flag on Sunday mornings, dutifully pledging allegiance and singing the national anthem in the company of the mayor, the priest, and local police.

In Peru today, primary schooling is nearly universal, and parents whose first language is Quechua speak to their children in Spanish "so they won't be held back" by their native language at school and in the workforce. Radio programs come through from nearby stations in Quechua, while television channels from Lima and beyond bring Spanish and urban middle-class cultures into one-bedroom adobe homes. Migrants call their parents on cell phones from Lima, send money and books for younger siblings, and invite teenage nieces and nephews to work or study in the city during school breaks.

The Language of Respect

One evening in a small highland town, I sit by the fire in Don Alejandro's kitchen and chat with him in Quechua, the language that I know he speaks and understands best: "Don Alejandro, *¿sapa kuti yanunkichu?*" [Mr. Alejandro, do you always cook?] When he doesn't respond, his eight-year-old daughter Iris leans toward him, asking more loudly and with better grammar in Quechua, "*¿Sapa kutichu yanunki, Pai?*" [Do you always cook, Papá?]

He mumbles, "*¿Ah?*" [Huh?] and Iris repeats the key word in the question, marked in Quechua with the morpheme *–chu*: "*¿Sapa kutichu?*" [Always?]

He asks again in Quechua, "*¿Imataq?*" [What?], and Iris repeats the entire question loudly, clearly, and patiently, to her elderly father. When he finally understands, he responds in Spanish with phrasing that mirrors the Quechua syntax: "*Sí, cada vez cocino yo.*" [Yes, every time I cook.]

We continue chatting as he prepares and spoons out the soup, switching casually between Quechua and Spanish depending on the topic and the words most readily available. Iris is unusually proficient in Quechua for children her age, having grown up with an elderly monolingual mother and a Quechua-dominant father.

In this town, what linguists call "code-switching" between Quechua and Spanish is the usual mode of communication. Every generation knows at least some words in each language, and it is only the proportion of speech in one language versus the other that shifts, depending on who is involved in the conversation.

Quechua speakers lack a single word for "respect," because it is implied in all thought and action. Native Quechua speakers add prefixes and suffixes to words and phrases to express respect in the form of special interest and concern for interlocutors and topics of conversation. However, appropriate use of these grammatical features, so ubiquitous in native Quechua speech, is difficult for non-native speakers to master. It is even dropping out of the speech of bilingual children who feel more comfortable with Spanish.

This suggests that explicit conversations about "respect" among Quechua speakers may have emerged through contact with the Spanish language and Hispanic cultural norms, which do not always imply "respect" in the ways that Quechua language and cultural practices do. In the Hispanic perspective, "respect" is an optional aspect of social life to the extent that one can choose to exercise it or not, and to the extent that it is talked about explicitly.

By contrast, the kind of "respect" that Quechua speakers invoke with the borrowed Spanish word *respeto* is considered vital and indeed is pervasive in Quechua linguistic and cultural practices. This is not to say that Hispanic and Christian notions of respect are irrelevant in Andean childrearing but, rather, that Andean families construct distinctly Quechua interpretations of the Spanish word *respeto* around which they orient their children's socialization.

When used by Quechua speakers in its various forms, the Spanish word *respeto* invokes a sense of reciprocal morality in interpersonal relations. It denotes an obligatory social code to which all community members are expected to conform, as well as a personal attribute – both "respected" and "respectful."

Although people rarely use the Spanish word *respeto* in southern Ayacucho, they convey many of these same moral imperatives through the Spanish compound verb, *hacer caso*. The word *kasuy*, used among Quechua speakers in southern Ayacucho, is borrowed from the Spanish *hacer caso* that has been integrated into Quechua. Depending on the context, the meaning of *hacer caso* can range from *obey* to *pay attention* or *listen*. Children and adults alike frequently state that children should *hacer caso* to adult and peer authorities, indicating that children should follow directions, help out when asked, and pay attention when spoken to.

Less commonly, the phrase is used to describe adults who *hacen caso* to children, or higher-status individuals who *hacen caso* to lower-status people, referring in this case to the act of listening to another person and taking what he or she says into account. When a mother *hace caso* to her child, it does not mean that she does whatever her child asks her to do but, rather, that she listens respectfully to her child and considers the child's perspective. No matter the context, the term *hacer caso* implies a relationship between two or more actors who communicate with one another, giving their full attention to that communication. With its emphasis on *hacer caso*, Andean notions of respect in childrearing thus seek to cultivate both respectful and respected children who conform to social norms and cooperate with others, thereby facilitating the daily activities of their families and neighbors.

In the childrearing manual that follows, a Quechua grandmother discusses her expectations for how and why children should be raised as both respectful and respected persons. Her guide is situated in a post-conflict context in which children are expected to play a key role in building a peaceful and prosperous society. Through the language of respect, the grandmother outlines her own understanding of both human rights and children's rights, ranging from the responsibilities of parents and family to nurture a newborn, to a young child's responsibility to behave like a human being – demanding his or her own human rights while also respecting the rights of others.

The primary fictional "author" of the chapter is a Quechua-speaking grandmother who dictates the manual to her literate daughter, who is bilingual in Spanish. The fictional daughter grew up during the internal armed conflict that afflicted Peru and is now raising two young children of her own. In writing down her mother's words in Spanish, the daughter inserts her own comments, illustrating generational shifts in childrearing by sharing her personal experiences.

In the grandmother's generation, many fathers were absent from family life due to the long-term war. Correspondingly, in the mother's generation, fathers are in effect emotionally absent – and sometimes physically, as well – because when they were growing up, they had no model for fatherhood.

The grandmother conveys to these parents the important role that children play in their families and communities, and the importance she sees in schooling. By asking her daughter to create a written, Spanish-language document that will serve as a guide for young parents, the grandmother negotiates old and new forms of knowledge and emphasizes the importance of integrating them, rather than choosing between them.

Her advice is directed toward parents currently raising children in highland communities of post-conflict Peru. This grandmother is distinctly aware of the limits of her knowledge and does not claim to know how children should be raised in other places or at other times. A sense of urgency is apparent in her efforts to try to make sure that the generation currently raising children knows and values the vital role that children play in their families and communities. She subtly reminds parents who have been fully socialized in Western-style education that Quechua language and childrearing principles still have a critical role to play in preparing children for school.

Quechua or Spanish? Farm or School?

The English prose of the manual reflects, to some degree, lexical and grammatical styles characteristic of oral Quechua mixed with Spanish, as people speak a combination of the two languages in contemporary Andean Peru. What follows should be read as a translated transcription of the grandmother's words, with the daughter's comments inserted in italics. The title of each section appears in Quechua after the English. The manual begins with an oral legend that is well known among grandparents in southern Ayacucho.

QUECHUA OR SPANISH? FARM OR SCHOOL?
NEW PATHS FOR ANDEAN CHILDREN
IN POST-CIVIL WAR PERU

About the Authors

A GRANDMOTHER AND HER DAUGHTER

I'm just a poor woman. I come from the *puna* – high up in the mountains, very far from here.

DAUGHTER'S NOTE: Puna *is what we call the highlands, way up where there are no trees, no corn, no barley, quinoa, or potatoes. Up in the* puna, *there are only animals – llamas, alpacas, vicuñas, sheep, and cows. Down here, where we live now, we are told that we are at 3,000 meters above sea level. We grow grains, potatoes, eucalyptus trees, vegetables, and even some fruits. Up in the* puna *it often snows, but down here it only rains. They say on the Internet that up there, it is 4,000 or 5,000 meters above sea level.*

When we lived in the *puna*, you and your brother were still very little. I would send you both to herd the animals while I stayed in our small hut to boil water and cook. Your father would help me dry the sheepskins and weave wool blankets for our beds, repair the thatched straw roof after a heavy snowfall, and gather cow dung and llama pellets to fuel the fire. There was always plenty to do.

A World of Babies

Our dwellings were very small. Inside, we only cooked and slept, and stored only whatever couldn't be left outside. It was impossible to stand up inside – well, children could, but not grown-ups. At night it was cold, and we all slept huddled together on the floor on top of sheep and llama skins, and under three, four, five wool blankets. We had to make the fire with cow dung and llama pellets, because there wasn't any wood so high up in the mountains. Your father and I would get up long before the sun rose, while you and your brother were still sleeping. That's when I would start the fire so we could boil water to drink, bathe, and cook. I had to stay by the fire all day to keep it going so we could cook our meals.

DAUGHTER'S NOTE: It takes a very long time to boil water at high altitudes. I've been to Lima, where everything cooks very fast, but here in the mountains it is slow, and up in the puna *it's even slower. Everything here has to be boiled. If you drink cold water or bathe in cold water, you will get sick. That's why my mother had to stay all day by the fire boiling water. There are no medicines or doctors in the* puna, *so you have to stay healthy and take care of yourself.*

Mostly we just ate meat. Sometimes, a visitor would come with potatoes or corn from their fields down below; in exchange, we would give them hides, leather ropes, and milk. Vegetables and fruits were a special treat for us.

That was all when you were very young. I moved down to this town for you, my children, so that you and your brother could go to school.

DAUGHTER'S NOTE: I was born in 1985, and we lived in the puna *until I was eight. My brother was two years younger. My mom doesn't know how old she is, but she was young when she had me – sixteen or seventeen, maybe. My dad must have been the same age.*

But it was also because of the terrorists that we came down from the *puna*. It was my uncle who told me that men with guns were coming. He said they were in other settlements already, and if we didn't leave, they would come to our house. He said I had to go, for the sake of my children.

I didn't want to leave. In the towns below, I didn't know anyone. All of my family was in the *puna*. But your father spoke with me. He said, "We have to listen to your uncle." He said, "We have to take our children and leave." He said, "There are schools down there, too, where our children can learn to read and write." Saying "Our children will learn and be better than us," your father convinced me to leave. But I was very afraid.

We took some of our animals, too, but we couldn't bring all of them. My uncle and my aunt stayed behind, saying they were too old to start over. They would take care of our animals, they said. It was a long walk with two small children, but you and your brother knew how to walk because you were always herding the animals.

Daughter's Note: I remember we used to stay out all day herding up in the puna. *Our cheeks would burn in the cold and the sun. While the animals grazed on highland brush, we would squat next to waterholes, hands hovering in stillness for hours, it seemed, waiting for the moment to plunge them in and catch a fish. When it was time to bring the animals back home, they would be almost specks on the horizon, and we would run across the fields, jumping over rocks and streams to catch every last one and lead it back to the corral. Sometimes a sheep or a llama wandered off, or we scared it, and we had to run again to bring it back. We didn't think anything of it. We were used to the air up there. Now, when I take my niece and nephew who live on the coast, they can't even run, because of the altitude. But for us, it was normal. We would run like it was nothing.*

Back then, there were no roads or buses in the *puna*. Even here in this town, you could only arrive on foot. (It wasn't like now, when a bus comes through our town every day, and another one goes up to the *puna* every week.) We had a donkey that we loaded with our food, water, and blankets. It took us around four days to get here, and, thank God, nobody bothered us along the way. We only saw fellow herders with their animals, who told us how to get to this town.

When we finally got here, it was only to discover that the people my uncle had warned us about were here, too. But I found the aunt whose name he had given me, and she took us in, so at least we had a roof over our heads, and you could go to school.

A World of Babies

Daughter's Note: It would have been the early 1990s when we came to this town. I started school in first grade with my brother, even though he was younger. It was normal – there were lots of kids like me who were older and had just come down from the puna *with their families.*

Some of the families who lived here were leaving, going down to the coast to escape the violence. But it was too far for us, and too much of a change to get to the big city. So we stayed. The town was run by the terrorists, but we got used to it. That's just how things were. What could we do?

We continued herding with the few animals we'd brought with us, and gradually our flocks grew. With the help of the aunt who took us in, we rented some land to grow crops, and we built another room on their house. That was where the four of us slept and cooked.

I had two more sons in those years. But then your father was killed, and I was alone with my four children. I didn't remarry, because in those times you couldn't trust anyone – neighbors, relatives, no one. You could never know who would turn on you, who would make up a story and report you to the terrorists or the military. It could even be your own siblings, your nephew, your uncle.

The soldiers had a base up on the hill where they could watch what went on in the town. They would sometimes come down into town, and they, too, would kill people. Sometimes I didn't know who was worse – the soldiers or the terrorists. The soldiers were supposed to kill the terrorists, but everyone was all mixed up, and anyone could say, "So-and-So is a terrorist," and the soldiers would kill you. Or someone might say, "So-and-So is against the movement," and the Shining Path would kill you.

That's what happened to your father, and that's why I couldn't trust anyone. So it was just you and your brothers and me, for many years, until the violence finally ended.

Daughter's Note: In the time of the violence, it was terrible. They were killing people everywhere. We would hear gunshots and, in fear for our lives, we would hide. My Mamá *would whisper,*

"Terrucos!" – *Terrorists! – and take us back behind the house, covering my little brothers' mouths so the* terrucos *wouldn't hear the crying. Sometimes we would hear everyone being called to the square through a megaphone, and we had to go. They would line us up and call out names, and if they called your name you had to go with them. One day they called my* Papá's *name. They took him, we heard a gunshot, and we never saw him again.*

Now, though, things are calm. There is no longer violence – no crime, either – not around here. It's calm like it used to be, a long time ago. You and your brothers are all grown up now. I have a new husband and two more sons who are still boys. They go to school with their nephew and niece – your children.

DAUGHTER'S NOTE: *Everyone pressured my mother to remarry, and then her new husband wanted more children, so now she has two more. One is even younger than my son. Women my age, we only want one or two. We take care of ourselves so we won't get pregnant. It's too expensive to send children to school, and too hard on our bodies to have so many babies. The older women, like my mother, had lots of children, but my friends are like me, with younger siblings who are children, and who play with our own sons and daughters.*

You have a little girl and a little boy now. They were born right here, like most of your brothers.

DAUGHTER'S NOTE: *Two of my brothers, the oldest ones, live in Lima with their families. My adult brother who is here still lives with* Mamá. *My husband and I have our own house next to my in-laws. My husband is from this town, too, but he went to Lima for high school. He's a professional – an agronomist. He teaches at the high school in town. That's where I finished studying – I never left here. My husband came back after the violence ended, to take care of his parents and his younger siblings. When he came back, we got to know each other, and then we started living together and had a family.*

You remember your father, and my first son remembers him too. But you're the only one here, close to me, who remembers. The men, sometimes they don't listen. They think childcare is only for their wives. Your husband should be here, and your brothers, but instead, they run away. They are afraid to be with their families and their children.

Daughter's Note: I think it's hard for all of us, growing up with so much uncertainty. I don't ask too much of my husband, because I know it's hard for him, too. I know that he had to leave his home town as a teenager, that he feared for his life growing up, like all the boys did. I just want him to stay, to be with his family like my father couldn't – but I don't want to ask too much of him. And sometimes I think I couldn't raise the children alone. I know my mother did, and I have her help, but she won't always be here. Besides, my husband is educated, and I want my children to learn from him. I want them to be professionals like him, so they can be even better than their parents, and better than their grandparents.

I am humble, just a poor woman. I am like the blind. I don't know how to read or write.

Daughter's Note: But my mother knows and understands everything. She has lived through so much. She is wise and incredibly courageous.

Write down what I know, my child – *Ñuqapa yachasqayta qillqapakuwaychik* – so you know how to raise the little ones. You know how to write. *Tukuy runanchikpaq, tukuy wawanchikpaq qillqapakuwaychik* – For all of our people, for all of our children, write for us.

THE AMARU LEGEND: *AMARUMANTA*

For our children to learn, we must start with a story. Our grandparents told us this story, and you will tell our children as well. You will tell them that they must remember our past. To create a more beautiful future, all of our children must remember. You will tell them that . . .

Ñawpaq kawsaypi – once upon a time – animals and people ran frantically, overwhelmed by sadness. The people sang prayers, praying for their hunger and thirst to be calmed. In those times long ago, the sky, which used to be blue with silver and white clouds pouring water, turned dark and cloudless. The fertile earth became black. It no longer bore flowers or fruit. Not even grains were among its provisions. And they say that all of this came to pass when people and animals sinned and offended, for they had forgotten that which was commanded and created to be just. With so much sadness and misery, not even tree trunks remained. They say, too, that the shape of golden corn was lost from memory.

They say that from the high mountains, tired of running, llamas, vicuñas, and other animals with worn-out feet came down to the valleys in search of food. They came to places that once were green and wooded ravines, and they found only ruins. Birds too weak to fly drifted into the dwellings, barely moving their wings. The situation was so severe that the bodies of people and animals were abandoned even by their shadows. Those among the survivors of such bitter pain awoke every morning with fear, for each dawn brought a day even more full of desperation than the last.

They say that to defend against this curse, old folks and youths from far-off villages who understood the trade of curing evils gathered together at the dried river bed. They tried all the secrets and rituals that were known in those times, but grieved upon discovering that there was no cure for such a great evil.

One day, they say the most elderly man of them all searched for good or bad omens with the last three coca leaves that remained on the earth. The leaves fell on their backs looking up at the man, and he trembled with joy to see the good omen they revealed. Despite his age, the old man ran and announced the good news.

They say it was then that a beautiful condor – the strongest and fastest of all the birds, who knew the world's mysteries – flew tirelessly for nights and days on end, searching for a cure. But the condor soon realized that her strength was leaving her. She felt death approaching and, not wanting to fall to the ground, she gathered her last bit of strength and threw herself down to die on the tallest peak of the region, Allakchiri.

Allakchiri has many paths that deceive by opening to deadly cliffs. It is our sacred guardian – our *apu* – watching over us wherever we go, and demanding the utmost respect. Only the condor can reach Allakchiri's peak.

They say that when Allakchiri saw the last breaths of the condor, who was his confidant and messenger, he said to her these words:

"My dear condor, my only friend. How would my days be without you? Only you reach my peak and relieve my solitude. For you I will divulge my secret, and you will go quickly to spread it. The cause of your evils began with the fierce *Amaru*, the Serpent endowed with human life who lives in the depths of the lake on the edge of town. In the waves of the lake, he devours all beings who dare to approach. The cruel Amaru disguised himself and stole the *sullawayta* – the pure and crystalline flower-of-frost that gives him life. The *sullawayta* holds all that is good and abundant, and when the Amaru devoured this precious flower, some feared him but others followed, and the people became full of evil."

As Allakchiri finished, he added, "To rescue the flower-of-frost, the most pure and crystalline of all people and animals must throw himself into the depths of the lake."

They say that the condor flew off at great speed despite her weakened state, and on reaching the village she recounted the news. Fearlessly, the people set off toward the lake and, upon arriving, each one assuming himself to be more pure than the others, they threw themselves into the water to drown. For many days, the sacrifices brought no result.

But when a young shepherd from far-off highlands drowned himself, the waters shook. The land trembled violently, the mountains fell, enveloped in dust, and erupted with thundering sounds. The wind blew with a fierce cracking, and the world screeched with rage.

They say that all of the people fainted, overcome with fear, and when they came to and regained their calm, they laid themselves down and promised to sin no more.

They say that from the waters of *Amaru Cocha*, the Serpent Lake, the people saw balls of black and white clouds rising into the sky. In the clouds were all those who had sacrificed themselves – the good people in the white clouds and the bad in the black. Only the young shepherd who had purified the world by being the most virtuous person of all remained forever at the bottom of the lake in exchange for the *sullawayta,* the flower-of-frost. They say that the clouds, full of such great sorrow, cried plentiful tears, which turned into rain.

From that time on, the clouds have ensured that the earth remains green with flowers and fruits, and the flower of the water dawns in the flowers of the earth. The condor, after so many years, has lost only the feathers of her neck, and only her feet have aged.

My child, I have lived a great deal. I have seen a great deal. There is so much sacrifice that we have to make in this life. People do so much evil. We must remember. We must respect our mountains, our *apus*, our rivers, our streams, our sisters and brothers, our alpacas, our cows, our trees and our grasses, our children and our grandparents. We must be like the young shepherd who knows that we must give to the earth so that the earth will provide for us in return.

Quechua or Spanish? Farm or School?

Daughter's Note: My mother cries every time she tells this story. I've never told it to my own children, because I don't speak to them in Quechua. They don't understand Quechua, and I didn't know how to recount the Amaru story in Spanish. But now, here it is, written in the language they know. Now I can make them understand.

Our children today, we must . . .

RAISE THEM TO BE LIKE PEOPLE
RUNA HINA WIÑACHINANCHIK

If our children do not act like people – like *runa,* or human beings – we have not raised them well.

Daughter's Note: We always scold our children to "be like people." My mother always used to say to me sharply, "Runa hina kay!" *in Quechua, and I always say to my children,* "Pórtate como gente!" *in Spanish.*

To "behave like a person" means we are not alone. I need you. You need me. We need our families. Our families need us. This is how it is with our children. They need their families, their school, their community, and their country. All of these people need our children, too. That's how it is. This is why all people must respect one another.

We must help one another, speak well to one another, work well for one another. Our children must greet their elders, they must speak well to their teachers, they must show respect for authorities. We must listen to our children, also. We must consider each child's perspective as we would any person's, as long as the child is behaving like a person. Children need to respect others and treat them like people so that they, too, will be respected. That is how we will live in peace, without violence, without weeping, without suffering. We must teach our children this.

They say that when you speak in Quechua, there is always respect for the other person, but in Spanish it isn't like that. You can't speak *without* respect in Quechua the way you can in Spanish.

Daughter's Note: It's true, what my mother says. She knows, even though she barely speaks a word of Spanish. When I greet an aunt or uncle with "Rimaykullayki" *in Quechua, I respect them as a person, saying, "Please would your honorable person kindly speak with me." When I say,* "Buenos días" *in Spanish, however, it might seem respectful, but it's not the same. I'm not considering their perspective and their dignity and the time I'm asking them to take to speak with me – well, I suppose it's possible that I might consider all this, but I don't have to, in order to speak with someone in Spanish, the way I do when I speak to them in Quechua. There are no words to express this kind of respect in Spanish. In Quechua, though, it's impossible to speak without respecting the person you're speaking to.*

And our children, when they don't speak Quechua, they lose this. They don't understand what it really means to respect, and be respected by, others.

Becoming a Person: *Runachakuy*

Giving Birth

When you were in my belly and you wanted to come out, your *Papá* brought the midwife from her house. She looked at my hand, and when the veins were hot and bursting, she knew that you were ready to come. She made me kneel like I was praying, and she made my husband go and hold me from the front. She made me lean back against her, and she massaged my belly from behind. She had a medicine made from herbs, and she massaged me with it to keep me warm and to put the baby straight.

After you came out, the midwife tied up my belly with my *chumpi* – the woven belt that we always wear. She took you in her arms and gave your *Papá* a sharp piece of ceramic, telling him to cut the umbilical cord. Then she made the placenta come out, so it wouldn't stay inside and harm me. She bathed me with rosemary water and then closed the windows and doors, wrapped me in blankets to keep me warm, and brought me warm foods and warm teas. Your *Papá* had to stay with me and keep me awake so I wouldn't slip away in my sleep.

That's how we used to have babies – at home, with a midwife. Now, everyone goes to the hospital – for us, the health post at the edge of our town. There are more hospitals now up here in the mountains, so it's easier for us to get to one. Now, the government even has laws that make everyone go to the hospital. If you don't go for your check-ups, you will be fined.

So everyone goes. But not everyone likes it. The hospitals are cold, and women need to be warm to give birth. The midwife knows how to make a baby come out just by massaging – she never puts her hands inside of you. The doctors, they don't even look at your hands to see if you're ready to give birth. They just shove their hands into you, saying they have to examine – over and over, they stick their hands into you. Their hands are cold, and they yank the baby out, not waiting until it's ready to come. The doctors say the hospitals are safe, that women don't die giving birth any more. So we have to go there, even though we don't like it. Now, our youth study to be doctors and nurses, but they should also learn from the midwives before their knowledge is lost.

There are still some midwives, but not too many. Most of them have grown old and died, and they haven't passed on their knowledge.

Daughter's Note: Both of my children were delivered by nurses at the health post. Everyone calls it a "hospital," but it's really just a health post, and there aren't always doctors on duty. Thank God, my children came out nice and healthy, and everything went well with both of their births. It's important these days to go to the health post, but it would be better if they let the midwives help there, too.

The Birth Godparents

When a woman has her belly, it is necessary to look for birth godparents for the baby. *Mamá* and *Papá* should choose good godparents who are able to set a good example for their child. The godparents will bring the child gifts, and when they can, they will come to visit. They will support and guide the baby as it grows.

DAUGHTER'S NOTE: My son's godparents are his uncle and aunt who live in Lima – my oldest brother and his wife. We asked them to be his godparents because in Lima they have more than we have here. Maybe they can buy clothes and school supplies for him. Maybe we can send him to Lima to stay with them when he's old enough to work, or when he wants to go to college. But it depends on them, on their will to help out.

My daughter, she just has a godmother, a cousin of my husband. My daughter's godmother is not married – she's alone – but she's a professional. Maybe she can teach my daughter things that I can't. Maybe she can help my daughter see that women, too, can go to college and be professionals. And maybe she will earn more at her job, and be able to contribute to my daughter's education.

These godparents are like part of the family. With your own godparents, you greet them by saying *Madrina* (Godmother) or *Padrino* (Godfather); and the godparents of your children, you greet saying *Comadre* (Co-mother) or *Compadre* (Co-father). They will always be part of your family.

The godparents must be invited over often and spend time with the family, even before the baby is born. When they come to visit, they must be well received. Just as the godparents support the baby with little gifts like clothing, you have to give the godparents some of your harvest.

DAUGHTER'S NOTE: Whenever my children's godparents are in town, we always go find them and ask them to come to our house. We give them the best of what we have cooked for the day, and we send them home with a nice full bag of potatoes, corn, and fresh cheese. When they are in Lima, we call them on our cell phones. Even when we don't have much money, we buy a few minutes of phone time so the godparents know we are thinking of them – so they don't forget their godchildren.

Only like this, treating godparents with the utmost respect, can parents expect them to support their godchild. Some godparents don't provide much support, and others do. That's why it's important to make good choices and then treat the godparents well.

Quechua or Spanish? Farm or School?

The External Womb

When the baby is born, it remains in the mother's belly. Whether it's a boy or a girl doesn't matter – for the first two years after birth, it's like the baby is still part of its mother. As a mother, you wrap your baby up in a cloth, and you let his or her hair grow as long as the baby is breastfeeding, because it is still part of you.

Or at least that is how it used to be. But I know, my daughter, that it's not always like this any more. When you have a baby boy in the city, many people there make you feel bad if he has long hair and wears a cloth that looks like a skirt. On the streets, the city people call you *Indian* and give you dirty looks, like you're a bad person. Even in some churches, the preachers say you are sinful and will confuse your baby boy if you dress him like a little girl. But the people who say this, they don't understand that the baby is not yet a girl or a boy, but is still part of you, part of the mother.

DAUGHTER'S NOTE: *It was like this for me. I didn't let my son's hair grow out when he was a baby, because I said to myself, "The neighbors will give me dirty looks. They will call me 'backwards.' Later, they will say it's my fault that my family doesn't get ahead." Even though we live here in the mountains, I worried, when my son was born, about what people would say if I let his hair grow long. There is no privacy here. In a small town, everyone talks, and we have to live with our neighbors' judgments.*

When I was a young mother, it was different. Back then, the neighbors would talk if you *didn't* let your baby's hair grow. They would talk if you raised a little baby like a boy when it was still too young, still just a part of its mother. But these days, we've been taught to hate our own traditions. The schoolteachers, the preachers, the politicians, the television – they all tell us that we are holding ourselves back with our traditions. So now, the neighbors talk behind your back if you speak to your children in Quechua or let your baby boy's hair grow long.

Well, my daughter, I know that it's difficult. You young people know better than me, because you've lived in the city and you've been criticized for following our traditions. Sometimes, even the father of your children doesn't want to let his little son's hair grow long, saying that the world is changing and that it's not right any more to do this. I think that God will understand. But fathers and mothers, when they look at their little baby, they should still see it as part of its mother. When it's very small, it can't yet be treated like a girl or a boy. Even though it is part of the family, it is not yet a person.

In these first two years, when the baby is not yet a person, it goes wherever you go, as if there were an external womb. You wrap your child in a carrying cloth and take it everywhere – to the fields, to church, and so on. Even at home, when you're cooking or sweeping, you bind the child in its cloth so that it stays close to you. Sometimes, too, your baby's father, or its older brothers or sisters, will carry the baby in a cloth on their backs. Even though babies are part of their mothers, sometimes we mothers get tired and need other family members to help.

Daughter's Note: When my children were babies, I carried them this way everywhere I went. When I got tired, my mother would help, carrying her grandchildren on her back. Mamá *says that when she got too tired, my* Papá *used to help carry us on his back. I don't very often see boys and men carrying babies on their backs these days.*

My husband helps in the ways he knows how: he works and he takes care of his family, bringing rice, sugar, sometimes vegetables or meat, from the corner store. He also helps me cook and do laundry. He's a good husband.

Together with your baby's father and everyone else in your household, you have to take care of your baby. Everyone has to help, because the baby belongs to the entire household. We all have to take care of our family's baby so that it can survive to be its own person, and contribute to our household like everyone else. In these first two years, we have to give our baby lots of love and affection. *Mamá, Papá*, grandparents, brothers and sisters – we all have to play with the baby and treat it with affection. When the baby is still small, it doesn't know anything yet. The baby doesn't know right from wrong, so we can't punish or blame it for getting in the way. Even the young men know how to play and laugh with our babies. Everyone knows how to laugh, even those who have been through so much in their lives. Our babies give us hope – they are our future, and we have to love them and make sure they survive to be people and contribute to the family.

The Protective Water

When your child is still a baby you have to do the *agüita de socorro*, the protective water, and the baby has to have its *agüita* godparents, too. Just like with the birth godparents, you don't have to choose a married couple – your baby can have just a godmother or just a godfather, if there is an unmarried woman or man who cares for the baby very much.

The *agüita* is like a baptism, but without the Church and without a priest. Up high in the mountains, there are no priests, and even here, sometimes there is no money for a Mass and a Catholic baptism, so in the meantime the *agüita* protects the baby. We do the *agüita de socorro* with water because water is sacred. Because the water comes from the mountains that nourish us and give us life, the *agüita de socorro* protects the baby. I believe we have always done this ritual, even before there were priests and churches.

DAUGHTER'S NOTE: Both of my children have their birth godparents and their agüita de socorro. *There is a priest here in town, and if we had money we would have baptized my children when they were babies. But no one has money here, so babies are never baptized until they're already school-age children. My children are protected, though. They have people who care for them – godparents of birth and godparents of water. I know that if something happened to me, they would be taken care of.*

Even if I could have baptized my son and daughter in the church when they were babies, we still would have given them their agüita de socorro, *too. We do it at home with close family and the godparents – no one else. It's different from baptism, because it's just in the family. Once we have done this ritual, our children are part of their families and part of the earth.*

The First Haircut

While the baby is still in the external womb, you let its hair grow long, because it is still part of you. But when it has been two or three years and the baby no longer needs your milk, you cut its hair as if you were cutting the umbilical cord. With this act, your baby becomes a person. This is the way it has been done, they say, for all of time.

After the haircut, we must give our child clothes for a girl or a boy, not a baby. When we lived up in the *puna*, I used to make all of our clothing myself. I wove the cloth that wrapped our babies – first you, when you were born, and then your brothers when they came along. Then, when you didn't like my milk so much any more, my mother told me that it was time to make you a skirt. At the same time that I weaned you, we took off your baby cloth, put on the skirt that made you a girl, and cut your hair. Then, you were no longer part of me. We did the same thing with your brothers, but I made them pants instead of a skirt, and I cut their hair shorter. Even with my youngest sons, who are still children, I have done this, although I don't make their pants myself any more, because their godparents send us clothes from Lima.

Some people don't do this ritual haircut, and sometimes their babies grow up spoiled and don't listen to anyone. They don't learn to support the family, and instead of helping *Mamá* and *Papá*, they make their parents' lives harder. They can be too smart, manipulating their parents instead of respecting and supporting them. This is why I think there should always be some sort of ritual when the baby is weaned; we have to do something to introduce our children into society. It doesn't have to be cutting their hair, but we have to do something.

Daughter's Note: When some parents my age don't want to let our babies' hair grow for the first two years, we end up treating them like babies longer. My son, for example – he's seven years old, and since we didn't let his hair grow as a baby and never did the hair-cutting ritual for him, we still don't make him do a lot of chores, and he never listens to his grandmother or me or his father. With my little daughter, on the other hand, we're stricter. We did the ritual for her, because it's easier to let a baby's hair grow long when it's a little girl. She's four years old now, and I already make her help milk the cows and take care of the animals. She's obedient and respectful – unlike her brother, who is whiny and spoiled.

Quechua or Spanish? Farm or School?

Once your baby's hair has been cut, he or she is no longer a part of you but already an independent person. Now you must raise the child like a boy or a girl. If the child is a boy, he needs to start spending more time with the men – his *Papá*, his uncles, grandfathers, nephews, and brothers-in-law.

Most importantly, your child needs to respect you, and you in turn need to respect your child.

The Catholic Baptism

You must protect the baby with its *agüita de socorro* until a priest can conduct the baptismal rite. It's better to baptize two of your children at the same time, because that way it's more affordable. Again, you have to find godparents, and they have to help pay for the Mass, the baptism clothes, and everything else. And you have to kill one of your cows so you can invite the whole community to a feast, and you have to give lots of food and alcohol to the godparents to show them your gratitude.

It is said that, with this baptism, your child's sins are washed away. The priest says that all babies are born in sin and that once they're baptized they can ask forgiveness for their sins. You still have to help them, though, because they don't yet know how to do this. Once they've been baptized, they can be with God when they die.

Daughter's Note: It's getting to be time for us to baptize my children together. My son is getting big; he'll soon be in second grade, and he has still not been baptized. I think this year we will be able to do it.

The priest says that baptism is absolutely necessary – one of the "seven sacraments." The schoolteachers talk about it, too. They say that everyone has to get baptized. You can't be a person if you aren't baptized. That's just how it is.

Later, around fourth grade, the schoolteacher will take the whole class to a Confirmation Mass. Then, once your children are "confirmed," they will be permitted to take Holy Communion and confess their sins, just like full members of the Church.

Being a Person in the Family and Community

Once children have been weaned from their mothers, they are expected to obey their elders and contribute to the family. We are very strict with them. You always have to be loving and caring with children, but when they don't listen, you have to hit them, because if children don't do their part, the whole family suffers.

Today, the schoolteachers and the psychologists that the government sent after the violence tell us that you shouldn't hit children, that it goes against children's rights. But we still punish misbehaving children severely, so they'll listen. For example, if you say to a child, "Bring me firewood for the stove," and they don't listen and obey, how are you going to prepare the food? The entire family won't eat because of a child who doesn't listen. And without eating, how is *Papá* going to go do the hard labor necessary to tend his fields or build a house or repair the roads? The whole family is going to suffer because of the child who didn't listen to *Mamá* and didn't bring firewood. This is why you have to punish a misbehaving child by saying, "Watch out, I'm going to hit you!" even if it's just a threat you don't intend to carry out.

An important value for us is that the family is not just the people, but also the animals that belong to us, and the land where we grow our crops and vegetables and build our houses. That's why we tell the children who play in the town square not to step on the flowers, and why we get angry when a child runs through our garden and tramples the plants. And that's why we give children a pet lamb or pet puppy, so they learn to be kind to animals and nurture them.

Daughter's Note: My son and daughter have a little lamb that we bought from the neighbors who raise sheep. My husband named the lamb Tukicha, *which means "little and restless" in Quechua, because the lamb never stays still – she is just like my son. Tukicha always comes with us when I take my children to milk the cows, and the children have to play with her and keep her safe, so she doesn't get stepped on by the cows or fall off a cliff. She drinks the fresh cows' milk and grazes on the plants in the pastures. But we have to make sure she doesn't eat too much, because little lambs can die if their bellies get too full. The children have to watch Tukicha at home, so she doesn't get into trouble. We lost two little lambs before her – they are so delicate and vulnerable when they're small.*

It is good for young children to care for animals. When I was very small like your daughter, I took care of our sheep in the highlands. You and your brother did the same when you were small. Here in this town, we can't send the children out alone any more, because there are bad people who might harm them, and because the children need to prepare for school. But it is good that they still milk and herd the cows with you, because children are talented at working with animals, and it is much easier for you when you have a good little helper.

As children grow, their social surroundings also expand. The respectful and respectable behaviors that the child has learned in the family are carried with them to the community, the school, and eventually the nation. Just as children have to listen to their elders so that the elders will listen to them, the family also has to be respectful to their neighbors so that others will respect the family. Even though children are always in their community and neighborhood, their behavior is primarily oriented toward the immediate family that they live with – *Mamá, Papá*, brothers and sisters.

All children have to obey their own *Mamá* and *Papá* – that's how everyone else will judge them. If the neighbors are aware of a problem with a child's behavior, they have to tell the child's *Mamá* so she can punish them. Since children represent their family any time they interact with the neighbors, one doesn't want to hear from a neighbor that their child has been misbehaving.

RAISING A GOOD WORKER AND GOOD PERUVIAN CITIZEN: *ALLIN LLAMKAQ ALLIN PIRU RUNA HINA WIÑACHIY*

Working for the Family and Community

Once the child has become a person, he or she has to learn to work well. Children learn a great deal just by watching and helping out others. Sometimes you have to tell them with words, but usually you can communicate by example and with gestures.

Children shouldn't bother adults. When you're working and a child misbehaves and gets in the way, you have to reprimand them with a gesture or with one simple word, quickly and clearly, without interrupting your work or your conversation with adults.

Most importantly, children have to contribute to the family. It's the first thing they learn to do, because their first responsibility is always to the family so that they can all live together well and thrive. Girls have to help their mothers collect firewood and water, cook, take care of the animals, make cheese, and wash clothes (see Figure 8.1). Boys also have to help *Mamá* when they're little, but as they grow older they help *Papá* more and more by working the land, taking care of the vegetable garden, driving the oxen, and repairing the house when necessary.

Figure 8.1 Peruvian children are expected to help with household and farm tasks from an early age. After washing clothes in a canal, this girl is taking home laundry (and a radio by which she entertained herself).
Photograph by Thomas Riddle.

Girls can also help with men's work, and boys can help with women's work. If there's no woman to wash clothes and cook, it still has to be done, so a man does it. If there's no man to water the garden and fix the roof, then a woman will.

Sometimes *Mamá* or *Papá* can send their child to buy something from a neighbor's store, or to borrow a tool. Or sometimes the child is just playing outside the house, and a neighbor comes down the road with her sheep. The child has to greet the neighbor, saying, "Good afternoon, Auntie." Then the child has to help herd the neighbor's sheep, because if he or she doesn't help, the sheep might run away.

Girls shouldn't be on the streets much, but it's okay if they play right outside of their houses. Boys can range further. Girls are more helpful to the family, because they stay close to home and are easy to find when we need them.

From the time that they're very small, we take our children to *faenas*, where we work together with the whole community.

Daughter's Note: Faenas *are work sessions that are organized by the Community Government. The President can call a* faena *to accomplish all kinds of things – plant and harvest crops on communal land, clean the irrigation ditches, renovate the Community Center, fix the road, and so on. When there is a* faena, *every community member has to participate. Usually the father will register as a member for the whole family. If you join the community, you get rights to irrigation water, but you also have to pay your dues and go to the work sessions. If you aren't there when they take attendance, you will be fined, and everyone will talk about your family, saying that you never contribute your part.*

At the *faenas*, we all represent the family. If you are a community member and you can't go to the work session, you can send your child, if they are already a teenager – or you can send anyone you want – but that person must represent the family well so that everyone else will respect the family. For the work sessions, usually the men or boys go when it's something like construction or hard labor with tools. But women and girls take care of planting seeds, bringing and serving food and drink, or clearing out irrigation canals by pulling weeds.

A World of Babies

DAUGHTER'S NOTE: In my household, we're not community members. We don't own land, so we don't need the irrigation water. Also, the community marginalizes women – they don't want us to go take our husbands' places when they're unable to work. So for people like us, with my husband working at the school and my son still small, it's hard to fulfill the communal obligations.

In contrast, my mother and her husband are community members. He owns land here, passed down by his family. He almost always goes to the work sessions, or sometimes he sends my brother – the older one who lives with him and Mamá.

When it is a really important work session, like a community festival or agricultural ceremony, the whole family goes. Babies attend on their mothers' backs. Older children help take care of the younger ones. The children play with each other, too, staying out of the way of the adults. The older children make sure that the little ones don't get in the way. Often children imitate adults when they play, and that's how they learn to do the communal work that adults do. For example, the boys play at lassoing and branding the bulls until they're old enough to help out a little bit. They gradually get involved more and more until they are able to do it well and can actually be of help to the men. As for the girls, they play at serving corn cider and food, marking the cows with ear ribbons, and planting corn seeds. That's how our children learn to contribute to their community – by playing, observing, and participating.

Early Schooling

Once your children are three or four years old, you need to send them to preschool. There was no preschool around here until recently, but we now have classrooms for three-, four-, and five-year-olds where teachers get the children ready for elementary school. We used to keep children of this age at home so they could help out in the fields. By staying at home, they learned a great deal about farming just through observation so that when they were older they could help.

But now, it's important for our children to get an education so they can be something other than farmers. They have to go to college, or at least to an institute, because now we depend not just on the fields to support us, but also on the city, and on the money that we get from our older sons and daughters who have gone to the coast and become professionals. Our older children also send notebooks and schoolbooks, some of them in English, so their younger brothers and sisters can learn. The ones who are professionals tell us that English is the most important subject to learn.

Nowadays, only a few of our children stay to work in the fields like their parents and grandparents did. It is beautiful here, and we love our land, but those of us who work the fields – well, we are just poor farmers. From the preschool teachers, the little ones learn important things that I don't know how to teach them, like the alphabet and mathematics. I don't know those things, and that's what the teachers are there for.

Figure 8.2 "All of us will weed the fields." Three generations of a Peruvian family rest on a Saturday, before getting back to work. Photograph by Kate Feinberg Robins.

DAUGHTER'S NOTE: The teachers actually say that the children in the mountains are very good at math. It's because we use it every day: counting our animals, planting our fields, and buying food at the corner store (see Figure 8.2).

My husband studied at the oldest university in Peru – Universidad Nacional Mayor de San Marcos. There, they taught him that the Inca were very advanced – they were great agricultural engineers, and they governed a vast empire with a complex system of roads, irrigation, trade, and tribute – long before there were cars or telephones. They had their own system of math, but now we don't understand it – it was so complex that even the scientists can't figure it out.

They also teach our Quechua language at San Marcos, and the university professors say it is very complex. They have ways to write it now, but we never wrote or read Quechua growing up. So my mother knows many things, even though she never went to school.

The teachers are there for Spanish, too, so our children can learn to speak well, and not get confused with Quechua. It's true that our young people now, like you and your husband, should already know these things from having gone to school. But you're busy with your own work, and you depend on the teachers who are trained for this. Everyone has their profession, and teachers should know best how to prepare our children for school. All of the parents – even mothers like me who don't know much – have to help our children with their schoolwork at home.

Even the littlest children leave school with work from their teachers to do at home. The teachers tell us that our children need their own little table where they can work at home, and we have to set a time when we make them do homework every day before they can play. For our families here in the mountains, this is not hard, because we've always made our children work. We used to take you to the fields or send you on your own to take care of the animals; now, instead, we make our children do their homework, because by doing that, they also support the family.

Sometimes children don't understand why they need to do homework. But if they don't do it, we have to punish them, just like we punish them when they don't bring the firewood. The family is sacrificing to send them to school, so the children need to do their part. If children don't do their schoolwork, how will they be able to contribute to the family? What will be the point of so much family sacrifice? We will have sent them every day for their whole lives to preschool, then primary school, then high school, and for what, if they don't work hard to get an education and don't become professionals, and don't come back to support their family and community with everything they know?

But education takes place in the home, too, where you must teach children to respect others and demand respect in return. If you make them work hard at home, they'll also work hard at school. If you make them listen to their parents, grandparents, aunts, and uncles, then they'll also listen to their teachers. If you teach them to take care of their own family, including making sure their brothers and sisters do their part, then they'll also take care of their classrooms and make sure their classmates always do their best. If you teach them to love their animals and their fields and their gardens, they will also love the gardens and fields and flowers at their school.

Children who grow up speaking Quechua understand this. When you don't speak to your children in Quechua, you may make them forget how to behave like people. We can't expect teachers to speak to our children in Quechua, because they're here for a different purpose – to teach our children what they need to succeed in school. We are the ones who know how to speak with respect, how to listen with respect, how to treat our children with respect, and how to make our children respect others so that our families will be respected. We must pass on our language to our children.

DAUGHTER'S NOTE: *All of the parents that I know who are of my age have stopped speaking Quechua to their children. When we were in school, the teachers punished us for speaking Quechua, and we don't want our children to suffer like we did. Most parents now think that it's bad to speak Quechua to our children, that it will make them struggle with Spanish and fall behind in school. Even though my husband went to university and learned about Quechua from the linguistics professors, we still have to live with the gaze of our neighbors and the uncertainty of doing the right thing for our children. Now, our children don't understand when we speak to them in Quechua, and it's easier just to use Spanish. Still, it isn't good when they can't understand their grandmother and don't know how to treat elders with the respect they deserve.*

At school, your children will learn how to raise the flag and serve their country. They will learn what it means to be Peruvian. "Citizenship" is what the teachers call it, saying, "You have to contribute to your country." Children put on their uniforms, and they learn their Spanish language and their Peruvian history. The teachers make them learn about other parts of our country – the coast and the rainforest – saying, "We have to progress" and "We're all one people." Even though no one ever taught me this, I understand it because of what I learned from my *Mamá* and *Papá*. Just like I make my family respected, when our children go out into the world they have to make their country respected, too.

There are teachers who aren't respectful to children and parents, and that's another reason why *you* have to teach your children well – so they won't be influenced by a bad role model. We are just poor people, and they send us any old teacher – some are very good, but others are very bad. Teachers need to be patient and explain things to mothers like me who didn't go to school. We must teach our children to make themselves respected so that they can tell us if someone disrespects them.

When there's a parent meeting for your child's classroom or the Parent Teacher Association, it's important to go. Mostly it is mothers who go, but fathers should go too. Fathers need to know what happens at school so they can make sure that their children are respected. Sometimes teachers listen more to men, and sometimes they're more respectful to parents who are better educated. Because so many of our men went off to Lima and studied there in the time of the terrorists, mostly it's the fathers who are professionals – engineers, doctors, and professors – so often, teachers respect them more than they respect mothers. Also, since the fathers who went to college are the ones who have spent the most time in school, they're the ones who know best how a school should be run.

MOVING FORWARD: *QIPAMAN QATIY*

That's how it is, my daughter. The world is very different today from when I was raising you. Now, we have peace, and we have to keep it that way. Before, it was terrible, and it can't be like that again. Now, there are opportunities to get ahead – something we all want for our children. We have to send them to be educated, and we also have to support them with a good education at home. From the time a woman has her belly, she and the baby's father must plan to bring the child into a world where he or she is welcomed, respected, and taught to respect others. As a parent, you must make sure that your child has godparents at birth, their protective water, their first haircut, and their baptism, so that they become a person in the family, a person in the community, and a citizen in their country.

My children – you and your brothers – are better than me, and you must raise your children to be better than you.

Daughter's Note: *If our children work hard in school, they will be able to study at the National University of San Marcos, just like my husband did. The test to get in is very difficult, but if they pass, they will study for free. This is what we want them to aspire to – to be better than their parents, to study at the best university, and to practice their professions so they can support our family and lift up their community and their country. Of course, we also want them to be happy.*

Fathers have to take responsibility, too. They can't be afraid. They need to spend time with their children, help their wife, teach their little boys how to do men's work, and help teach their little girls how to do women's work – and men's work, too, when it's necessary. Fathers should teach their children to study, to work, to get ahead.

Our children are going to be "Peruvians" – citizens of their country. Maybe they'll even travel around the world. Who knows? But they will always have to come back to support their own family and their own people. That is what we, the blind grandparents who can't even read or write or speak, can give you, the parents of a new generation. And you are going to need it, my daughter. Your children – our children – have to remember where they come from, and who they come from, in order to move forward.

CHAPTER 9

"Equal Children Play Best"

Raising Independent Children in a Nordic Welfare State

Mariah G. Schug

LIFE IN THE FAROE ISLANDS

One of the most remote European societies, the Faroe Islands consist of an eighteen-island archipelago located in the North Atlantic – north of Scotland and west of Norway (see Figure 9.1). Modern Faroese are descended from Vikings who first settled the islands around 800 AD; with this maritime heritage, the Faroese people have long relied on the sea for their subsistence. Of their current population of 48,000, about 20,000 live in or near the capital city of Tórshavn. Most other people live in tiny villages, often consisting of about 200–500 individuals, located throughout the islands.

Faroese culture is often described as emphasizing emotional and physical resilience, and closeness with nature. After centuries of rule by Denmark, since 1948 the islands have become a largely self-governing, autonomous province of Denmark. They have their own parliament and prime minister, although Denmark still handles much of their foreign affairs. Nevertheless, although Denmark belongs to the European Union, the Faroes have chosen not to join, in order to protect their

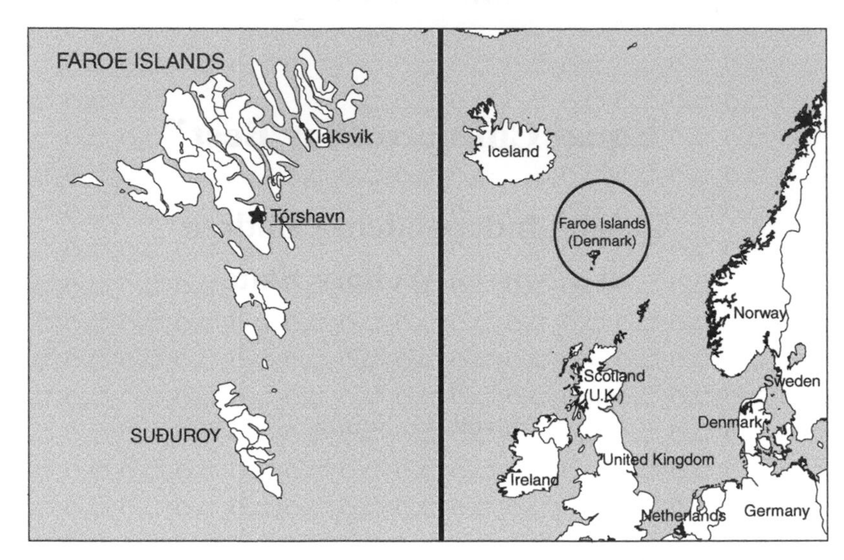

Figure 9.1 While nominally part of Denmark, the Faroe Islands' location in the North Atlantic promotes a rugged sense of independence in its residents.

fishing rights. In spite of their small population, they have their own native language – Faroese (a northern Germanic language descended from Old West Norse, and mostly closely related to Icelandic). Today's Faroese lifestyle combines traditional and modern values to create a unique culture. At the same time that they remain proud of their identity and continue to value family and community ties and other traditional practices, Faroese also increasingly seek a more progressive way of life.

The classic Faroese mindset emphasizes individual hardiness and an understanding of the natural world, developing from the islands' isolation and harsh landscape. Before the twentieth century, food imports to the Faroes were very limited, although they became much more common after World War II. Before that, people relied almost exclusively on the sea for survival. Fish, seabirds, and whale meat were the basis of the diet.
Pursuing these food sources meant fishing in the unpredictable seas, or scaling down cliff walls to birds' nests. Because the islands are rocky and subject to strong sea winds, the Faroes are almost entirely without trees. The few crops that can grow there –

primarily potatoes – formed an important additional component to the traditional diet. Sheep were the final critical element in Faroese survival. They provided wool and meat and required little care – roaming the rocky cliffs freely most of the year.

Despite making optimal use of the resources available to them, throughout most of Faroese history, survival was a struggle. When weather patterns made food from the sea less available, people remained hungry and reportedly lived on seaweed. Strong storms regularly forced families indoors for days and killed countless fishermen. Because fishing was cooperative, sometimes most of the men in a single village would be on a fishing expedition together – and then be wiped out in an unexpected storm. Even today, people indulge in stories featuring women left behind who had prophetic dreams predicting these tragedies. In addition to risk of hunger, travel between villages and islands was difficult and dangerous, making communication with the outside world rare. Over the course of the last hundred years, this situation slowly improved, with the building of better roads and tunnels. It was in this environmentally difficult landscape that Faroese culture developed to emphasize hardiness and independence – while, at the same time, recognizing the critical importance of family and community relationships for survival.

Because of the islands' isolation, this difficult lifestyle was slow to change. The Faroe Islands' entry into the modern world was driven, in large part, by their role as an important fish supplier for the British during World War II. Nonetheless, even as late as the 1970s, the more remote villages lacked electricity. Today, in contrast, life is comfortable in the Faroes. Almost everyone has not only electricity but satellite television. Travel between villages and islands is easy via car, ferries, bridges, and inter-island tunnels. Moreover, an array of social services provided by the national government allows for a tremendous level of security for the modern Faroese. While in the past one's survival depended on the elements, today almost everyone is guaranteed a place to live and food to eat.

Nevertheless, the influence of the Faroe Islands' past remains strong today. Traditional subsistence practices continue to contribute to many families' diets. Most fishing is conducted on large commercial vessels, but much of the Faroese economy continues to depend on the fishing industry, with approximately 30 percent of the annual GDP coming from fishing, fish processing, and aquaculture. Although controversial at the international level, a more humane version of the traditional whale hunt continues and is cherished as one of the Faroes' oldest traditions. (The pilot whale – not an endangered species – is the aim of the contemporary hunt. The technique for killing the whales has been modified to be more humane: the spinal cord is directly cut, providing a fast death for the whales. In order to be allowed to kill the whales, Faroese people must take a certification course to ensure they use this method appropriately.) The products of the whale hunt are not sold. Rather, following historical practices, whale meat is distributed for free to villagers, regardless of whether they participated in the hunt.

Many families continue to maintain small garden plots in which potatoes, rutabaga, and rhubarb are grown. Sheep remain omnipresent. Indeed, there are more sheep than humans in the Faroes, and one cannot travel through a village without seeing sheep roaming freely. Heavy woolen sweaters are worn in place of rain jackets in wet weather, and wool remains one of the islands' primary exports, following fish. Although many Faroese now work in offices, people remain very attuned to their environment. But, whereas the fast-changing weather patterns may have once threatened life or subsistence, today they simply influence the day's activities.

Perhaps because of their isolation and strong valuing of tradition, the Faroese people remain far more religious today than their fellow northern Europeans. Although a small number of Faroese are atheist or secular, over 90 percent belong to some form of the Lutheran Evangelical Church. Most belong to the National Church, although there are several "independent" Lutheran churches, whose members are among the most zealous of the Faroese. A small percentage of people are non-Lutheran Christians (e.g., Catholics) or non-Christian. For instance, in 2011 there were 1,397 people who self-identified as having "no religious belief," along with sixty-six Buddhists and twenty-three Muslims. The strong commitment to religion in the Faroes contrasts starkly with mainland Denmark, where only 28 percent of people report believing in God.

Although most Faroese claim some affiliation with the Lutheran Church, there is diversity in the extent to which people participate in church activities and define themselves through their religiosity. Especially in the northern city of Klaksvík, a strong religious community promotes a conservative lifestyle and resists what is perceived to be the damaging influences of outside forces – including the LGBT rights movement. Despite their religiosity, Faroese parents commonly raise children without being married, with about 50 percent of Faroese children born to single mothers in a typical year. (Many of these mothers are, however, in long-term committed relationships with their children's fathers.) This rate of single parents is just as high as in the other – far less religious – Nordic countries.

While intergroup tensions in the Faroes frequently revolve around religious differences, the more secular Denmark is coping with divides over the place of immigrants in its society. Throughout Scandinavia, xenophobia has been growing along with increasing immigrant populations. Although many Scandinavians find such developments distressing, xenophobic sentiments have gained momentum and have led to the increasing power of political parties – particularly the Danish People's Party – that are based on anti-immigrant platforms. Some Danes' discomfort with immigration appears to stem from a fear that their very secure lives, guaranteed by the welfare state, may now be threatened, as more people in need of social services enter the country and potentially put stress on this supportive system. Similar tensions have emerged throughout Europe, resulting in the rise of xenophobic parties in France, Germany, and Greece, and elsewhere. Denmark's neighbor, Norway, was home to the most shocking event in this trend. In the summer of 2011, a gunman killed eighty-seven people, many of whom were teenagers with ties to the progressive and multicultural Labor Party, with the killer apparently driven by fear of multiculturalism in general and Muslim immigration in particular. Other Nordic countries – including Denmark – joined Norway in mourning after this attack. Nevertheless, a social and political divide remains among northern Europeans as to how welcoming they should be to outsiders.

The relative homogeneity of the Faroe Islands has long sheltered them from such dramatic intergroup tensions. However, the Faroes are now home to a growing immigrant population – and, with it, a growing potential for intergroup tension. Nowadays, many more Faroese women than men choose to move (or remain) abroad, leaving far more men than women in the Faroes. In response to what is deemed by many a social and demographic crisis – contributing to the islands' dropping birthrate – some Faroese men have invited women from overseas to come to the Faroes and become their wives. Hence, the Faroes has seen the emergence of "imported brides." Most of these brides have come from the Philippines, Thailand, and Russia. Since 2000, the number of women from these three countries who now live in the Faroe Islands has increased more than fivefold.

Because this is a new trend, it is difficult to assess whether and how these newcomers may influence life and intergroup interactions in the Faroe Islands. Most of the immigrants are entering families and filling a locally acknowledged need, therefore it is possible that they will be readily accepted. But in other parts of the world, even when there has been a need for immigrant labor, intergroup tensions have still tended to emerge, as immigrant populations grow. Whether this new population will be welcomed in the Faroe Islands, or relegated to a stigmatized status of outsiders, will likely become clear in the coming years. At present, it appears many Faroese are comfortable with the immigrant population, so long as the immigrants are willing to integrate into Faroese culture.

Although subsistence practices provide some insights into Faroese values, understanding the Faroese emphasis on interpersonal relationships is essential to understanding

Faroese culture. People's identities are strongly linked to their villages. People not only know their neighbors, they are very aware of their neighbors' activities. Visiting one's neighbors and family members in the evening is common and, indeed, expected, with cultural norms surrounding the practice. For instance, people are expected to leave their doors unlocked – to do otherwise would be to rudely reject visitors. One does not knock when coming to visit a neighbor; rather, one opens the door and yells out, "Hallo!" When visitors arrive, they should be offered tea and something to eat, in a practice called *drekkamunnur*, literally translated as "drink-mouthful." Together with their hosts, guests are likely to rehash gossip about others in the community.

Even more than maintaining strong relationships with one's neighbors, relationships with one's family members are primary. Children see their grandparents, aunts, uncles, and cousins at least weekly, if not daily (Figure 9.2). They are expected to be present at family events, and extended family members frequently fill in as caregivers. Many Faroese adults who choose to stay in Denmark after completing their education decide to return to the Faroes when they have children. Raising children without the help of family is considered a daunting task to those who grew up in the Faroes, and parents view building relationships with family members as critical to a child's healthy social development. Given the close family relationships, and the fact that children have many opportunities to enjoy the natural environment, many parents consider the Faroe Islands a paradise for children.

Nowadays, one of the many advantages that Faroese children have is that the state provides many resources for them and their families. One example of this support comes in the form of "maternity nurses." These nurses visit new mothers and their infants regularly in their homes during the year after the child's birth. They check on the child's health and give advice to the mothers. The childrearing guide provided here is written from a fictional maternity nurse's perspective.

Figure 9.2 These Faroese grandparents are walking in the countryside with their young grandchild.
Photograph by Mariah G. Schug.

"EQUAL CHILDREN PLAY BEST": RAISING INDEPENDENT CHILDREN IN A NORDIC WELFARE STATE

About the Author

I am one of many maternity nurses in the Faroe Islands. Here on these islands – as in Denmark – we recognize that providing children with a good start in life helps them to be better citizens and to require fewer government resources over the course of their lives. Scandinavian countries developed the idea of maternity nurses. We began the practice in the Faroe Islands in 1980. Maternity nurses need a great deal of education. I first went to nursing school in the Faroe Islands, where (like all of our maternity nurses) I was born and raised. After finishing my nursing degree, I spent two years working as a nurse and specialized in child-related practice. After gaining that experience, I went to Denmark for an additional eighteen months of specialized training for home-health visitors. It was only after all of this training that I was qualified to be a maternity nurse, and I returned to the Faroe Islands. When giving advice, I follow the recommendations of the Danish health authorities and the World Health Organization. My fellow maternity nurses and I have offices all over the islands and often share office space with a village doctor.

We maternity nurses often meet with women when they are pregnant, but much of our job focuses on home visits after the child is born. After mothers give birth, I visit them in their homes about once a month until each child is eighteen months old. We try to have our first visit in the infant's first week of life. I have many duties, including looking after a child's physical and mental health. I weigh the infant and make sure she or he is developing appropriately. If he isn't, I'll be sure he gets the extra care he needs. If a child has a serious health problem, I may continue to visit a family for years. I also visit children again once they reach school age. I'm proud to think that visits from nurses like myself are one of the reasons that the Faroe Islands have an even lower infant mortality rate than the US.

I'm also proud to think that I am an important resource for mothers. Teaching parenting skills is a big part of my job. I teach mothers about breastfeeding and help them cope with the challenges. I also give them advice on any problems they're having with their babies – such as getting them to sleep, or knowing when they need to eat.

But I can't provide all of the support a mother may need. In the Faroes, we recognize that having a community can be extremely helpful for mothers. So, like all maternity nurses, I organize mothers' groups in which mothers with infants of about the same age meet up every few weeks. I attend the first couple of meetings of each group, but then they meet on their own. Many lasting friendships have been built in these groups. Mothers remain a resource for each other throughout their children's lives and continue their friendships even once their children have grown.

I provide my services for native Faroese families as well as for immigrants and long-term visitors. More and more women are moving to the Faroe Islands from other countries to marry Faroese men. I know that our childrearing practices in the Faroes may be very different from what the members of our immigrant community are used to seeing. I have written the following guide as a resource for these new immigrant wives and mothers. I hope that, with my help, they can learn more about Faroese traditions and the values we choose to share with our children.

RELATIONSHIPS AND MARRIAGE

One of the most important choices you make for your child is the choice of your partner. Although most Faroese people agree that it is not important to actually get married – a piece of paper means very little when a couple is truly committed to each other – marrying a Faroese person makes it easier for foreigners to live here permanently. Finding a good partner is ideal so you have someone to help you with childcare and extra income. It is also good for the child to see a loving relationship between parents. It is possible to be a single parent without help from a partner, but this can be very difficult.

Many of our new immigrants to the Faroe Islands have, like you, moved here because they have married a Faroese man. It may surprise you to learn that, while women from the Philippines, Thailand, and Russia often find moving to the Faroes appealing, many native Faroese women have chosen to leave the islands. You see, many young Faroese go abroad – most often to Denmark – to attend university. However, when their studies are complete, the women are much less likely than the men to return to the Faroes. Many young men still find the traditional jobs related to fishing and sheep-rearing appealing, whereas many young women now prefer the more cosmopolitan lifestyle they experience overseas. As a result, we now have far fewer Faroese women than men of childbearing age on the islands.

Your husband may be one of the many Faroese men who have solved this problem by finding a partner from overseas. Often these couples meet online and, after many months of correspondence, they decide to meet. The man may go to the woman's home country and meet her family. If all goes well, they are likely to marry and return together to the Faroe Islands.

If this is, indeed, how you met your husband, adjusting to life in the Faroe Islands may be difficult. You should know that we have resources for you here. The Faroese government funds a minimum of twenty hours of language and culture training for immigrants. There is, however, no established system for providing these courses, and they are of variable quality. Therefore, you might want to ask your husband, his family, or your neighbors to help you find a good one.

If you and your husband are among the many happy immigrant–Faroese couples, you might be comforted to learn that you are not the only relationship trailblazers in the Faroe Islands. The LGBT community in the Faroe Islands has become much more visible and active in just the last few years. For instance, there are now monthly "out nights" in Tórshavn where LGBT individuals can meet. In fact, the LGBT community recently had a major legislative victory, after years of battling the conservative members of the Faroese Parliament. Same-sex marriage was legalized in April 2016, and same-sex marriages are also now recognized from Denmark and abroad. This is very different from the situation in Denmark, where same-sex unions were legitimized twenty-five years ago. The LGBT community continues to fight for rights, including employment protections.

Having a child poses another challenge for LGBT couples that you and your husband have likely been spared. Married same-sex couples are, as of 2016, allowed to adopt. However, few Faroese children are available for adoption. Often heterosexual couples in the Faroes adopt from abroad. Yet, many countries are reluctant to allow LGBT couples to adopt their children. So, while this has become a legally available option, it is difficult for couples to take advantage of it. Another challenge for LGBT families is the cost of fertility treatments. Although the Faroese government gives financial support to heterosexual couples who need reproductive treatments, at this point lesbians wishing to undergo in vitro fertilization may not have their expenses covered. Same-sex male couples face further challenges, as hiring surrogate mothers is illegal. As you can see, members of the Faroese LGBT community now have some options as they start families, yet they continue to work for all of the rights provided to heterosexual couples.

PREGNANCY

Here in the Faroe Islands, we have had a slowly declining birthrate. Because it is important to maintain our population, and because we care about children's health and families' quality of life, we have tried to make starting a family in the Faroes an appealing prospect. If you and your husband decide that you would like to have children, you will find that you have access to many resources.

While parenting in the Faroe Islands is easier than in many countries because of the resources we provide, you and your husband do not need to rush to have children immediately. Take some time to build a healthy relationship together. When you are ready for the commitment of parenthood and have become pregnant, it is time to think about your health and the health of your developing child. It is important that you receive regular prenatal care. Because complete medical care is free to all Faroese people, there is no excuse for you not to do this. What may be more difficult are the changes you must make to your diet and lifestyle.

It is important that you do not drink any alcohol or smoke cigarettes when pregnant. Both of these practices are very harmful to your child's development. Most expectant mothers don't think of this as a big sacrifice. In fact, alcohol used to be difficult to obtain in the Faroe Islands. We were only allowed to order a limited amount each year, shipped in from Denmark.

Back then, people did not have very healthy drinking habits. They would order the drinks that had the highest content of alcohol and often drink it all at once when it arrived. As a result, people would occasionally be very drunk for a few days and then not drink at all for a long time. This changed in the 1990s when the laws limiting access to alcohol were lifted and alcohol began to be sold in local stores. Today, young people – in their early twenties – may drink a lot on weekends. But adults with families tend to drink in moderation. In fact, Faroese people take very seriously recent laws making it illegal to have even one drink when driving. The exception to our moderate drinking may be on our national holiday, Ólavsøka, in July. On Ólavsøka, we pass around a sheep's horn that has been fashioned into a shot glass and drink a strong form of schnapps from it. On the night of Ólavsøka, many people become intoxicated. But even on Ólavsøka, pregnant women are not likely to drink, and no one would dream of driving unless completely sober.

Aside from the temptations of Ólavsøka, avoiding alcohol and cigarettes will probably be less difficult than avoiding pollutants in your diet. Although we have always relied on seafood for nutrition in the Faroe Islands, because our waters are now polluted by emissions from fossil fuel combustion, mining, and the use of fertilizers, many fish have high levels of mercury and other toxic substances such as PCBs. This pollution is the result of international activity, and there is little we Faroese can do to stop it. These toxins are very dangerous for pregnant women to eat, as they can stunt brain development in the growing fetus. In addition to limiting your intake of fish, you must also avoid the whale meat and blubber that we call *grind* (which rhymes with "wind"). Because whales have so much fat, they absorb a great deal of mercury. At any time in life, it is important to limit your intake of whale meat, but during pregnancy you must avoid it entirely. I know this may be very difficult – *grind* meat is a cherished delicacy among our people – but you can resist the temptation knowing that you are doing what is best for your child.

It is also important that you get enough rest during your pregnancy, especially toward the end, when you will be tired from carrying all the extra weight. I understand that many immigrants come to the Faroe Islands with high levels of education and strong work experience. But, perhaps because they have difficulty learning Faroese, once immigrants are here, they work long hours in jobs that are physically challenging, such as custodial work, or processing fish in a factory. If you have one of these difficult jobs, you may be especially relieved to get a break toward the end of your pregnancy.

Your paid maternity leave from whatever job you hold on the islands will begin four weeks before your due date. If you have any special health needs, your doctor can even require that you be given leave eight weeks before your due date. During your maternity leave, regardless of whether you are working part-time or full-time, you are paid your full salary up to about $3,700 per month. These benefits are paid for by a small tax on all Faroese people's wages. Being able to take this time off at the end of your pregnancy will allow you to rest and prepare for your new family member under minimal stress. Faroese people don't mind paying taxes for maternity leave. We recognize that it's important for children's health, and for the whole family's quality of life. We also know that it's important to make it easier for mothers to have children.

GIVING BIRTH

You should plan to give birth in a hospital. The hospital in Tórshavn is best equipped to handle births and has a maternity ward, so if you can get to Tórshavn in time, that would be best. But, for women on the far-off islands, this may be too difficult. Especially if you live in Suðuroy, because it is only connected to the other islands by ferry, you might need to go to the local hospital.

During the birth, you will likely want to have a midwife and your husband present. If you'd like your mother or another family member there, that is also okay. If there are any complications with the birth, a doctor and nurse will also be present.

Many Faroese women choose to give birth without any painkillers. Recently some women have been taking classes on how to cope with the pain of natural childbirth. If you and your doctor decide you should have painkillers, you will likely receive an inhaled sedative, nitrous oxide, or morphine. However, the baby may not suckle well in the few hours after birth if you use morphine, so it is best to try to do without. It is not common to use an epidural in the Faroe Islands, and our doctors also work hard to avoid giving Caesarean sections. It is best to do things the natural way, if at all possible.

Most women stay in the hospital for a few days before returning home to recover. One of the maternity nurses will visit you the day after you return home.

NAMING YOUR CHILD

Naming your child in the Faroe Islands is not as difficult as it is in some other Western countries. Faroese parents do not have to worry about trying to come up with a completely unique name. Instead, in order to maintain Faroese traditions, our government has created a list of approximately five hundred names from which Faroese parents must select their child's name. (Similar laws exist in several other European countries, including Denmark, Iceland, and Portugal.) Our approved names are mostly Scandinavian or have Christian origins. The most popular men's names are Hans, Jógvan, and Jákup (like the English Jacob); the most popular women's names are Anna, Maria, and Katrin. They are all either traditional northern European names, or names from the Bible.

For most Faroese people, the only way you would be allowed to choose a name that is not on the list is if you want to give your child an old family name. If you can provide documentation of your family member's name, you can petition to the government for approval. People file such petitions frequently, and their requests are often approved. Typically, requests are for European names that are not very different from those on the list. For instance, some people want to choose a different spelling of a name on the list because that is how a family member spelled it. Because you are not originally from the Faroes, the government may allow you to give your child a name from your native country. In fact, the law states that people from other countries are allowed to name their child – with special permission – according to their native country's practices. Therefore, although you may prefer to give your child a Faroese name, you can still maintain your traditional practices in the Faroe Islands if you so choose.

We have one more naming custom that might interest you. Often people do not name their children until they have been christened. In the old days, people believed that, before christening, children are at risk of being kidnapped by the pagan *huldufólk* – mythical hidden people said to live in the mountains. It's said that it's easier for the *huldufólk* to steal the baby if they know its name, so it's best to keep the name a secret until after the child receives the protection of the christening. Almost no one really believes this old-fashioned idea any more, but some people still wait to announce the name because of this superstition.

PARENTING AND PROFESSIONAL LIFE

Faroese mothers are very fortunate in being legally guaranteed a long period of paid maternity leave – about nine months. They receive the same pay as they do during pregnancy leave: up to $3,700 a month, based on their usual salary. If women choose to forgo pay after their nine months of paid leave are up, they may still take another three months off without worrying about losing their job. Although you are allowed to put your child in the government daycare from as early as six months of age, I recommend that you take the full twelve months of leave allowed, if you can afford it. This is ideal for infant development – especially because it facilitates breastfeeding. Most women take at least the paid nine months off.

Your husband, however, is not so lucky. He is only guaranteed four weeks of paternity leave. Even so, he may choose to do as many fathers do – which is to transfer half of this time to you, the child's mother. New laws also allow you to transfer some of your three months of unpaid leave to him, if you choose to give it up. Increasingly, people recognize that this is a discriminatory system, and I am hopeful that it will change someday.

Once your child gets older, you may decide to return to work full-time. However, you may also find that you prefer part-time work. About half of working women in the Faroes only work part-time. Although businesses and government offices are not required to allow mothers to work part-time, most try to be accommodating. Employers can pay a little less in benefits when they have part-time staff, so it is good for them, as well. Many women view part-time work as providing an ideal balance between the professional and parenting life, and unless a woman runs her own business, it works for most careers. Nonetheless, most Faroese believe – and I agree – that a mother can have a successful professional life and be a great parent. So, you should simply make the choice that you believe is best for yourself and your family.

Unlike many Faroese women, Faroese men tend to continue to work full-time even after they have children. It would be very unusual for a father to work part-time in order to spend more time with his family.

Fathers may not receive as much parental leave as mothers, but mothers and fathers both play important roles in the household. In the old days, when most men went on long fishing excursions, women were left to run the villages on their own for weeks at a time. As a result, women's contributions to families and to our society at large have always been appreciated. But that's not to say that everything is equal between the sexes. Some roles, like being fishermen and farmers, traditionally belonged to men. Today we see a few female farmers and fishers, but they are still very uncommon.

In spite of these traditional divisions, Faroese men are increasingly involved in childcare and housework. Modern Faroese women expect their children's fathers to be equal partners in childcare. If your husband is a fisherman, you might be anxious if he is gone for weeks at a time. But remember, he will also be at home for weeks at a time. During those times, he is likely to be a devoted partner and father.

FEEDING AND SLEEPING

Almost all Faroese mothers breastfeed their infants, recognizing that this is best for the infant's healthy development. I recommend that you breastfeed for at least the first six months of your child's life. After that, many Faroese mothers choose to breastfeed while giving their child solid food until one year of age and beyond. The only thing you need to be careful about during this time is your consumption of whale meat, oily fish, and alcohol. Because toxins can be passed on to your infant in your breastmilk, I urge you to avoid or severely limit the amount of these substances while breastfeeding. If you have refrained from all these during pregnancy, you will already be used to living without them.

Part of my job is not only to make sure you understand the benefits of breastfeeding, but to help you with the practice. Some women have difficulties getting their infants to suckle, or are worried about whether their infants are getting enough nutrition. When I come to your home for medical visits, we can discuss all of your concerns. I am here to help you with these questions, and together we will make certain your child's needs are being met.

From between four and six months of age, you should start introducing solid foods to your infant. Most families make their own food for their infants – for instance, by putting cooked vegetables in a blender. Because you have a long maternity leave and will therefore be home more than your husband, you'll probably be the one to make this food most of the time. But some Faroese men really enjoy cooking and are eager to be active fathers. If your husband offers to help, accept graciously. For times when you are out and about, you might want to have some store-purchased, jarred baby food with you – but we don't use those very often. You can also buy cereals for your infant that you mix with water. Make sure to limit the amount of fatty fish your child eats. The toxins in them can be harmful to the developing child.

You may also wonder where your infant should sleep. We recommend that your child sleep in a crib next to your bed instead of having her or him sleep in a separate room. This will help you to be aware of your infant's needs and respond quickly. Be sure that your infant sleeps on her back – this reduces the risk of sudden infant death syndrome. An infant should not have a heavy comforter, which can cause her to overheat, or a pillow, which makes it harder for her to turn her head. You should also make sure your infant's head is not always turned in the same direction, to the left or right, when she goes to sleep. If her head is always facing the same direction as she sleeps, flat spots may form on her skull.

Like some parents, you might prefer to have your infant share your bed early on. This makes breastfeeding at night much easier, and many parents enjoy the feeling of closeness they experience with their infant during the night. But if you want to do this, you must be very cautious. Your child should not sleep between you and your husband, where she could be smothered. Instead, she should sleep on the side of one of you. You should put her crib next to the mattress to prevent her from rolling off the bed. But, be sure that there is no space between your bed and her crib – you don't want her to fall into the space between the two pieces of furniture. If you are bedsharing, you also need to be aware of your own physical state. If you are taking medication that makes you tired, or if you have been drinking alcohol, you may not be sensitive enough to your infant's presence and could roll onto her. Also, if your child is sharing the bed with you, your pets and other children cannot. They are likely to wake often, take up too much space in the bed, and prevent your infant from getting enough sleep. If it is too difficult for you to live by these restrictions, then I suggest you have your infant sleep in a crib in your bedroom.

If your child has any difficulty falling asleep, you might sing some traditional Faroese children's songs. At your child's baptism, you will probably receive a book called *Barnarímur*, or "Children's Rhymes," by the Faroese poet Hans Andrias Djurhuus. This book was written one hundred years ago and is full of Djurhuus's poems, which are often sung to music. We still sing these songs to children today. In one of these songs, a butterfly who lives in the flowers falls in love with a fly who lives on a dung heap. The fly rejects the butterfly and chooses to be with another insect from the dung heap because "líka børn tey leika best"–"equal children play best." Although this expression can have many meanings, in the children's song it implies that, when choosing a partner, it is best to find someone from a similar background to your own. As an immigrant to the Faroes, you may not believe that to be true! But this song, along with the others by Djurhuus, are part of any Faroese childhood, and I recommend that you share them with your child.

In addition to sleeping at night, your infant will need to take frequent naps. It's important that you have your child sleep outside for at least a few hours each day. If it's cold out, you should bundle her or him up in several layers of clothing. Then park your baby carriage outside your front door with your baby inside, and cover the top of the carriage with a blanket. Do not leave loose blankets in the carriage, as they can pose a smothering risk.

Having your child nap outdoors is important for many reasons. The cool air and the sounds of the sea and wind help the infants to sleep. Your infant will take longer naps while sleeping outside, and this promotes healthy development. Being outdoors will also help protect your baby's health by reducing exposure to the many germs indoors. I'm sure you've noticed that it doesn't get severely cold in the Faroe Islands, but parents in even the coldest Nordic countries (like Sweden and Finland) also have their infants sleep outdoors. Some people think that this practice prepares children to withstand cold temperatures and claim that it develops their immune systems.

The only time sleeping outdoors is dangerous for an infant is when it is very hot. Although the weather is usually very mild in the Faroes, if there is a hot day, be sure to park the carriage in the shade, and don't cover it with a blanket. Although we often cover the stroller with a blanket in cool weather, doing so when it's hot out can cause the carriage to fill up with hot air and become much too warm. So long as you are aware of the temperature and take the right precautions, having your child nap outdoors during the daytime is highly beneficial.

Perhaps you are worried that your child will not be safe sleeping alone outside. One of the wonderful things about the Faroes is how safe it is. Children are not kidnapped here, and we have limited traffic from cars. In our small villages, we all know each other's children and notice every stranger, should one happen to come through. But if you remain worried, just park the carriage next to your kitchen window. That way, you can peek out frequently and be reassured that your baby is safe.

I understand that this practice is very different from that in other societies, and that it may surprise some foreigners. I remember being shocked by a story of a Danish woman who was arrested in New York City for leaving her infant outside a restaurant while she dined. The New York authorities thought leaving an infant alone outdoors was child abuse. In the Faroe Islands, we think it's completely natural.

FAMILY RELATIONSHIPS

It is important that you and your partner have a close relationship with your child. As he gets older, you do not have to be overly affectionate and tell him that you love him all the time, but do let him know that he can count on you. Beyond the nuclear family, it is also extremely important that your child have strong relationships with all of her grandparents, uncles, aunts, and cousins. You will be expected to bring your child to frequent family gatherings. She will be welcome and, often, the center of attention. Try to have your child see her uncles, aunts, and cousins at least once a week. If there are no family gatherings planned, just call on your family during the evening.

Your child will likely see his or her grandparents several times a week. Grandparents are ideal caregivers. Any time you need to run to the store or would like to have a night out, just call your parents-in-law, and they will be happy to take your infant for a few hours. Not only will this give you a needed break, but it will help build an important relationship between your parents-in-law and your child. This relationship, and the extra help that comes with it, is so important that many Faroese couples who have settled in Denmark decide to move home when they have a child. Even though we have daycare centers in both Denmark and the Faroe Islands, trying to raise children without help from extended family is just too difficult, especially in a large and busy place like Copenhagen. Faroese people have always relied on family to help raise their children, and we feel overwhelmed at the idea of trying to get by without our extended family network.

Domestic Abuse and Divorce

Some Faroese officials are concerned that a minority of immigrant wives are experiencing domestic violence. Because women often hesitate to report this sort of crime, it is difficult to say how common the problem is. In fact, many immigrant women appear to be very happy in their marriages. But in case you face this situation, you should know that any sort of abuse – emotional or physical – is illegal in the Faroe Islands. There is a women's shelter in Tórshavn. If you are experiencing emotional abuse or physical violence, you can go there and they will provide you with shelter, information, and resources.

While you and the Faroese LGBT parents may face different challenges, there is one that unites you. If you should get divorced and become a single parent, having a good social and family network to help you raise your child will be important. As an immigrant, your family may be far away. For that reason, it will be especially important for you to maintain a good relationship with your husband's family and develop relationships with other mothers. I encourage you to become active in the mothers' groups that I organize so that you can build local friendships. The government will provide you with considerable financial assistance as a single parent. However, the Danish government provides more resources for single parents than the Faroese government does, so some single parents choose to move to Denmark in order to have even greater security.

Although the government provides a great deal of help for single parents, as an immigrant to the Faroe Islands you may also face some additional challenges if you get divorced. Your residence permit – granted by the Danish government – has likely been given to you only because you are married to a Faroese person. These permits are renewed annually and so, if you get divorced, you may have to leave the country in less than a year. Because child custody is decided on a case-by-case basis, having to leave the country may be especially stressful to mothers who fear they will not be allowed to take their children with them.

Once you have been married to your husband for three years, however, you can apply for permanent residence. If you obtain permanent residence, then you may remain in the country even if you get divorced. If you and your husband are considering divorce before you qualify for permanent residence, I suggest that you contact the Legal Aid Office and the Self-Help Office (a counseling service). These offices provide free resources and advice to people in difficult situations. Although there are guidelines about who is allowed to stay in the country, Danish officials ultimately make their decisions based on individual circumstances. They may be more likely to allow you to stay if your child has a Faroese father who will be remaining in the country. They are also likely to extend residence permits to women who are victims of domestic violence and leave their husbands before qualifying for permanent residence. So, if you are in a very difficult situation, getting good legal advice could help you make a strong case to the immigration officials.

ENJOYING CHILDHOOD

With or without a husband, a great benefit of raising children in the Faroe Islands, instead of in busy cities in Denmark, is that it allows children to experience freedom and nature. If you live in a village rather than the capital city of Tórshavn, you have probably already discovered that everyone knows each other, and there is limited traffic. So there is nothing for children to fear in the villages. Of course, you should teach them to watch out for cars, but, as your child grows, you can allow him or her to play outside with the other children of the village. If there are older children in the group, your child can play outside without you from as early as two or three years of age. Just look out the window every now and then to make sure they are okay.

As a toddler, your child will probably just want to play around your house and in the street out front. If you've told them to watch out for cars, don't worry if they are playing directly in the street. Although there are signs warning drivers about children around daycare centers and schools, they are unnecessary in the villages. The neighbors know that children play there. People will drive slowly and give the children time to get out of the way. In fact, your neighbors will probably enjoy having the opportunity to greet your children, as they would any member of the community. Neighbors will likely wave to your children as they drive past and, if they are close to your family, they may even stop and roll down their window to say "Hello."

Once your child is about four or five, then he can run freely with the other children around the mountains and beaches. You do not need to worry about strangers hurting your child, as we do not have many strangers in the Faroese villages. You only need to warn your child to be careful around the many cliff edges on our mountains. When a sudden fog comes in, it can be easy to get too close to the cliffs. Also tell your child to be careful on the beaches: she should not go into the sea, which is usually very cold, and the surf is often much too rough for swimming. If she avoids these things, she should be perfectly safe.

By allowing children to run freely, we allow them to develop their independence. Although it is important that your child have strong relationships with your family and other people in the village, he also needs to be self-reliant. Our emphasis on self-reliance is not so different from the old Puritan values still taught to many American children. Freedom granted early on lets Faroese children explore and discover their own abilities and interests – instead of just relying on their parents, or the television, to entertain them. When playing outside, groups of children make up their own games and use their imaginations. In these children's games, a large boulder may become a table, and flowers may become a pie. Groups of children also play games something like the American versions of tag or hide-and-seek.

Another benefit of the Faroese childhood is that it allows children to develop a relationship with nature. Here in the Faroes, we are very sensitive to the weather and how it affects our lives. We are also very aware of how reliant we are on nature for our livelihood. By playing outdoors much of the day, your child will learn to recognize changes in the wind, sun, clouds, and air. She will also see how the sheep behave on the mountainsides, notice where the birds fly and nest, and learn about the fish that come in close to shore. Children playing outdoors will learn the distinctive call of our national bird, the oystercatcher, which arrives in the spring and leaves in the fall. Or they might see the puffins – one of the seabirds that we frequently eat – when they create their burrowed nests on the sea-facing hillsides in the summer. As they explore their beautiful natural environment, our children learn many lessons from nature all day long.

DISCIPLINE AND RESPONSIBILITIES

Although your child should have the opportunity to explore freely and independently, there will be times when they make mistakes that need to be corrected. It is your job as a parent to make sure that they behave in a socially appropriate manner. For instance, they need to be respectful of others.

When problems with behavior arise, do not hit or spank your child. By physically disciplining your child, you may damage your relationship. Indeed, it is important that your child learn to control feelings of anger – it is never appropriate to lose one's temper. If you become angry with your child, you will be setting a bad example. Instead, you need to help her understand why her behavior was wrong. Talk with her about what she did, why it was wrong, and what she might do differently in the future. This helps your child to develop the reasoning skills needed to make good decisions throughout her life. By talking through the issues, you will also treat your child with the respect that every individual deserves. Finally, by not losing your temper or hurting your child, you will express that you only want what is best for her, and she will understand that she is loved, even when she makes mistakes.

If your child has behaved in a selfish way, you must also remind him that getting along with the group is important in Faroese society. We Faroese have many practices that maintain social order and equal statuses among community members. We do not have many rich or poor people here – almost everyone lives comfortably. Even if someone does make more money than their neighbors, you might not guess it. There is not much to spend money on in the Faroes, and we frown upon making yourself look better than others. In fact, when individuals appear to think too highly of themselves, we tease them publicly, in a practice we call *rukka*, which brings them back down to size. People who are not good at controlling their tempers may also be subject to *rukka*. In our egalitarian society – where all people are viewed as important, and where, in the old days, we had to rely on our neighbors for survival – we view one person putting himself above others, or disturbing relationships, as a threat to social stability, and we do not tolerate this.

As your child grows, he or she will also need to take on some responsibilities around the home. From a very young age, boys and girls can be taught to clean up after themselves. If you have a farm or go fishing, you can begin involving your child in these practices when they are about three or four years old. We sometimes teach boys more about fishing and sheep slaughtering, and girls more about preparing food from sheep products. But it is okay to teach both girls and boys all of these practices. We also often teach our girls one of our most important crafts: knitting with traditional Faroese patterns. Although knitting remains popular, many children today do not learn the traditional ways of fishing or sheep rearing. If you are able to teach your child some of these older practices, they will benefit from learning more about nature, survival, and Faroese culture. You will also help to keep Faroese traditions alive.

RELIGION

You and your husband can decide together the extent to which you should raise your children with religion. Most families belong to a church, but you do not have to go often if you do not wish to. Only the most conservative people will judge you harshly if you choose not to attend church regularly. Still, many parents say that teaching their children about religion helps to give them good values. If you agree, I suggest that you take your child to Sunday School from age five. This will also help him to develop relationships in the community. Many families say the bedtime prayer with their children every night before they go to sleep, even if they are not religious. This can help give children a sense of routine at the end of the day and can help them to feel protected while they sleep. If the practice is tolerable to you, I recommend it.

Even if you choose not to take your child to church or to pray, she will be exposed to Christian values. In fact, the official primary school code states the goal of giving children a "Christian and ethical" education. There are lessons in Christianity beginning in the first grade, although many teachers expand these courses to provide more multicultural religious perspectives. But if you do not want your child to attend these religious classes, she can sit in the hall at this time. Another important part of our Christian education is reflected in the practice of the "morning song." When children first arrive at school, they all gather in the assembly room and spend about fifteen minutes singing Christian songs. Some schools also have the children pray together during this time.

The continuation of the morning song practice is somewhat controversial. Some Faroese argue that this is a cherished tradition, of which they have many fond memories. They also claim that the practice is about more than just religion – it is also a part of Faroese history and identity. Few people worry about how the practice might affect children from non-Christian religions simply because we have so few non-Christian families in the Faroes. However, we do have non-religious families. Some people view the morning songs as intolerant of non-religious families, and a form of indoctrination. Children who are not being raised with religion are, with their parents' permission, allowed to not participate. However, this can be difficult for the children who do not take part. They may feel pressure from their teachers to be there, and they may miss important school-wide announcements that happen during this time. They may also feel stigmatized because all of the other children attend. In spite of this controversy, the practice continues. Thus, you must be prepared to have your children receive some religious education unless you choose, in spite of the potential for ostracism, to deliberately remove them from such experiences.

EDUCATION

Faroese children are very well educated beginning from preschool, which many children attend, starting from around the age of six. Unlike some Western preschools, we do not pressure our children to achieve any academic milestones in preschool. Instead, we view this as a time for children to build healthy social and emotional foundations for later academic learning.

Before your child starts primary school, I suggest that you practice walking to school with her. That way she can learn how to safely walk to school by herself. The size of the school your child attends will depend on how large your village is. Some primary schools in the smaller villages have as few as ten students. Children enter kindergarten at age seven. Compared to some countries, this is a little late. But, academically, our children catch up with their other Western peers soon enough. Our schoolteachers are Faroese, and although Faroese is the language we all speak at home, your child will begin learning Danish at age eight and English at age ten. School is mandatory through the ninth grade, and about 80 percent of Faroese complete high school, which ends when students are nineteen or twenty years old. By the time they graduate, children will have studied at least four foreign languages (Danish, English, German, and either French or Spanish), and many will go on to attend university. Those who do not graduate from high school tend to be boys who are not very academically inclined. These boys are often more tempted by the money they can make on fishing boats than the knowledge that comes with an education.

Our educational system is not without controversy. More conservative members of Faroese society worry that schools may have a corrupting influence. They are concerned about the emphasis on science in the classroom – particularly when science lessons contradict things children have learned at church or at home. In contrast, more secular parents feel their children should be receiving a stronger science education, pointing out that the schools begin teaching Christianity years before they begin teaching science. A similar debate exists over the extent to which children should receive education on human sexuality and reproduction. In the end, many do not receive much education on sexuality. As they enter the teen years, if you are concerned that your child may not be receiving adequate education in the sciences and in matters of sexuality, you may need to supplement their schooling at home.

We also have two private schools in the Faroe Islands that give parents more options. One of these schools has a progressive approach and is not as focused on Christianity. It may be a better fit for children with secular parents. On the other hand, if you are concerned that your child is not receiving adequate education concerning religion, the other Faroese private school has a strong Christian focus and is valued by some members of our very religious community.

Another issue in our educational system concerns how much we focus on Faroese traditions at school. Under Danish colonial rule, teaching in Faroese was forbidden, and only Danish was allowed – one of many ways in which we have often felt disrespected by the Danes. Some Faroese people believe the Danes think of them as backward. Many Faroese argue that the Faroe Islands should become a completely independent nation, instead of remaining an autonomous province of Denmark. After 1938, when the Faroe Islands gained the right to govern themselves, the Faroese language started being used as the main language in the schools. Although the Faroese language has borrowed many words from Danish, our language belongs to the West-Nordic family of languages, which means that, beyond these Danish words, our language is more similar to Icelandic. In fact, Faroese and Icelandic people claim they can understand each other's written languages, even if it is hard to understand each other when speaking.

Just as Faroese was not taught in schools for many decades, schools did not teach anything about Faroese cultures or traditions. Happily, today's schoolchildren learn our traditional Faroese ballads and dances, including the Faroese chain dance and various ballads to which it is performed. This dance and the accompanying ballads are an essential part of our identity. During our national holiday, Ólavsøka, crowds of people flood the streets of Tórshavn, where the old ballads are played shortly after midnight. People sing together in the streets, and during the chain dance we take the hand of whoever is standing next to us, take steps to the left and right in unison, and wind through the streets forming rings. You can dance with any group – no one will reject you – and you can leave the dance at any time. Yet, as the dance continues, more and more dancers join together, and it feels like we are all truly one long chain. Often, by the end, we have formed a single large ring. So you see, passing on these traditions to our children is very important to the Faroese.

With globalization, some Faroese fear that these precious cultural practices will disappear. As a parent, you can address this potential problem by educating your child at home about Faroese cultural and subsistence practices. Although the schools will provide some training, there is much more that you can teach. For instance, if you or your neighbors raise sheep, you can involve your child in the summer shearing. Children also have time off from school for the week in autumn when we slaughter sheep. If you know someone who rears sheep, you can easily include your child in the slaughter, and the food preparation that follows.

You might also teach your child about our traditional belief in the "hidden people," or *huldufólk* . Most young people do not believe in these supernatural beings any more, but older people still share stories in which they claim to have seen them. The *huldufólk* are said to look like humans but are very large and gray, with black hair. They live in the mountains, hedges, and rocks, where they behave just like humans – they raise cows and go fishing – but they can turn themselves and their possessions invisible at will. They differ from the human Faroese in one important way: They are not Christian – they are heathens. There are only a couple of ways in which they may harm people: they may try to kidnap unchristened infants, and the *huldufólk* girls may try to seduce human boys. Although most people don't believe in the *huldufólk* today, some still do. Moreover, we still respect some of the related traditions. For instance, people are still careful not to move large boulders in which they reportedly live. But you don't want to scare your children when you tell them these stories: they should be entertaining and are important to remember only as a part of our history.

A World of Babies

CHILDREN'S PARADISE

You are very fortunate to be raising your family in this ideal location! As I have described, we have arranged it so that every child's needs are met here in the Faroe Islands. Between your husband's family and the government, your child will have medical care, nutritious food, warm shelter, fresh air, security, and a loving community.

However, if you find you have concerns, do not hesitate to contact me at any point. I know that, because the Faroe Islands are new to you, you may need more assistance than other new mothers do. You can always call me or send a text message. I am available all day during the week, and if you need help at night or on a weekend, my office can also send additional staff to you. And don't forget about asking advice from the other women in your mothers' group. We are all here to help you and your baby!

About the Contributors

Bree Akesson is Assistant Professor at Wilfrid Laurier University, where she holds appointments in the Lyle S. Hallman Faculty of Social Work, and the Social Justice and Community Engagement Graduate Program. She is also a faculty affiliate with the Child Protection in Crisis (CPC) Learning Network at Columbia University, and a research associate for the Columbia Group for Children in Adversity. She is a licensed social worker with the Child Psychiatric Epidemiology Group, providing clinical support to children and families. Her most recent research project was a qualitative study of children and families living under Israeli occupation in the West Bank and East Jerusalem. She is currently conducting research that explores experiences of pregnancy and childbirth for Syrian refugee women and their families.

Judy S. DeLoache is the Kenan Professor of Psychology Emerita at the University of Virginia. She has published extensively on cognitive development in infants and young children. She has served as President of the Developmental Division of the American Psychological Association and as President of the

Cognitive Development Society. Dr. DeLoache's research has been funded by a Scientific MERIT Award from the National Institutes of Health, as well as by a National Science Foundation grant. She is a Fellow of the National Academy of Arts and Sciences. In 2013, Dr. DeLoache received the William James Award for Lifetime Distinguished Contributions to Psychological Science from the American Psychological Society, as well as the Distinguished Research Contributions Award from the Society for Research on Child Development.

Deborah Golden is a social anthropologist specializing in education, with interests in Israeli society, including the inculcation of national identity, citizenship, and temporal order among adult immigrants and children. She is a senior lecturer in education at the University of Haifa (Faculty of Education), where she is Head of the Program in Education, Society and Culture. In the early 1990s, she conducted extensive fieldwork on newcomers to Israel from the Soviet Union; in 2000, she conducted an in-depth ethnography of an Israeli preschool in which a third of the children were from the former Soviet Union; and she has an ongoing research project in Israel with Jewish and Palestinian mothers as well as mothers from the former Soviet Union.

Alma Gottlieb is Professor Emerita of Anthropology and Gender and Women's Studies at the University of Illinois at Urbana-Champaign. She conducted long-term fieldwork in Beng communities between 1979 and 1993 and now connects with young Beng people through social media. A full-length ethnography of Beng childrearing practices appeared as *The Afterlife Is Where We Come From: The Culture of Infancy in West Africa*; she has also written a *Beng–English Dictionary* (with M. Lynne Murphy) and *Under the Kapok Tree: Identity and Difference in Beng Thought*. With proceeds from two memoirs of their lives with the Beng (*Parallel Worlds: An Anthropologist and a Writer Encounter Africa*; and *Braided Worlds*), Gottlieb and co-author Philip Graham have co-founded the Beng Community Fund, a non-governmental, 501(c)(3) organization that funds locally requested development projects in Beng villages.

Michelle C. Johnson is Chair of the Department of Sociology and Anthropology and Associate Professor of Anthropology at Bucknell University. She is a cultural anthropologist specializing in religion in West Africa, and has conducted fieldwork with Mandinga and Fula peoples in Guinea-Bissau and Portugal, and with Inuit peoples in the Canadian Arctic. She has held research grants from Fulbright-Hays, the Social Science Research Council, and the Woodrow Wilson Foundation, and has published numerous scholarly articles and book chapters. She has served as an expert witness on asylum cases involving African women and genital cutting, and is completing a book on the religious lives of Guinean Muslims in Portugal. She and her husband, an Arctic anthropologist, have two children, a daughter and a son.

Erin Raffety is a cultural anthropologist and a Lecturer in the Writing Program at Princeton University, where she currently teaches courses on modern childhood and disability. Her doctoral dissertation, *Morality on the Margins: Fostering Disabled Children in Contemporary China* (2015), argues that seemingly marginal foster families in China comprised of poor, elderly women and abandoned, disabled children disrupt mainstream, biological understandings of family propagated by Chinese society and the state. In the dissertation, Raffety also profiles conflictual, intergenerational approaches to Chinese childrearing. Her publications include work critically discussing participatory strategies of doing research with children. Complementing her research, Raffety is also an advocate for children and adults with disabilities.

Kate Feinberg Robins holds a PhD in anthropology from University of Illinois at Urbana-Champaign. She has lived throughout South America and is fluent in Spanish and

Portuguese, and conversational in Quechua. She has led sustainable development projects in community-based education and has taught English as a Second Language and dance to children, teens, and adults. She received a Fulbright-Hays fellowship (2010–11) to conduct doctoral research with children and their families in a post-conflict community of Ayacucho, Peru, and received an Honorable Mention for the Outstanding Dissertation Award of the Council on Anthropology and Education (2013). As a Lecturer in Global Studies at University of Illinois at Urbana-Champaign (2013–15), she taught courses on research methods, international development, and children's rights. She serves as Editor for *Neos,* a publication of the Anthropology of Children and Youth Interest Group.

Mariah G. Schug is an assistant professor of psychology at Widener University (in Chester, Pennsylvania). With a PhD in anthropology, her long-term research in the Faroe Islands (ongoing since 2008) includes studying Faroese childhood, parenthood, and adults' and children's ideas about "different" groups, including immigrants and the Faroese gay rights movement. Dr. Schug also applied her knowledge of evolutionary biology as a project scientist for the 2010 Faroese exhibit *It's Only Natural: Diversity of the North*, which combined Dr. Schug's scientific research with the work of Nordic artists to describe the homosexual, bisexual, and transgendered behaviors observed among animals of the Nordic countries. Beyond her work in the Faroes, Dr. Schug has also conducted research on childhood in Germany, and parenting styles in Greece and Italy.

Sirad Shirdon is a trained speech language pathologist with research interests in early childhood language, literacy development, and special education. Currently completing her doctorate in Language, Education and Society at Ohio State University, Shirdon is a Visiting Scholar at the Minnesota Center for Reading Research (University of Minnesota). A Somali-

American, Shirdon also has interests in migration in general, and the Somali diaspora in particular. An advocate of using the power of scholarship to promote grassroots change and improve the lives of marginalized communities, Shirdon co-founded the Somali Literacy Project, which prepares Somali children and their families for school, and trains early childhood professionals in providing culturally responsive services for Somali children.

Authors' Acknowledgments

CHAPTER 1 BY ALMA GOTTLIEB AND JUDY S. DELOACHE

We are tremendously grateful to the Jacobs Foundation (Zurich) for providing us with a precious week of intensive work at the delightful Marbach Castle on Lake Constance, Germany, where we completed this book amidst stimulating conversations with Marc Bornstein, Ken Dodge, Jennifer Lansford, Kirby Dieter-Deckard, Viara Mileva, Robert Volpe, and other colleagues in residence. Additional thanks go to Andrew Winnard (CUP editor extraordinaire), James McKellar (CUP publicist extraordinaire), and Erica Sheeran (research assistant extraordinaire).

AG: For inspiring me by their own writings to engage with broader publics, I am grateful to Meredith Small and Paul Stoller. On the home front, Philip Graham – devoted co-parent, family DJ, gourmet chef-in-residence, and all-around husband extraordinaire – suggested the original idea behind the first edition; Hannah Gottlieb-Graham, daughter extraordinaire, cheerfully provided all manner of research help; and Nathaniel Graham, son extraordinaire, cheerfully solved all computer crises, great and small. Our charmed family circle of baby love now includes Emily Graham, daughter-in-law extraordinaire, and Dean and Mona Graham, grandchildren extraordinaire.

JD: I wish to thank my three favorite babies in all the world for their inspiration in many aspects of my life, including my research in developmental psychology. My son, Benjamin Clore, has always been a delightful presence from birth to adulthood, and many of my best research ideas came from observations of surprising and fascinating things he did as an infant. One of my early publications was based on seeing him try to pick up a picture of an object off the page of a book. Observing him do this led me to conduct a study of infants' exploration of pictures, and that led to years of rewarding research on the early development of the understanding and use of symbolic objects. My other favorite babies are my delightful granddaughter Waverly Aimone Clore and grandson Wilder Lewis Clore.

CHAPTER 2 BY MICHELLE C. JOHNSON

Field research in Guinea-Bissau and Portugal was generously funded by the Social Science Research Council, Fulbright-Hays, the University of Illinois, and Bucknell University. A Scholarly Research Grant from Bucknell University in Summer 2014 supported the writing of the first draft of the chapter. I benefited greatly from the expertise of several people at Bucknell's Bertrand Library: Carrie Pirrman, the Social Science Librarian, provided expert assistance with bibliographic sources and citations and Debra Cook-Balducci scanned and prepared the photographs. I am also grateful to the following people, all of whom provided me with helpful comments on the chapter and/or encouragement at various stages of the project: Debbie (Deb) Baney, Chris Boyatzis, author Beth Fantaskey, and Edmund (Ned) Searles. I also thank the editors, Alma and Judy, for including me in the project and for their invaluable editorial comments. Contributing to *A World of Babies* was even more enjoyable the second time around! My greatest debt is to my Mandinga and Fula informants in both Guinea-Bissau (Bafata-Oio and Bissau) and Lisbon, Portugal, who have so openly shared their lives with me over the past nineteen years. I dedicate the chapter to Aminata Baldé, who inspired the fictive author, and to my namesake, "White Fatumata" in Bafata-Oio.

CHAPTER 3 BY ERIN RAFFETY

I would like to thank the Princeton University Department of Anthropology and the Princeton Institute for International and Regional Studies, both of which provided generous funding and support for my research and writing projects. I would also like to thank Yang Xiaoli, Huang Siqi, Xiao Xiao, and Yanling Qin, all of whom provided valuable insight into my understanding of childrearing in contemporary China. Finally, I'd like to thank the countless foster families with whom I worked in Guangxi, China – your devotion and commitment to children with special needs defies all logic and flies in the face of the modern challenges many in this chapter name. Such love not only touched me, but changed me; thank you for inspiring me to become a parent.

CHAPTER 4 BY BREE AKESSON

This research was funded with the support of the Social Sciences and Humanities Research Council (SSHRC) of Canada. My sincerest thanks go to the Palestinian women (especially my good friend N.) who welcomed me into their homes, sharing their stories of motherhood and childrearing under great adversity.

CHAPTER 5 BY DEBORAH GOLDEN

The teacher in this chapter is inspired by a real-life teacher in the preschool in which I carried out fieldwork in the early 2000s.

I cannot name her without breaching confidentiality but nevertheless thank her for generously sharing with me her professional world. I appreciate the useful suggestions from my colleagues: Freema Elbaz-Luwisch, Lauren Erdreich, Lotem Perry-Hazan, and Avihu Shoshana. I also thank my friend Yaffa Adari Moore for sharing scenes from her family life, including recollections of her mother, Rachel Adari.

CHAPTER 6 BY ALMA GOTTLIEB

This chapter is based most directly on fieldwork in Beng villages in Côte d'Ivoire that I conducted in summer 1993 and, more indirectly, on previous fieldwork in 1979–80 and summer 1985. For intellectual support during my research, I am ever grateful to Véronique Amenan Akpoueh and Yacouba Kouadio Bah; other Beng friends who shared with me their insights into Beng infancy include Kouakou Bah and the late Kouassi Kouassi, as well as dozens of Beng women whose gracious motherhood in the face of grinding poverty I found humbling. That summer, Véronique Amenan Akpoueh, Augustin Kouakou, Dieudonné Kwame Kouassi, and Bertin Kouadio also served as research assistants. Updates on Beng lives since my last residence in Côte d'Ivoire have been provided by Bertin Kouadio, Kouadio Honoré Yao, and other old and new Beng friends on social media.

For financial support of my research in and about Bengland over the years, I acknowledge with gratitude the John Simon Guggenheim Memorial Foundation, National Endowment for the Humanities, Wenner-Gren Foundation for Anthropological Research, Social Science Research, United States Information Agency, Woodrow Wilson Foundation, and American Association of University Women, as well as several units at the University of Illinois (Center for Advanced Study, Research Board, International Programs and Studies, Center for African Studies, College of Liberal Arts and Sciences, and Department of Anthropology).

I am forever grateful to Philip Graham for inspiring me, through the wisdom of his own writing, to seek the power and poetry in language.

Authors' Acknowledgments

CHAPTER 7 BY SIRAD SHIRDON

I want to begin by thanking Allah (God) for making this publication possible. I am thankful for the patience and love of my husband, Yasir, and I am grateful to my beloved mother, Amina, who patiently answered all of my questions about childrearing in diasporic Somali communities. Finally, I extend my deepest gratitude to Somali mothers globally, who have demonstrated resilience, strength, and an unyielding optimism despite the challenges of displacement.

CHAPTER 8 BY KATE FEINBERG ROBINS

I wish to acknowledge the many families who shared their lives, stories, and friendship with me during my fieldwork in Peru. I am particularly grateful to the Cáceres Salazares, the Clares Cusis, the Clares Lópezes, the de la Cruz Bendezús, the Dumets, the García Riveras, the Marcacusco Palominos, the Mejía Chinchays, the Mendoza Vegas, and the Poma Cubas. For their comments on an early version of this chapter, I thank Pilar Egüez, Anthony Jerry, Katie O'Brien, and Monica Santos. This research was funded at its various stages with a Fulbright-Hays Doctoral Dissertation Abroad Fellowship (United States Department of Education), Marion Morse Wood Fellowship (Graduate College, University of Illinois at Urbana-Champaign), Foreign Language and Area Studies Fellowships (United States Department of Education and Center for Latin American and Caribbean Studies, UIUC), Tinker Summer Field Research Grant (Center for Latin American and Caribbean Studies, UIUC), and a Summer Research Assistance Award (Department of Anthropology, UIUC). I received institutional support in Peru through affiliation with the Instituto de Estudios Peruanos. This chapter is dedicated to my son Ahanu, who provided extra inspiration for my research on pregnancy and childbirth by coming into our lives somewhere between draft 7 and draft 11.

Authors' Acknowledgments

CHAPTER 9 BY MARIAH G. SCHUG

I am deeply indebted to my closest Faroese friend, Eiler Fagraklett, for his unwavering and generous support of my work. This chapter would not be possible without him. I'd also like to thank Amy Johannesen, Siw Mary Thomsen, Femja Petersen, and Sóleyð P. Hansen, for always finding time for me. I'm grateful to Wesleyan University, Widener University, the Culture and the Mind Project, and the UK Arts and Humanities Council for their financial support. I give thanks also to my delightful colleagues, Erika Hayfield and Richard McElreath, for sharing in my research passions. Finally, I'd like to thank my wonderful husband, Sahr Conway-Lanz, for his constant encouragement of all of my professional endeavors.

Citations and Sources Cited

1 Raising a World of Babies

Citations

The numbers in the citations below refer to the numbered references in the Sources Cited section immediately following for this chapter.

Page

3	skyrocketing US interest in "other" childrearing strategies – 86; TED talk – 16; China-inspired parenting book – 17; France-inspired parenting book – 22, 89, 95; willingness to "parent in public" – 74; books about comparative parenting styles – 31, 46
4	what people accept as "common sense" in one society is often considered odd, exotic, or even barbaric in another – 25; on Benjamin Spock as "the world's most famous baby doctor" – 48; Dr. Spock's book has sold over 50 million copies – 85; similar childrearing challenges for all parents – 52
5	infant mortality rates by country – 90; effects of European colonialism on populations of the global south – 27
6	3.1 million children die from hunger each year – 101; the world's farmers produce enough food to feed the world's population – 65
7	wet nurses in the ancient world, and elite families in western Europe from the eleventh to the eighteenth century – 23; wet

nursing: in Paris of 1780 – 42, in Europe until World War I – 23; "milk kin" – 19, 43; cow's milk and death in Iceland – 33; recommended length of breastfeeding: by the American Academy of Pediatrics – 3, by the World Health Organization – 98

8 rates of breastfeeding: in US – 13; globally – 98; population lacking access to safe water – 100; diluting infant formula from poverty – 75

9 lawsuits against employers and restaurants in the US to support public breastfeeding – 38, 54, 102; call for a return of "wet nurses" to help working mothers – 68

11 older children take care of babies: effective in "traditional" societies – 93

11–12 impossible in contexts of extreme poverty – 20; dangerous in the *favelas* of northeastern Brazil – 75

12 adoption on Ifaluk – 49; international adoptions within communities spanning national borders – 18; interracial and international adoptions: increasingly popular – 76, sometimes becoming human trafficking schemes – 15

13 emotional ties of young children: with older siblings – 93, with daycare teachers – 37; infants' ties to ancestors: via reincarnation – 27, among Baganda 44, among Warlpiri – 66; Portuguese concept of *saudade* – 29; recent comparative work by developmental psychologists: on children's lives – 77, on "attachment theory" – 64, 72

14 young children learn as apprentices: weaving – 70, washing laundry, cooking, weeding, hoeing, and harvesting – 97, doing errands – 61

16 co-sleeping: throughout human history – 36, 79

17 co-sleeping: in modern societies – 78; co-sleeping: in Mayan families – 60, in Japanese families – 1, 12; babies sleep solo: rare cross-culturally – 79, recommended by American pediatricians – 53, recommended by public health campaigns in Milwaukee – 58, recommended by public health campaigns in New York City – 63, 92; co-sleeping among Asian versus White parents in the US – 62; "attachment theory" mischaracterized in popular discussions – 91; co-sleeping stigmatized and under-reported in the US – 55; co-sleeping: claimed to increase the risk of SIDS – 4, claimed to reduce the risk of SIDS – 55

19 infants sleeping solo seen as shocking mistreatment by Mayan mothers – 60, and by others elsewhere – 78; "cultural intimacy" – 35

20 effects of long-term political strife and poverty on parents and children – 21

21 relatives no longer available to advise many new mothers in US – 96; pediatricians and books as common sources of information about parenting in Western nations – 32

22 "Parenting Industrial Complex" – 69; eager readership of parenting books – 39; parenting books appeal to what readers already know – 57

23 Penelope Leach's advice on gender – 50, 51

24 article spoofing Spock – 26

25 societies with a long tradition of literacy having earlier parenting manuals – 5; contemporary Chinese mothers seek parenting advice online – 14

26 changing American ideas about blue and pink – 56

27 experimental writing among scholars – 2, 8, 11, 24, 28, 59, 67, 71, 82, 83, 84, 87; parenting manuals: in Renaissance Italy – 9, in China – 5, 79, in contemporary Western societies – 30, 94

28 dramatic changes in children's lives globally: positive health indicators – 99, recruitment of child soldiers – 80

30 work by developmental psychologists acknowledging cultural differences – 10, 40; WEIRD research subjects – 34, 41; new cross-cultural studies of childhood by psychologists – 47; new interest in children by anthropologists – 6, 7, 73

Sources Cited – Chapter 1

(1) Abelmann, Nancy (1999). Personal communication.

(2) Allen, Catherine J. and Nathan Garner (1997). *Condor Qatay: Anthropology in performance*. Longview Heights, IL: Waveland Press.

(3) American Academy of Pediatrics (2012). AAP reaffirms breastfeeding guidelines. February 27. www.aap.org/en-us/about-the-aap/aap-press-room/Pages/AAP-Reaffirms-Breastfeeding-Guidelines.aspx.

(4) American Academy of Pediatrics (2014). Bed sharing remains greatest risk factor for sleep related infant deaths. American Academy of Pediatrics, July 14. www.aap.org/en-us/about-the-aap/aap-press-room/pages/Bed-Sharing-Remains-Greatest-Risk-Factor-for-Sleep-Related-Infant-Deaths.aspx#sthash.Hflb2QEC.dpuf.

(5) Anagnost, Ann (1997). The child and national transcendence in modern China. In Kenneth Lieberthal, Shuen-fu Lin, and Ernest Young (eds.), *Constructing China: The interaction of culture and economics*. Michigan Monographs in Chinese Studies 78. Ann Arbor: Center for Chinese Studies, University of Michigan, pp. 195–222.

Citations and Sources Cited

(6) *AnthropoChildren* (n.d.). University of Liège (Belgium). http://popups.ulg.ac.be/2034-8517/index.php?page=presentation.

(7) Anthropology of Childhood and Youth Interest Group (n.d.). American Anthropological Association. www.aaanet.org/sections/acyig/.

(8) Balakian, Sophia (n.d.). Mapping a lost friend. www.google.com/maps/d/viewer?ie=UTF&msa=0&mid=zKCba1oFPteg.kJvHABRwjL44.

(9) Bell, R. (1999). *How to do it: Guides to good living for Renaissance Italians*. Chicago: University of Chicago Press.

(10) Brofenbrenner, Urie, Frank Kessel, William Kessen, and Sheldon White (1986). Toward a critical social history of developmental psychology: A propaedeutic discussion. *American Psychologist* 41 (11), 1218–30.

(11) Burde, Mark (2014). Social-science fiction: The genesis and legacy of Horace Miner's "Body ritual among the Nacirema." *American Anthropologist* 116, 549–61.

(12) Caudill, William and David W. Plath (1966). Who sleeps by whom? Parent–child involvement in urban Japanese families. *Psychiatry* 29, 344–66.

(13) Centers for Disease Control (2013). *Breastfeeding report card – United States* 2013. www.cdc.gov/breastfeeding/pdf/2013breastfeedingreportcard.pdf.

(14) Chen, Huiyi (2014). Personal communication, November 20.

(15) Cheney, Kristen E. and Karen Smith Rotabi (2015). "Addicted to orphans": How the global orphan industrial complex jeopardizes local child protection systems. In C. Harker, K. Horschelmann, and Tracey Skelton (eds.), *Conflict, violence, and peace*. Singapore: Springer, pp. 1–19.

(16) Choi, Amy (2014). How cultures around the world think about parenting. July 15. TED Talk. http://ideas.ted.com/how-cultures-around-the-world-think-about-parenting/.

(17) Chua, Amy (2011). *Battle hymn of the tiger mom*. New York: Penguin.

(18) Coe, Cati (2012). Transnational parenting: Child fostering in Ghanaian immigrant families. In Randy Capps and Michael Fix (eds.), *Young children of black immigrants in America: Changing flows, changing faces*. Washington, DC: Migration Policy Institute, pp. 265–96.

(19) Delaney, Carol (1991). *The seed and the soil: Gender and cosmology in Turkish village society*. Berkeley: University of California Press.

Citations and Sources Cited

(20) Dornan, Paul and Kirrily Pells (2015). Building strong foundations for later livelihoods by addressing child poverty: Evidence from young lives. *Enterprise Development and Microfinance* 26 (2), 90–103, early online publication, DOI: 10.3362/1755-1986.2015.009.

(21) Dornan, Paul and Martin Woodhead (2015). How inequalities develop through childhood: Life-course evidence from young lives. Office of Research Discussion Paper No. 2015-01. Florence: UNICEF Office of Research.

(22) Druckerman, Pamela (2012). *Bringing up bébé: One American mother discovers the wisdom of French parenting*. New York: Penguin.

(23) Fildes, V. A. (1995). *Breasts, bottles, and babies: A history of infant feeding*. Edinburgh: Edinburgh University Press.

(24) Galman, Sally Campbell (2007). *Shane, the lone ethnographer: A beginner's guide to ethnography*. Lanham, MD: AltaMira Press/ Rowman & Littlefield.

(25) Geertz, Clifford (1983). Common sense as a cultural system. In *Local knowledge*. New York: Basic Books, pp. 73–93.

(26) Gottlieb, Alma (1995). Of cowries and crying: A Beng guide to managing colic. *Anthropology and Humanism* 20 (1), 20–28.

(27) Gottlieb, Alma (2004). *The afterlife is where we come from: The culture of infancy in West Africa*. Chicago: University of Chicago Press.

(28) Gottlieb, Alma (2005). Dancing a jig with genre. *Anthropology News* (American Anthropological Association), April 2005, 27–28.

(29) Graham, Philip (2009). *The moon, come to earth: Dispatches from Lisbon*. Chicago: University of Chicago Press.

(30) Grant, Julia (1998). *Raising baby by the book: The education of American mothers*. New Haven: Yale University Press.

(31) Gross-Loh, Christine (2013). *Parenting without borders: Surprising lessons parents around the world can teach us*. New York: Penguin.

(32) Harkness, Sara, Charles Super, Constance H. Keefer, Chemba S. Raghavan, and Elizabeth Kipp Campbell (1996). Ask the doctor: The negotiation of cultural models in American parent–pediatrician discourse. In Sarah Harkness and Charles M. Super (eds.), *Parents' cultural belief systems: Their origins, expressions, and consequences*. New York: Guilford, pp. 289–310.

(33) Hastrup, Kirsten (1992). A question of reason: Breast-feeding patterns in 17th and 18th century Iceland. In Vanessa Maher (ed.), *The anthropology of breast-feeding*. Oxford: Berg, pp. 91–108.

(34) Henrich, Joseph, Steven J. Heine, and Ara Norenzayan (2010). The weirdest people in the world: How representative are experimental findings from American university students? What do we really know about human psychology? *Behavioral and Brain Sciences* 33 (2–3), 61–83.
(35) Herzfeld, Michael (2004 [1997]). *Cultural intimacy: Social poetics in the nation-state*. Second edition. New York: Routledge.
(36) Hewlett, Barry S. and Jennifer W. Roulette (2014). Cosleeping beyond infancy: Culture, ecology, and evolutionary biology of bedsharing among Aka foragers and Ngandu farmers of Central Africa. In D. Narvaez, K. Valentino, A. Fuentes, J. McKenna, and P. Gray (eds.), *Ancestral landscapes in human evolution: Culture, childrearing and social wellbeing*. New York: Oxford University Press, pp. 129–63.
(37) Howes, C. and C. E. Hamilton (1993). The changing experience of child care: Changes to teachers and in teacher–child relationships and children's social competence with peers. *Early Childhood Research Quarterly* 8, 15–32.
(38) Huffington Post (2012). Dawn Holland, breastfeeding mom, asked to nurse in Applebee's bathroom. *Huffington Post*, September 18. www.huffingtonpost.com/2012/09/18/dawn-holland-breastfeeding_n_1893681.html.
(39) Hulbert, Ann (2003). *Raising America: Experts, parents, and a century of advice about children*. New York: Knopf.
(40) Jensen, Lene Arnette (2012). *Bridging cultural and developmental psychology: New syntheses for theory, research and policy*. Oxford: Oxford University Press.
(41) Karasik, Lana B., Karen E. Adolph, Catherine S. Tamis-LeMonda, and Marc H. Bornstein (2010). WEIRD walking: Cross-cultural research on motor development. *Behavior and Brain Sciences* 33 (2–3), 95–6. www.ncbi.nlm.nih.gov/pmc/articles/PMC3175590/.
(42) Kessen, Frank (1965). *The child*. New York: John Wiley & Sons.
(43) Khatib-Chahidi, J. (1992). Milk kinship in Shi'ite Islamic Iran. In Vanessa Maher (ed.), *The anthropology of breast-feeding: Natural law or social construct*. Oxford: Berg, pp. 109–32.
(44) Kilbride, Philip L. and Janet E. Kilbride (1990). *Changing family life in East Africa: Women and children at risk*. State College: Pennsylvania State University Press.
(45) Lancy, David (2012). Why *anthropology* of childhood? A brief history of an emerging discipline. *AnthropoChildren* 1. http://popups.ulg.ac.be/AnthropoChildren/document.php?id=918.

Citations and Sources Cited

(46) Lancy, David (2015 [2008]). *The anthropology of childhood: Cherubs, chattel, changelings*. Second edition. Cambridge: Cambridge University Press.

(47) Lansford, Jennifer E. and Marc H. Bornstein (2011). Parenting attributions and attitudes in diverse cultural contexts. *Parenting: Science and Practice* 11, 87–101.

(48) Lapidus, Faith and Steve Ember (1998). Dr. Spock, 1903–1998: The world's most famous baby doctor. *Voice of America*, Oct. 20, 2015. http://learningenglish.voanews.com/content/dr-spock-1903-1998-the-worlds-most-famous-baby-doctor-131321239/115370.html.

(49) Le, Mimi (2000). Never leave your little one alone: Raising an Ifaluk child. In Judy S. DeLoache and Alma Gottlieb (*eds.*), *A world of babies: Imagined childcare guides for seven societies*. Cambridge: Cambridge University Press, pp. 199–220.

(50) Leach, Penelope (1977). *Your baby and child: From birth to age five*. New York: Alfred A. Knopf.

(51) Leach, Penelope (1983 [1976]). *Babyhood: Stage by stage, from birth to age two: How your baby develops physically, emotionally, mentally*. Second edition. New York: Knopf.

(52) LeVine, Robert (1988). Child psychology and anthropology: An environmental view. In Catherine Panter-Brick (ed.), *Biosocial perspectives on children*. Cambridge: Cambridge University Press, pp. 102–30.

(53) Lozoff, Betsy, A. Wolf, and N. S. Davis (1984). Cosleeping in urban families with young children in the United States. *Pediatrics*, 74, 171–82.

(54) McCardle, Elaine (2015). N.H. woman sues to breastfeed at work. *UU world: Liberal religion and life*. February 2. www.uuworld.org/articles/woman-sues-breastfeed-work.

(55) McKenna, James (2015). *Mother–baby behavioral sleep laboratory*. University of Notre Dame. http://cosleeping.nd.edu.

(56) Maglaty, Jeanne (2011). When did girls start wearing pink? *Smithsonian.com*, April 8. www.smithsonianmag.com/arts-culture/When-Did-Girls-Start-Wearing-Pink.html?c=y&page=1.

(57) Maier, T. (1998). *Dr. Spock: An American life*. New York: Harcourt Brace.

(58) Milwaukee Health Department (n.d.). Safe sleep campaign. http://city.milwaukee.gov/health/Safe-Sleep-Campaign#.VeGohbSTSzA.

(59) Miner, Horace (1956). Body ritual among the Nacirema. *American Anthropologist* 58, 503–07.

(60) Morelli, G., B. Rogoff, D. Oppenheim, and D. Goldsmith (1992). Cultural variation in infants' sleeping arrangements: Questions of independence. *Developmental Psychology*, 28, 604–13.
(61) Morton, H. (1996). *Becoming Tongan: An ethnography of childhood*. Honolulu: University of Hawaii Press.
(62) National Sleep Foundation (2010). Sleep differences among ethnic groups revealed in new poll. *ScienceDaily*, March 27. www.sciencedaily.com/releases/2010/03/100308081740.htm.
(63) New York (2015). Mayor de Blasio announces "safe sleep" campaign to reduce infant fatalities caused by unsafe sleep. New York City Administration for Children's Services. www.nyc.gov/html/acs/html/about/baby_safe_sleep_campaign.shtml.
(64) Otto, Hiltrud and Heidi Keller (eds.) (2014). *The different faces of attachment: Cultural variations on a universal human need*. Cambridge: Cambridge University Press.
(65) Oxfam (2015). There is enough food to feed the world. www.oxfam.ca/there-enough-food-feed-world.
(66) Pierroutsakos, Sophia (2000). Infants of the dreaming: A Warlpiri guide to child care. In Judy S. DeLoache and Alma Gottlieb (eds.), *A world of babies: Imagined childcare guides for seven societies*. Cambridge: Cambridge University Press, pp. 145–70.
(67) Price, Richard and Sally Price (1995). *Enigma variations*. Cambridge, MA: Harvard University Press.
(68) Robb, Alice (2014). Parenting: Bring back the wet nurse! A solution for working mothers that has been around for centuries. *The New Republic*, July 22. www.newrepublic.com/article/118786/breastfeeding-wet-nurses-mommy-wars.
(69) Roberts, David (2015). Most parenting advice is worthless. So here's some parenting advice. *Vox – Science & Health*, August 12. www.vox.com/2015/8/11/9127769/parenting-advice-worthless.
(70) Rogoff, Barbara (1990). *Apprenticeship in thinking: Cognitive development in social context*. New York: Oxford University Press.
(71) Rosaldo, Renato (2003). "Invisibility," "Wild men," "The force in women." In *Prayer to Spider Woman*. Saltillo, Coahuila, Mexico: Gobierno del Estado de Coahuila/Instituto Coahuilense de Cultura, pp. 12, 30, 98.
(72) Rothbaum, Fred, John Weisz, Martha Pott, Kazuo Miyake, and Gilda Morelli (2000). Attachment and culture: Security in the United States and Japan. *American Psychologist* 55 (10), 1093–1104.
(73) Rutgers University (n.d.). Department of Childhood Studies. http://childhood.camden.rutgers.edu.

(74) Sandberg, Sheryl (2011). The 2011 TIME 100: Amy Chua – Tough-love mother. *Time Magazine*, April 21.
(75) Scheper-Hughes, Nancy (1993). *Death without weeping: The violence of everyday life in Brazil*. Berkeley: University of California Press.
(76) Seligmann, Linda (2013). *Broken links, enduring ties: American adoption across race, class, and nation*. Stanford: Stanford University Press.
(77) Serpell, Robert and A. Bame Nsamenang (2015). The challenge of local relevance: Using the wealth of African cultures in ECCE programme development. In P. T. M. Marope and Y. Kaga (eds.), *Investing against evidence: The global state of early childhood care and education – Education on the move*. Paris: UNESCO Publishing, pp. 231–48.
(78) Shweder, R., L. Jensen, and W. Goldstein (1995). Who sleeps by whom revisited: A method for extracting the moral goods implicit in practice. *New Directions for Child Development: Cultural Practices as Contexts for Development*, 67, 21–39.
(79) Small, Meredith (1998). *Our babies, ourselves*. New York: Anchor Books.
(80) SOS Children's Villages UK (n.d.). Children in conflict: Child soldiers. www.child-soldier.org.
(81) Spock, Benjamin and S. Parker (1998 [1946]). *Dr. Spock's Baby and Child Care*. Seventh edition. New York: Pocket Books/ Simon & Schuster.
(82) Stern, Daniel (1990). *Diary of a baby: What your child sees, feels, and experiences*. New York: Basic Books.
(83) Stern, Larry (2013). Psychological hijinks: Hailed as a "scientific *Playboy*," for 20 years the *Worm Runner's Digest* poked fun at the pomposity of science, with spoofs by B. F. Skinner, James V. McConnell and other psychology luminaries. *APA Monitor* 44 (1), 22.
(84) Stoller, Paul (1999). *Jaguar: A story of Africans in America*. Chicago: University of Chicago Press.
(85) Talbot, M. (1999). The lives they lived: Benjamin Spock, M.D.; A Spock-marked generation. *New York Times* Magazine, January 3, 3.
(86) Taylor, Elizabeth (2011). Power of a "tiger." Books. *Chicago Tribune*, February 11.
(87) Taylor, Julie (1998). *Paper tangos*. Durham, NC: Duke University Press.

Citations and Sources Cited

(88) Tomlinson, Mark and Leslie Swartz (2003). Representing infancy across the world: Does Osama Bin Laden love his children? *Culture & Psychology* 9 (4), 487–97.

(89) Tree, Oliver (2012). Bringing up bébé: Why French children don't throw food – Author says American's [sic] need to learn French parenting skills. *International Business Times*, February 8. www.ibtimes.com/bringing-bebe-why-french-children-dont-throw-food-author-says-americans-need-learn-french-parenting.

(90) United States Central Intelligence Agency (2014). *The World Factbook, 2015*. New York: Skyhorse Publishing.

(91) Vicedo, Marga (2013). *The nature and nurture of love: From imprinting to attachment in Cold War America*. Chicago: University of Chicago Press.

(92) Wartik, Nancy (2015). Stay close, sleep apart? Motherlode: Living the family dynamic. *New York Times*, June 29. http://parenting.blogs.nytimes.com/2015/06/29/stay-close-sleep-close-or-stay-close-sleep-apart/?_r=0.

(93) Weisner, Tom S. and R. Gallimore (1977). My brother's keeper: Child and sibling caretaking. *Current Anthropology* 18, 169–89.

(94) Weiss, N. (1978). The mother–child dyad revisited: Perceptions of mothers and children in twentieth century child-rearing manuals. *Journal of Social Issues* 34 (2), 29–45.

(95) West Hawaii Today (2012). This week's best-sellers from *Publishers Weekly*. *West Hawaii Today*, March 25. http://westhawaiitoday.com/sections/news/wire-features/week's-best-sellers-publishers-weekly.html.

(96) Whiting, Beatrice (1974). Folk wisdom and child rearing. *Merrill Palmer Quarterly* 20, 9–19.

(97) Whiting, Beatrice and C. Edwards (1988). *Children of different worlds: The formation of social behavior*. Cambridge, MA: Harvard University Press.

(98) World Health Organization (2015). 10 facts on breastfeeding. World Health Organization, July. www.who.int/features/factfiles/breastfeeding/en/.

(99) World Health Organization (2015). *Statistics 2015*. Geneva: World Health Organization.

(100) World Health Organization and UNICEF Joint Monitoring Programme (2014). Progress on drinking water and sanitation, 2014 Update. www.who.int/water_sanitation_health/publications/2014/jmp-report/en/.

Citations and Sources Cited

(101) World Hunger Education Service (2015). World child hunger facts. www.worldhunger.org/articles/Learn/child_hunger_facts.htm.

(102) Yarrow, Allison (2014). Pumped up: Breastfeeding mothers fight for rights at work. *NBC News*, January 10. http://usnews.nbcnews.com/_news/2014/01/10/22257760-pumped-up-breastfeeding-mothers-fight-for-rights-at-work?lite.

2 Never Forget Where You're From

Citations

The numbers in the citations below refer to the numbered references in the immediately following Sources Cited section for this chapter.

Page

33 religious profile of Guinea-Bissau – 23, 26; population of Fula in Guinea-Bissau – 26

34 "if the cattle die . . ." – 15, p. 25; population of Mandinga in Guinea-Bissau – 26; description of Muslim versus indigenous societies in Guinea-Bissau – 5

35 migration from Guinea-Bissau to Portugal – 1, 6, 24; Guinean Muslims migrated from rural areas in Guinea-Bissau – 25

36 population of Muslims in Europe and in Portugal – 30; number of Guinean Muslims outnumber Indian Muslims from Mozambique – 31

37 Guineans in Lisbon are becoming critical of polygyny – 2

40 infant and maternal mortality rates in Guinea-Bissau and Portugal – 7; Allah fixes the time and place of death at birth – 20

41 how a belly is made, and contributions of male and female sexual fluids – 18

43 obtaining Portuguese citizenship for your baby – 14

44 hospital births rising in Guinea-Bissau – 16; a laboring woman may have a birthing companion in Portugal – 27

45 excision prepares a woman for childbirth pain – 17; true sweetness must entail suffering – 17; African women's labors are easier, due to absence of chemicals in food, and to farm work – 21

46 bodily substances should be buried in the ground – 20, 32

50 rely on mobile phone to "visit" – 22

52 spirits move easily between Guinea-Bissau and Portugal – 29

54 magical practices for protecting White Portuguese babies from witches – 11; child fostering in Africa – 13

55 many Portuguese babies are weaned by 3–6 months – 10; children acquire personality traits and habits through breastfeeding – 28;

breastmilk is a "kinship glue" – 32, p. 47; children of one mother are close and trusting, while children of one father are distant and competitive – 3; "milk kin" – 4, p. 100; 9, p. 136

56 avoiding pork is difficult in Portugal – 12; colostrum "thin and weak" and not fed to Mandinga babies – 32, p. 51

57 avoid sex until baby begins walking – 32; breastmilk during pregnancy belongs to fetus – 32; "Let go of the breast!" and threaten to put hot pepper on your nipples – 32, p. 56

58 the importance of three rituals (name-giving ritual, circumcision, writing-on-the-hand ritual) for Mandinga identity – 18

62–65 writing-on-the-hand ritual – 18

64 parents must keep channels of communication open between children and angels – 18; waking sleeping children disrupts communication with angels – 18; female nudity and keeping dogs in apartment scare away angels – 18

65 writing-on-the-hand ritual as magical safeguard against alcoholism – 18; "big initiation" and "little initiation" are changing – 17, 19

66 *Kankuran* protects initiates from witches – 8

67 today girls are circumcised earlier – 17, 19; when a girl's clitoris is cut, God can hear her prayers – 17, 19; many Guinean Muslim men in Lisbon now oppose female circumcision – 19

68 female circumcision tames a girl's sex drive – 17, 19; danger of circumcising a sexually active girl – 19

70 news travels fast by mobile phone in Guinean immigrant community in Lisbon – 19, 22

Sources Cited – Chapter 2

(1) Abranches, Maria (2007). Muslim women in Portugal: Strategies of identity (re)construction. *Lusotopie* 14 (1), 239–54.

(2) Abranches, Maria (2014). Remitting wealth, reciprocating health? The "travel" of the land from Guinea-Bissau to Portugal. *American Ethnologist* 41 (2), 261–75.

(3) Bird, Charles S. and Martha B. Kendall (1980). The Mande hero: Text and context. In Ivan Karp and Charles S. Bird (eds.), *Exploration in African systems of thought*. Washington, DC: Smithsonian Institution Press, pp. 13–26.

(4) Boddy, Janice (1989). *Wombs and alien spirits: Women, men, and the Zar cult in northern Sudan*. Madison: University of Wisconsin Press.

(5) Brooks, George (1993). Historical perspectives on the Guinea-Bissau region, fifteenth to nineteenth centuries. In Carlos Lopes

(ed.), *Mansas, escravos, grumetes e gentio: Cacheu na encruzilhada de civilizações*. Bissau: Institutio Nacional de Estudos e Pesquisa, pp. 27–54.
(6) Carvalho, Clara (2012). Guinean migrant traditional healers in the global market. In Hanjörg Dilger, Abdoulaye Kane, and Stacey A. Langwick (eds.), *Medicine, mobility, and power in global Africa: Transnational health and healing*. Bloomington: Indiana University Press, pp. 316–36.
(7) Central Intelligence Agency (2014). *The World Factbook, 2015*. New York: Skyhorse.
(8) de Jong, Ferdinand (2007). *Masquerades of modernity: Power and secrecy in Casamance, Senegal*. Edinburgh: Edinburgh University Press.
(9) Delaney, Carole (2000). Making babies in a Turkish village. In Judy S. DeLoache and Alma Gottlieb (eds.), *A world of babies: Imagined childcare guides for seven societies*. Cambridge: Cambridge University Press, pp. 117–44.
(10) Figueiredo, Bárbara, Claudia C. Dias, Sónia Brandão, Catarina Canário, and Rui Nunes-Costa (2013). Breastfeeding and postpartum depression: State of the art review. *Jornal de Pediatra* 89 (4), 332–38.
(11) Gallop, Rodney (1961). *Portugal: A book of folk-ways*. Cambridge: Cambridge University Press.
(12) Graham, Philip (2009). 365 days of pork surprise. In *The Moon, come to Earth: Dispatches from Lisbon*. Chicago: University of Chicago Press, pp. 12–16.
(13) Grosz-Ngaté, Maria (2014). Social relations: Family, kinship, and community. In Maria Grosz-Ngaté, John H. Hanson, and Patrick O'Meara (eds.), *Africa*. Bloomington: Indiana University Press, pp. 56–82.
(14) Healy, Claire (2011). *Portuguese citizenship: The new nationality law of 2006 (summary and English translation by the author)*. Lisbon: ACIDI.
(15) Hopen, C. E. (1958). *The pastoral Fulbe family in Gwandu*. Oxford: Oxford University Press.
(16) Integrated Regional Information Networks (2014). Guinea-Bissau: Hospital births on rise. *Humanitarian News and Analysis*, July 21.
(17) Johnson, Michelle C. (2000). Becoming a Muslim, becoming a person: Female "circumcision," religious identity, and personhood in Guinea-Bissau. In Bettina Shell-Duncan and Ylva Hernlund (eds.), *Female "circumcision" in Africa: Culture, controversy, and change*. Boulder, CO: Lynne Rienner.

Citations and Sources Cited

(18) Johnson, Michelle C. (2006). The proof is on my palm: Debating Islam and ritual in a new African diaspora. *Journal of Religion in Africa* 36 (1), 50–77.

(19) Johnson, Michelle C. (2007). Making Mandinga or making Muslims? Debating female circumcision, ethnicity, and Islam in Guinea-Bissau and Portugal. In Ylva Hernlund and Bettina Shell-Duncan (eds.), *Transcultural bodies: Female genital cutting in global context*. New Brunswick: Rutgers University Press, pp. 202–23.

(20) Johnson, Michelle C. (2009). Death and the left hand: Islam, gender, and "proper" Mandinga funerary custom in Guinea-Bissau and Portugal. *African Studies Review* 52 (2), 93–117.

(21) Johnson, Michelle C. (2013). "Children of Muslims eat rice": Food, identity, and Islamic piety among Guinean Muslims in Lisbon. Paper presented at the Annual Meeting of the American Anthropological Association. Chicago, November 20–24.

(22) Johnson, Michelle C. (2013). Culture's calling: Mobile phones, gender, and the making of an African migrant village in Portugal. *Anthropological Quarterly* 86 (1), 163–90.

(23) Johnson, Michelle C. (2014). Guinea-Bissau. In *Worldmark encyclopedia of religious practices*. Second edition, ed. Thomas Riggs, vol. 3: *Countries, Greece to Philippines*. Detroit: Gale, pp. 40–49.

(24) Machado, Fernando Luís (1994). Luso-Africanos em Portugal: Nas margens de etnicidade. *Sociologia: Problemas e Práticas* 16, 111–34.

(25) Machado, Fernando Luís (1998). Da Guiné-Bissau a Portugal: Luso-Guineenses e imigrantes. *Sociologia: Problemas e Práticas* 26, 9–56.

(26) Mendy, Peter Karibe and Richard A. Lobban, Jr. (2013). *Historical dictionary of the Republic of Guinea-Bissau*. Lanham, MD: Scarecrow Press.

(27) Portugal (1985). Lei 14/85, de 6 de Julho. Acompanhamento da mulher gravida durante o trabalho. *Diario da Republica*, 1a Serie, no. 153.

(28) Riesman, Paul (1992). *First find your child a good mother: The construction of self in two African communities*, ed. David L. Szanton, Lila Abu-Lughod, Sharon Hutchinson, Paul Stoller, and Carol Trosset. New Brunswick: Rutgers University Press.

(29) Saraiva, Clara (2008). Transnational migrants and transnational spirits: An African religion in Lisbon. *Journal of Ethnic and Migration Studies* 34 (2), 253–69.

(30) Tiesler, Nina Clara (2008). No bad news from the European margin: The new Islamic presence in Portugal. In Andrew Rippin (ed.), *World Islam: Critical concepts in Islamic studies*, vol. 4. London: Routledge, pp. 189–216.
(31) Tiesler, Nina Clara (2011). Happy at home and going international: Young Portuguese Muslims. *Checks and Balances* 7 (4), 30–35.
(32) Whittemore, Robert D. and Elizabeth A. Beverly (1998). Mandinka mothers and nurslings: Power and reproduction. *Medical Anthropology Quarterly* 10 (1), 45–62.

3 From Cultural Revolution to Childcare Revolution

Citations

The numbers in the citations below refer to the numbered references in the Sources Cited section immediately following for this chapter.

Page

71	description of Chinese society – 9; studies of lineage – 10
72	collectivization – 29; women's roles and experience during Communism – 21; women in Communism and family violence during Communism – 21, 29
73	One Child Policy and modernity – 5; modernity and birth planning – 16, 17, 18; only children and family's hope – 13
74	household registration system, legality, and social stratification – 26; family separation – 14, 15, 41, 42, 43; migration and Spring Festival – 8; government and "high quality" citizens – 1, 2, 3, 11, 16, 20, 27, 28, 32, 33, 34, 46
74–5	immorality of Chinese society – 38, 39, 40
75	fosterage and adoption of abandoned, female, and disabled children – 7, 22, 23, 28, 30, 31, 34, 37
75–6	reinterpretation of filial piety – 4, 6, 44, 45
76	intergenerational relationships – 14, 15, 30; argumentative communication – 47
77–8	prevailing importance of intergenerational relations – 4, 6; children as parents' hope for security – 13
81–2	local marriages under Communism – 29
83–5	intergenerational tension over prenatal vitamins – 47
84	Chinese personhood – 28

Sources Cited – Chapter 3

(1) Anagnost, A. (1997). Neo-Malthusian fantasy and national transcendence. In *National past-times: Narrative, representation, and power in modern China*. Durham, NC: Duke University Press, pp. 117–37.

(2) Anagnost, A. (2004). The corporeal politics of quality (*suzhi*). *Public Culture,* Spring (2), 189–208.

(3) Bakken, B. (2000). *The exemplary society*. Oxford: Oxford University Press.

(4) Chen, F., G. Lu. and C. A. Mair (2011). Intergenerational ties in context: Grandparents caring for grandchildren in China. *Social Forces* 90 (2), 571–94.

(5) Chen, Junjie (2011). Globalizing, reproducing, and civilizing rural subjects: Population control policy and constructions of rural identity in China. In Carole Browner and Carolyn Sargent (eds.), *Reproduction, globalization and the state: New theoretical and ethnographical perspectives*. Durham, NC: Duke University Press, pp. 38–52.

(6) Croll, E. (2010). The intergenerational contract in the changing Asian family. *Oxford Development Studies* 34 (4), 473–91.

(7) Dorow, S. (2006). *Transnational adoption: A cultural economy of race, gender, and kinship*. New York: New York University Press.

(8) Fan, L. (2010). *The last train home*. Canada: EyeSteelFilm.

(9) Fei, X. T. (1992 [1947]). *From the soil: The foundations of Chinese society*. Berkeley: University of California Press.

(10) Freedman, M. (1966). *Chinese lineage and society: Fukien and Kwangtung*. London: Athlone.

(11) Friedman, S. (2006). *Intimate politics*. Cambridge, MA: Harvard University Asia Center.

(12) Fong, V. (2002). China's one-child policy and the empowerment of urban daughters. *American Anthropologist*, 104 (4), 1098–1109.

(13) Fong, V. (2004). *Only hope: Coming of age under China's one child policy*. Stanford: Stanford University Press.
(14) Goh, E. C. L. (2009). Grandparents as childcare providers: An in-depth analysis of the case of Xiamen, China. *Journal of Aging Studies* 23, 60–68.
(15) Goh, E. C. L. (2011). *China's one-child policy and multiple caregiving: Raising little suns in Xiamen*. New York: Routledge.
(16) Greenhalgh, S. (2003). Planned births, unplanned persons: "Population" in the making of Chinese modernity. *American Anthropologist*, 30 (2), 196–215.
(17) Greenhalgh, S. (2010). Governing Chinese life: From sovereignty to biopolitical governance. In E. Y. Zhang, A. Kleinman, and W. Tu (eds.), *Governance of life in Chinese moral experience: The quest for an adequate life*. New York: Routledge, pp. 146–62.
(18) Greenhalgh, S. and E. A. Winckler (2005). *Governing China's population*. Stanford: Stanford University Press.
(19) Hu, Y. (2007). Baby born with birth defects every 30 seconds. *China Daily* (October 30), 3.
(20) Jacka, T. (2009). Cultivating citizens: Suzhi discourse (quality) in the PRC. *Positions: East Asia Culture Critique* 17 (3), 523–35.
(21) Johnson, K. A. (1985). *Women, the family, and peasant revolution in China*. Chicago: University of Chicago Press.
(22) Johnson, K. A. (2004). *Wanting a daughter, needing a son*. St. Paul, MN: Yeong & Yeong Book Co.
(23) Keyser, C. (2009). The role of the state and NGOs in caring for at-risk children: The case of orphan care. In J. Schwartz and S. Hsieh (eds.), *State and society responses to welfare needs in China: Serving the people*. New York: Routledge, pp. 45–65.
(24) Kohrman, M. (1999). Grooming "Que Zi": Marriage exclusion and identity formation among disabled men in contemporary China. *American Ethnologist* 26 (4), 890–909.
(25) Kohrman, M. (2005). *Bodies of difference*. Berkeley: University of California Press.
(26) Liang, Z. P. (2011). The death of a detainee: The predicament of status politics in contemporary China and the way out. In E. Y. Zhang, A. Kleinman, and W. Tu (eds.), *Governance of life in Chinese moral experience: The quest for an adequate life*. New York: Routledge, pp. 83–102.
(27) Murphy, R. (2004). Turning peasants into modern Chinese citizens: "Population quality" discourse, demographic transition, and primary education. *China Quarterly*, 177, 1–20.

Citations and Sources Cited

(28) Naftali, O. (2014). *Children, rights, and modernity in China*. London: Palgrave Macmillan.
(29) Potter, J. and Potter, S. H. (1990). *China's peasants: The anthropology of a revolution*. Cambridge: Cambridge University Press.
(30) Raffety, E. (2015). *Morality on the margins: Fostering disabled children in contemporary China*. Doctoral dissertation, Princeton University.
(31) Shang, X. Y. (2011). *Zhongguo ertong fuli qianyan wenti [The frontlines of Chinese children's welfare]*. Beijing: Social Sciences Academic Press.
(32) Sigley, G. (2009). Suzhi, the body, and the fortunes of technoscientific reasoning in contemporary China. *Positions: East Asia Cultures Critique* (17) 3, 537–66.
(33) Solinger, D. (1999). *Contesting citizenship in urban China: Peasant migrants, the state, and the logic of the market*. Berkeley: University of California Press.
(34) Wang, L. (2010). Importing Western childhoods into a Chinese state-run orphanage. *Qualitative Sociology* 33, 137–59.
(35) Wolf, M. (1970). Child training and the Chinese family. In Maurice Freedman (ed.), *Family and kinship in Chinese society*. Stanford: Stanford University Press, pp. 37–62.
(36) Wolf, M. (1972). Uterine families and the women's community. In *Women and the family in rural Taiwan*. Stanford: Stanford University Press, pp. 32–41.
(37) Wu, Y. P., X. Y. Han, and Q. Gao (2005). *Jiating Jiyang: Dongji yu Jixiao [Family fostering: Motivation and effect]*. Beijing: Social Sciences Academic Press.
(38) Yan, Y. X. (2003). *Private life under socialism*. Stanford: Stanford University Press.
(39) Yan, Y. X. (2011). The individualization of the family in rural China. *Boundary 2: An International Journal of Literature and Culture* 38 (1), 203–29.
(40) Yan, Y. X. (2011). The changing moral landscape. In A. Kleinman et al. (eds.), *Deep China: The moral life of the person – what anthropology and psychiatry tell us about China today*. Berkeley: University of California Press, pp. 36–77.
(41) Ye, J. Z. (2011). Left-behind children: The social price of China's economic boom. *Journal of Peasant Studies* 38 (3), 613–50.
(42) Ye, J. Z. and P. Lu (2011). Differentiated childhoods: Impacts of rural labor migration on left-behind children in China. *Journal of Peasant Studies* 38 (2), 355–77.

(43) Ye, J. Z., J. Murray, and Y. Wang (2005). *Left-behind children in rural China: Impact study of rural labor migration on left-behind children in mid-west China*. Beijing: Social Science Academic Press.
(44) Zhang, H. (2004). "Living alone" and the rural elderly: Strategy and agency in post-Mao rural China. In C. Ikels (ed.), *Filial piety: Practice and discourse in contemporary East Asia*. Stanford: Stanford University Press, pp. 63–87.
(45) Zhang, H. (2005). Bracing for an uncertain future: A case study of new coping strategies of rural parents under China's birth control policy. *China Journal* 54, 53–76.
(46) Zhang, L. (2001). *Strangers in the city: Reconfigurations of space, power, and social networks within China's floating population*. Stanford: Stanford University Press.
(47) Zhu, J. F. (2010). Mothering expectant mothers: Consumption, production, and two motherhoods in contemporary China. *Ethos* 38 (4), 406–21.

4 A Baby to Tie You to Place

Citations

The numbers in the citations below refer to the numbered referencing in the following Sources Cited section of this chapter.

Page

94 expelled from their homes – 47, 59; *al-Nakba*, meaning "the catastrophe" – 24; longest military occupation – 34; increasingly criticized – 13; the second *intifada* – 56; illegal by the United Nations General Assembly – 68

95 Israelis and Palestinian injured or dead – 23, 41; separation wall – 22, 69; checkpoints – 70; the permit system – 3, 66; demolition of Palestinian homes – 6; violation of international humanitarian law – 27; Fourth Geneva Convention – 43; decrease in public support for "settlements" – 62; others who are more distantly related – 44; strong ties with the *hamula* – 35; members numbering in the thousands – 15

95–6 daily interaction and socialization – 31

96 relatives beyond those in the *'a'ila* – 44; strengthened family ties – 65; socialize within the confines of the *hamula* – 42; levels and

structures of mobility – 36, 37; central to Arab culture and practice – 73; Israel citing security risks – 16, 63

97 since the 1948 *Nakba* – 2; internal deficiencies within the Palestinian Authority – 60

98 money to support the *hamula* – 2; weakening the economic situation in the West Bank and East Jerusalem – 67; pools its resources for family needs – 42; 161 Palestinian dead and another 700 injured – 53; Palestinian killed by other Palestinians – 21; targeted each other's activists, leaders, and supporters – 18, 19, 53; accused of being "collaborators" – 20; death for being a "collaborator" – 14; human rights organizations have documented instances – 14; collaboration has been broadly defined – 20

99 collaboration includes acts that are deemed immoral – 20; marriage is often central to a family's survival – 2; members of *'a'ila* consulted in decision-making process – 15; women tend to join their husband's families – 15; Palestinian society is young – 25; responsibility often falls upon the oldest son – 42; "honor" is reflected in the "virtuous" behaviors of its women – 42; "honor" has expanded to include other elements – 42

100 maintenance of traditional values and customs – 42; women are considered to be some of the most educated women – 58

104 marriage governed by customary orthodox Sunni Islamic law – 30; legally seek divorce – 30; 4.5 percent of families in the West Bank practiced polygamy – 71; psychological and economic distress – 52; stressful for children – 9, 10

105 *dayat* – 46; discouraged home delivery births – 17; 3.2 percent of births in the West Bank – 54

106 eating dates during the last month of pregnancy – 11

107 "checkpoint" – 70; pregnant women stuck at checkpoints – 49; pregnant and laboring women were refused passage – 12; exposed to tear gas – 40

111 depression because of the political situation – 4, 7; breastfeed up to two years – 51

112 symbol of Palestinian resistance – 64

114 maternity leave – 55

116 food allergies – 33

117 *Qabr Yūsuf* – 57, 72; considered a holy place – 25, 56; site of intense conflict for centuries – 48, 57, 61; Israeli army prohibits Palestinian Muslims – 1, 28, 29, 38, 39

118 in the company of older siblings or cousins – 50; protect them from violence – 5, 7

119 resist the Israeli occupation and its violence – 8

Citations and Sources Cited

Sources Cited – Chapter 4

(1) Abu El Haj, N. (2001). *Facts on the ground: Archaeological practice and territorial self-fashioning in Israeli society*. Chicago: University of Chicago Press.

(2) Abu Nahleh, L. (2006). Six families: Survival and mobility in times of crisis. In L. Taraki (ed.), *Living Palestine: Family survival, resistance and mobility under occupation*. Syracuse: Syracuse University Press, pp. 103–84.

(3) Abu-Zahra, N. (2008). Identity cards and coercion in Palestine. In R. Pain and S. J. Smith (eds.), *Fear: Critical geographies and everyday life*. Burlington, VT: Ashgate, pp. 175–91.

(4) Akesson, B. (2008). Addressing the psychosocial needs of pregnant women affected by war. *Refuge* 25 (1), 55–59.

(5) Akesson, B. (2014). Castle and cage: Meanings of home for Palestinian children and families. *Global Social Welfare* 1 (2):81–95.

(6) Akesson, B. (2014). "We may go, but this is my home": Experiences of domicide and resistance for Palestinian children and families. *Journal of Internal Displacement* 4 (2):8–22.

(7) Akesson, B. (2015). Holding everything together: Experiences of Palestinian mothers under occupation. In T. Takseva and A. Sgoutas (eds.), *Mothers under fire: Mothering in conflict areas*. Bradford, Ontario: Demeter Press, pp. 40–56.

(8) Akesson, B. (2015). School as a place of violence and hope: Tensions of education in post-intifada Palestine. *International Journal of Educational Development* 41, 192–99.

(9) Al-Krenawi, A., J. R. Graham, and V. Slonim-Nevo (2002). Mental health aspects of Arab-Israeli adolescents from polygamous/monogamous families. *Journal of Social Psychology* 142, 446–60.

(10) Al-Krenawi, A. and V. Slonim-Nevo (2008). Psychosocial and familial functioning of children from polygamous and monogamous families. *Journal of Social Psychology* 148, 745–64.

(11) Al-Kuran, O., L. Al-Mehaisen, H. Bawadi, S. Beitawi, and Z. Amarin (2011). The effect of late pregnancy consumption of date fruit on labour and delivery. *Journal of Obstetrics and Gynaecology* 31 (1), 29–31.

(12) Allen, L. (2008). Getting by the occupation: How violence became normal during the second Palestinian intifada. *Cultural Anthropology* 23 (3), 453–87.

(13) Allen, L. (2013). *The rise and fall of human rights: Cynicism and politics in occupied Palestine*. Stanford: Stanford University Press.

(14) Al-Mughrabi, N. (2013). Hamas looks to root out Israel's spy networks. Reuters, May 8. www.reuters.com/article/2013/05/08/us-palestinians-hamas-spies-idUSBRE9470LF20130508.
(15) Alternative Tourism Group (ATG (2008). *Palestine and Palestinians*. Beit Sahour, Palestine: Alternative Tourism Group.
(16) Ashkar, A. (2006). *Perpetual limbo: Israel's freeze on unification of Palestinian families in the Occupied Territories (Joint report with Hamoked – Center for the Defence of the Individual)*. Jerusalem: B'Tselem.
(17) Barnea, T., and R. Husseini (eds.) (2002). *Separate and cooperate, cooperate and separate: The disengagement of the Palestine health care system from Israel and its emergence as an independent system*. Westport, CT: Greenwood Publishing Group.
(18) Bronner, E. (2008). 9 dead in Hamas raid on pro-Fatah clan in Gaza. *The New York Times*, August 3.
(19) Bronner, E. (2009). 6 die as Palestinian Authority forces clash with Hamas. *The New York Times*, June 1.
(20) B'Tselem (2011). *Harm to Palestinians suspected of collaborating with Israel*. Jerusalem: B'Tselem.
(21) B'Tselem (2011). *Severe human rights violations in inter-Palestinian clashes*. Jerusalem: B'Tselem.
(22) B'Tselem (2011). *The separation barrier – statistics*. Jerusalem: B'Tselem.
(23) B'Tselem (2013). *Statistics: Fatalities*. Jerusalem: B'Tselem.
(24) Caplan, N. (2010). *The Israel–Palestine conflict: Contested histories*. Oxford: Wiley-Blackwell.
(25) Central Intelligence Agency (CIA) (2014, June 20). West Bank. www.cia.gov/library/publications/the-world-factbook/geos/we.html
(26) Condor, C. R. (1889). *Tent work in Palestine: A record of discovery and adventure*. London: Alexander P. Watt.
(27) Defence for Children International (DCI) (2010). *Under attack: Settler violence against Palestinian children in the Occupied Palestinian Territory*. Jerusalem: DCI.
(28) Dor, D. (2004). *Intifada hits the headlines: How the Israeli press misreported the outbreak of the second Palestinian uprising*. Bloomington: Indiana University Press.
(29) Dumper, M. and B. E. Stanley (2007). *Cities of the Middle East and North Africa: A historical encyclopedia*. Santa Barbara, CA: ABC-CLIO.
(30) El Alami, D. and D. Hinchcliffe (1996). *Islamic marriage and divorce laws of the Arab world*. New York: Springer.

(31) Ghabra, S. (1988). Palestinians in Kuwait: The family and the politics of survival. *Journal of Palestine Studies* 17 (2), 62–83.

(32) Giacaman, R., N. Abu-Rmeileh, and L. Wick (2007). The limitations on choice: Palestinian women's childbirth location, dissatisfaction with the place of birth and determinants. *European Journal of Public Health* 17 (1), 86–91.

(33) Graif, Y., L. German, I. Livne, and T. Shohat (2012). Association of food allergy with asthma severity and atopic diseases in Jewish and Arab adolescents. *Acta Paediatrica* 101 (10), 1083–88.

(34) Hajjar, L. (2005). *Courting conflict: The Israeli military court system in the West Bank and Gaza*. Berkeley: University of California Press.

(35) Harker, C. (2009). Spacing Palestine through the home. *Transactions of the Institute of British Geographers* 34 (3), 320–32.

(36) Harker, C. (2010). On (not) forgetting families: Family spaces and spacings in Birzeit, Palestine. *Environment and Planning A* 42 (11), 2624–39.

(37) Harker, C. (2011). Geopolitics and family in Palestine. *Geoforum* 42 (3), 306–15.

(38) Hassner, R. E. (2009). *War on sacred grounds*. Ithaca, NY: Cornell University Press.

(39) Hayden, R. M. (2002). Intolerant sovereignties and "multi-multi" protectorates: Competition of religious sites and (in)tolerance in the Balkans. In C. M. Hann (ed.), *Postsocialism: Ideals, ideologies, and practices in Eurasia*. London: Routledge, pp. 159–79.

(40) Infant Risk Center (2010, June 3). Tear gas and pregnancy. www.infantrisk.com/content/tear-gas-and-pregnancy.

(41) Institute for Counter-Terrorism (n.d.). An engineered tragedy: Statistical analysis of fatalities (Statistical Report Summary). Israel: Institute for Counter-Terrorism.

(42) Institute for Middle East Understanding (IMEU) (n.d.). Social customs and traditions. http://imeu.org/article/social-customs-and-traditions.

(43) International Committee of the Red Cross (ICRC) (1949). Geneva Convention relative to the protection of civilian persons in time of war. ICRC, August 12. www.refworld.org/docid/3ae6b36d2.html.

(44) Johnson, P. (2006). Living together in a nation in fragments: Dynamics of kin, place, and nation. In L. Taraki (ed.), *Living Palestine: Family survival, resistance and mobility under occupation*. Syracuse, NY: Syracuse University Press, pp. 51–102.

(45) Jones, R. (2012). *Border walls: Security and the war on terror in the United States, India, and Israel*. London: Zed Books.

Citations and Sources Cited

(46) Katvan, E. and N. Bartal (2011). A midwife's tale. *Haaretz*, September 26. www.haaretz.com/print-edition/features/a-midwife-s-tale-1.386740.

(47) Khalidi, R. (1997). *Palestinian identity: The construction of modern national consciousness*. New York: Columbia University Press.

(48) Kohen, E. (2007). *History of the Byzantine Jews: A microcosmos in the thousand year empire*. Lanham, MD: University Press of America.

(49) Long, J. C. (2006). Border anxiety in Palestine-Israel. *Antipode* 38 (1), 107–27.

(50) Matthews, M. (1992). *Making sense of place: Children's understanding of large-scale environments*. Hemel Hempstead and Lanham, MD: Harvester Wheatsheaf/Barnes & Noble.

(51) Musmar, S. G. and S. Qanadeelu (2012). Breastfeeding patterns among Palestinian infants in the first 6 months in Nablus refugee camps: A cross-sectional study. *Journal of Human Lactation* 28 (2), 196–202.

(52) Naser-Najjab, N. (2013). Polygamy, family law, and the crisis of governance in Palestine. *Journal of Family Issues* 36 (8), 1087–1111.

(53) O'Callaghan, S., S. Jaspars and S. Pavanello (2009). *Losing ground: Protection and livelihoods in the Occupied Palestinian Territory* (Humanitarian Policy Group Working Paper). London: Overseas Development Institute.

(54) Palestinian Central Bureau of Statistics (2005). *Demographic and health survey 2004*. Ramallah: Palestinian Central Bureau of Statistics.

(55) Palestinian Central Bureau of Statistics (2013). *Labor law*. Ramallah: Palestinian Central Bureau of Statistics.

(56) Pearlman, W. (2011). The organizational mediation theory of protest. In *Violence, nonviolence, and the Palestinian national movement*. Cambridge: Cambridge University Press, pp. 1–26.

(57) Pummer, R. (1993). Joseph's Tomb. In A. D. Crown, R. Pummer and A. Tal (eds.), *A companion to Samaritan studies*. Tübingen: Mohr Siebeck.

(58) Royal Academy of Science International Trust (2009). *Women and education in Palestine: Is education improving the status of women?* www.rasit.org/files/women_in_palestine_education.pdf.

(59) Sa'di, A. H. and L. Abu-Lughod (2007). *Nakba: Palestine, 1948, and the claims of memory*. New York: Columbia University Press.

(60) Safadi, N. S. and S. D. Easton (2014). The evolution of the social welfare system in Palestine: Perspectives of policymakers in the West Bank. *International Journal of Social Welfare* 23, 52–60.

(61) Sivan, H. (2008). *Palestine in late antiquity*. Oxford: Oxford University Press.
(62) Skop, Y. (2014). Support for West Bank settlements dropping among Israeli public, poll indicates – Diplomacy and defense. *Haaretz*, June 16. www.haaretz.com/news/diplomacy-defense/.premium-1.599003.
(63) Stein, Y. (2004). *Forbidden families: Family unification and child registration in East Jerusalem* (Joint report with Hamoked – Center for the Defence of the Individual). Jerusalem: B'Tselem.
(64) Swedenburg, T. (2003). *Memories of revolt: The 1936–1939 rebellion and the Palestinian national past*. Fayetteville: University of Arkansas Press.
(65) Taraki, L. (2006). Introduction. In *Living Palestine: Family survival, resistance and mobility under occupation*. Syracuse, NY: Syracuse University Press, pp. xi–xxx.
(66) Tawil-Souri, H. (2010). Orange, green, and blue: Color-coded paperwork for Palestinian population control. In *Surveillance and control in Israel/Palestine*. New York: Routledge, pp. 219–38.
(67) United Nations (UN) (2010). *United Nations seminar on assistance to Palestinian people analyses current state, future of economy* (General Assembly Meetings Coverage No. GA/PAL/1157). New York: United Nations.
(68) United Nations General Assembly (2012). *Resolution adopted by the General Assembly [on the Report of the Special Political and Decolonization Committee]* (No. A/RES/66/78). New York: United Nations.
(69) United Nations Office for the Coordination of Humanitarian Affairs (UNOCHA) (2009). *Five years after the International Court of Justice advisory opinion: A summary of the humanitarian impact of the barrier*. East Jerusalem: UNOCHA.
(70) Weizman, E. (2007). *Hollow land: Israel's architecture of occupation*. London: Verso.
(71) Welchman, L. (2004). Legal context: Shari'a courts and Muslim family law in the transitional period. In L. Welchman (ed.), *Women's rights and Islamic family law: Perspectives on reform*. London: Zed Books, pp. 99–101.
(72) Zangenberg, J. (2006). Between Jerusalem and the Galilee: Samaria in the time of Jesus. In J. H. Charlesworth (ed.), *Jesus and archeology*. Grand Rapids, MI: William B. Eerdmans, pp. 392–431.
(73) Zureik, E. (2001). Constructing Palestine through surveillance practices. *British Journal of Middle Eastern Studies* 28 (2), 205–27.

Citations and Sources Cited

5 Childrearing in the New Country

Citations

The numbers in the citations below refer to the numbered references in the Sources Cited section immediately following this chapter.

Page

123 construction of shared peoplehood in contemporary Israel – 11

124 Zionist ideology – 5, pp. 3–13; factors facilitating the spread of Hebrew as lingua franca among Jewish settlers in Palestine – 41

125 Palestinian population of Israel – 1, 25; occupied territories and Jordan Palestinian population of – 6, p. 5; creation of Palestinian refugee problem – 40

126 complex relations between the Jewish majority and the Palestinian minority – 3, 46, 51, 54, 56; Israel a "deeply divided society" – 52

127–8 surveys of religiosity – 4

128 evolving meanings of terms, *Sephardi* and *Mizrahi* – 18; increase of Mizrahi Jews to 40 percent – 47; construction of overarching "Mizrahi" identity that disregards internal diversity – 19

129 development towns – 51, pp. 80–1; rise of Mizrahi middle-class in Israel – 10, 38; Israeli "melting pot" as success or failure – 61; Ethiopian immigration statistics – 47, p. 4

130 recent education and employment trends among Ethiopian Israelis – 58; newcomer groups in Israeli society including Russians, Ethiopians, and labor migrants – 31, pp. 130–72; 51, pp. 308–34; implications for educational policy of lack of recognizing diversity among Russian-speakers – 8; what is "Russian" about diverse population of Russian-speakers in Israel? – 34

130–1 comparison between Mizrahi immigrants of the 1950s and Russian immigrants of the 1990s – 53

131 occupational fates of various professional groups among immigrants from former Soviet Union 14, 35, 42, pp. 73–93, 53, 55; Russian immigrants' social enclave and political mobilization – 42, pp. 138–42; adolescents' adaptation – 12; Mizrahi Jews' attitudes toward Russian immigrants – 42, pp. 153–6

132 familism – 16, p. vii; changes in family patterns over the past five decades and across socio-ethnic groups – 32; continuing centrality of familism in Israeli society – 15; family policy and

Sources Cited – Chapter 5

(1) Aderet, O. (2014). Israel by numbers, in 5774: Getting older, staying single, heading for the hills. *Haaretz*, September 23.

(2) Adler, C. (2008). Israel's system of education. In A. Stavans and I. Kupferberg (eds.), *Studies in language and language education:*

Essays in honor of Elite Olshtain. Jerusalem: Hebrew University Magnes Press, pp. 337–52.

(3) Al-Haj, M. (2002). Multiculturalism in deeply divided societies: The Israeli case. *International Journal of Intercultural Relations* 26, 169–83.

(4) Arian, A. and A. Keissar-Sugarmen (2011). *A portrait of Israeli Jews: Beliefs, observances, and values of Israeli Jews 2009*. Jerusalem: The Israeli Democracy Institute.

(5) Avineri, S. (1981). *The making of modern Zionism: The intellectual origins of the Jewish state*. New York: Basic Books.

(6) Beinin, J. and L. Hajjar (2014). *Palestine, Israel and the Arab–Israeli conflict: A primer*. Middle East Research and Information Project. www.merip.org.

(7) Berkovitch, N. (1997). Motherhood as a national mission: The construction of womanhood in the legal discourse of Israel. *Women's Studies International Forum* 20, 605–19.

(8) Bram, C. (2008). The Catch 22 of categorization: Soviet Jews, Caucasus Jews, and dilemmas of multiculturalism in Israel. In Z. Beckerman and E. Kopelowitz (eds.), *Cultural education – Cultural sustainability: Minority, diaspora, indigenous and ethnoreligious groups in multicultural societies*. New York and London: Routledge, pp. 31–50.

(9) Brody, D. (2007). Israeli kindergarten teachers cope with terror and war: Two implicit modes of resilience. *Curriculum Inquiry* 37 (1), 9–31.

(10) Cohen, U. and N. Leon (2008). The new Mizrahi middle class: Ethnic mobility and class integration in Israel. *Journal of Israeli History: Politics, Society, Culture* 27 (1), 51–64.

(11) Dominguez, V. R. (1989). *People as subject, people as object: Selfhood and peoplehood in contemporary Israel*. Madison: University of Wisconsin Press.

(12) Eisikovitz, R. (2000). Gender differences in cross-cultural adaptation styles of immigrant youths from the former USSR in Israel. *Youth and Society* 31 (3), 310–31.

(13) Feldman, J. (2002). Marking the boundaries of the enclave: Defining the Israeli collective through the Poland "experience." *Israel Studies* 7 (2), 84–114.

(14) Flug, K., N. Kasir and G. Ofer (1997). The absorption of Soviet immigrants into the labour market: Aspects of occupational substitution and retention. In N. Lewin-Epstein, Y. Ro'i, and P. Ritterband (eds.), *Russian Jews in three continents: Migration and resettlement*. London: Frank Cass, pp. 433–70.

(15) Fogiel-Bijaoui, S. (2002). Familism, postmodernity and the state: The case of Israel. *Journal of Israeli History: Politics, Society, Culture* 21 (1–2), 38–62.
(16) Fogiel-Bijaoui, S. and R. Rutlinger-Reiner (2013). Rethinking the family in Israel. *Israel Studies Review* 28 (2), vii–xii.
(17) Glassman, I. and R. A. Eisikovits (2006). Intergenerational transmission of motherhood patterns: Three generations of immigrant mothers of Moroccan descent in Israel. *Journal of Comparative Family Studies* 37 (3), 461–77.
(18) Goldberg, H. E. (2008). From Sephardi to Mizrahi and back again: Changing meanings of "Sephardi" in its social environments. *Jewish Social Studies* 15 (1), 165–88.
(19) Goldberg, H. and C. Bram (2007). Reflections on critical sociology and the study of Middle Eastern Jewry within the context of Israeli society. *Studies in Contemporary Jewry* 22, 227–56.
(20) Golden, D. (2003). A national cautionary tale: Russian women newcomers to Israel portrayed. *Nations and Nationalism* 9 (1), 83–104.
(21) Golden, D. (2005). Childhood as protected space? Vulnerable bodies in an Israeli kindergarten. *Ethos* 70 (1), 1–22.
(22) Golden, D. (2009). Fear, politics and children: Israeli Jewish and Israeli Palestinian preschool teachers talk about political violence. *Etnofoor* 21 (2), 77–95.
(23) Horowitz, T., S. Shmuel, and I. Zinaida (2008). The Russian immigrant community vs. the Israeli educational establishment: From extra-curricular activities to systemic change. In A. Stavans and I. Kupferberg (eds.), *Studies in language and language education: Essays in honor of Elite Olshtain*. Jerusalem: Magnes Press, pp. 379–94.
(24) Israel Central Bureau of Statistics (2010). *Women in Israel and in the world 2007/2008*, Statistilite 103. Jerusalem: Israel Central Bureau of Statistics.
(25) Israel Central Bureau of Statistics (2011). *Israel in figures, 2011*. Jerusalem: Israel Central Bureau of Statistics.
(26) Ivry, T. (2010). *Embodying culture: Pregnancy in Japan and Israel*. New Brunswick, NJ: Rutgers University Press.
(27) Kahn, S. M. (2000). *Reproducing Jews: A cultural account of assisted conception in Israel*. Durham, NC: Duke University Press.
(28) Kanaaneh, R. A. (2001). *Birthing the nation: Strategies of Palestinian women in Israel*. Berkeley: University of California Press.
(29) Katriel, T. (1991). *Gibush*: The crystallization metaphor in Israeli cultural semantics. In *Communal webs: Communication and*

culture in contemporary Israel. Albany: State University of New York Press, pp. 11–34.

(30) Kimhi, A. (2012). *Pre-primary education in Israel: Organizational and demographic perspectives*. Policy paper No. 2012.01. Report submitted to the Bernard van Leer Foundation. Jerusalem: Taub Center for Social Policy Studies in Israel.

(31) Kimmerling, B. (2001). *The invention and decline of Israeliness: State, society, and the military*. Berkeley: University of California Press.

(32) Lavee, Y. and R. Katz (2003). The family in Israel. *Marriage and Family Review* 35 (1–2), 193–217.

(33) Lemish, D. (2000). The whore and the other: Israeli images of female immigrants from former USSR. *Gender & Society* 14 (2), 333–49.

(34) Lerner, J. (2011). "Russians" in Israel as a post-Soviet subject: Implementing the civilizational repertoire. *Israel Affairs* 17(1), 21–37.

(35) Leshem, E. (2008). Being an Israeli: Immigrants from the former Soviet Union in Israel, fifteen years later. *Journal of Israeli History* 27 (1), 29–49.

(36) Lewin-Epstein, N., H. Stier, M. Braun, and B. Langfeldt (2000). Family policy and public attitudes in Germany and Israel. *European Sociological Review* 16 (4), 385–401.

(37) Michelovitz, R. (1999). Hinuch kedam yesodi beYisrael [Pre-school education in Israel]. In E. Peled (ed.), *Yovel lamaarechet hahinuch beYisrael* [Fifty years of education in Israel]. Jerusalem: State of Israel Ministry of Education, Culture and Sport, pp. 859–79.

(38) Mizrachi, B. (2013). *Paths to middle-class mobility among second generation Moroccan immigrant women in Israel*. Detroit: Wayne State University Press.

(39) Moin, V., M. Schwartz, and A. Breitkopf (2011). Balancing between heritage and host languages in bilingual kindergarten: Viewpoints of Russian-speaking immigrant parents in Germany and in Israel. *European Early Childhood Education Research Journal* 19 (4), 515–33.

(40) Morris, B. (1987). *The birth of the Palestinian refugee problem, 1947–1949*. Cambridge: Cambridge University Press.

(41) Nahir, M. (1988). Language planning and language acquisition: The "Great Leap" in the Hebrew revival. In C. Bratt Paulson (ed.), *International handbook of bilingualism and bilingual education*. New York: Greenwood Press, pp. 275–95.

(42) Remennick, L. (2007). *Russian Jews on three continents: Identity, integration, and conflict*. New Brunswick, NJ: Transaction.
(43) Roer-Strier, D. and M. Rivlis (1997). Israeli and Russian immigrant parents: Timetable of psychological and behavioral autonomy expectations. *International Journal of Psychology* 33, 123–35.
(44) Rosenthal, M. K. (2006). Early childhood care and education in Israel. In E. Melhuish & K. Petrogiannis (eds.), *Early childhood care and education: International perspectives*. London: Routledge, pp. 115–32.
(45) Rosenthal, M. K. and D. Roer-Strier (2001). Cultural differences in mothers' developmental goals and ethno theories. *International Journal of Psychology* 36 (1), 20–31.
(46) Saban, I. (2004). Minority rights in deeply divided societies: A framework for analysis and the case of the Arab-Palestinian minority in Israel. *New York University Journal of International Law and Politics* 36, 885–1003.
(47) Schafferman, K. T. (2008). *Israel: A society of immigrants*. Jerusalem: The Israeli Democracy Institute.
(48) Schwartz, M., V. Moin, M. Leikin, and A. Breitkopf (2010). Immigrant parents' choice of a bilingual versus monolingual kindergarten for second-generation children: Motives, attitudes, and factors. *International Multilingual Research Journal* 4, 107–24.
(49) Segal-Levit, K. (2003). Transforming the culture of scientific education in Israel. In K. Anderson-Levitt (ed.), *Local meanings, global schooling*. New York: Palgrave Macmillan, pp. 219–38.
(50) Sered, S. S. (1993). Religious rituals and secular rituals: Interpenetrating models of childbirth in a modern, Israeli context. *Sociology of Religion* 54 (1), 101–14.
(51) Shafir, G. and Y. Peled (2002). *Being Israeli: The dynamics of multiple citizenship*. Cambridge: Cambridge University Press.
(52) Smooha, S. (1978). *Israel: Pluralism and conflict*. Berkeley: University of California Press.
(53) Smooha, S. (2008). The mass immigrations to Israel: A comparison of the failure of the Mizrahi immigrants of the 1950s with the success of the Russian immigrants of the 1990s. *Journal of Israeli History: Politics, Society, Culture* 27 (1), 1–27.
(54) Smooha, S. (2010). Arab–Jewish relations in Israel: Alienation and rapprochement. *Peace Works No. 67*. Washington, DC: US Institute of Peace.
(55) Stier, H. and V. Levanon (2003). Finding an adequate job: Employment and income of recent immigrants to Israel. *International Migration* 41 (2), 81–105.

(56) Swirski, S. (2011). *Israel in a nutshell: A different introduction to present day Israeli society and economy*. Tel Aviv: Adva Center, Information on Equality and Social Justice in Israel.
(57) Taub Center for Social Policy Studies in Israel (2012). *The state of public preschool education in Israel*. Jerusalem: Taub Center Staff Bulletin Articles, August 21.
(58) Taub Center for Social Policy Studies in Israel (2015). *Education and employment trends among Ethiopian Jews*. Jerusalem: Taub Center Staff Bulletin Articles, October 15.
(59) Teman, E. (2010). *Birthing a mother: The surrogate body and the pregnant self*. Berkeley: University of California Press.
(60) Wolff, L. and E. Breit (2012). *Education in Israel: The challenges ahead*. University of Maryland, Institute for Israel Studies Research Paper. http://israelstudies.umd.edu/pdf/Larry%20Wolff%20Research%20Paper%20-%20May%202012%20-%20Updated.pdf accessed 06/07/2015.
(61) Ya'ar, E. (2005). Continuity and change in Israeli society: The test of the melting pot. *Israel Studies* 10 (2), 91–128.
(62) Ziv, Y., D. Golden, and T. Goldberg (2015). Teaching traumatic history to young children: The case of Holocaust studies in Israeli preschools. *Early Education and Development* 26, 520–33.

6 Luring Your Child into this Life of Troubled Times

Citations

The numbers in the citations below refer to the numbered references in the Sources Cited section immediately following this chapter.

Page

153–4 early Beng history – 10, 15

154 Ivorian groups who actively resisted colonization – 34; French colonial history of West Africa – 24; on Houphouët-Boigny's reign – 18, 24; early warning signs of economic and political trouble – 6, 16

155 vigilante justice – 17; civil war – 23; early structural causes of the civil war – 22

156 on increasing poverty under colonial domination in Africa – 28; fragility of post-conflict rebuilding of infrastructure and democracy – 4, 31; toxic waste dumping in Abidjan by multinational corporations – 2; problematic youth behavior – 26; religious and ethnic xenophobia – 1, 3, 25; religious extremism – 19;

	human rights abuses – 33; negative implications of the declining economy and weak infrastructure for children's lives – 29, 30
157	Beng regional and political structure – 8
158	extended families, clan structure, and arranged marriage rules – 10; rebellion against arranged marriage – 13, 14; indigenous Beng religion – 10, 13
159	newborns emerge from afterlife – 11, 12
160	religious and mundane not easily distinguished – 10
165	two worlds of people and animals remain connected – 10
170	slow process to leave the afterlife – 11, 12

Sources Cited – Chapter 6

(1) Akindès, Francis (2004). *The roots of the military-political crises in Côte d'Ivoire*. Research Report No. 128. Uppsala: Nordiska Afrikainstitutet.
(2) Amnesty International (2015). *UK giving green light for corporate crime*. July 23. www.amnesty.org/en/latest/news/2015/07/UK-giving-green-light-for-corporate-crime/.
(3) Bah, Abu Bakarr (2010). Democracy and civil war: Citizenship and peacemaking in Côte d'Ivoire. *African Affairs* 109 (437), 597–615.
(4) Banegas, Richard (2011). Post-election crisis in Côte d'Ivoire: The *gbonhi* war. *African Affairs* 110 (440), 457–68.
(5) Bassett, Thomas J. (2011). Briefing: Winning coalition, sore loser: Côte d'Ivoire's 2010 presidential elections. *African Affairs* 110 (440), 469–79.
(6) Chamley, Christopher (1991). Côte d'Ivoire: The failure of structural adjustment programs. In V. Thomas, A. Chhibber, M. Dailami, and J. deMelo (eds.), *Restructuring economies in distress: Policy reform and the World Bank*. Washington, DC: World Bank/Oxford University Press, pp. 287–308.
(7) Cohen, Herman (2015). *Moments in US diplomatic history: The Ivory Coast's Félix Houphouët-Boigny – "A master manipulator and destabilizer."* Association for Diplomatic Studies and Training. http://adst.org/2015/04/the-ivory-coasts-felix-houphouet-boigny-a-master-manipulator-and-destabilizer/.
(8) Gottlieb, Alma (1989). Witches, kings, and the sacrifice of identity; or, The Power of paradox and the paradox of power among the Beng of Ivory Coast. In W. A. Arens and I. Karp (eds.), *Creativity of power: Cosmology and action in African societies*. Washington, DC: Smithsonian Institution Press, pp. 245–71.

(9) Gottlieb, Alma (1995). Of cowries and crying: A Beng guide to managing colic. *Anthropology and Humanism* 20 (1), 20–8.
(10) Gottlieb, Alma (1996 [1992]). *Under the kapok tree: Identity and difference in Beng thought*. Chicago: University of Chicago Press.
(11) Gottlieb, Alma (1998). Do infants have religion? The spiritual lives of Beng babies. *American Anthropologist* 100 (1), 122–35.
(12) Gottlieb, Alma (2004). *The afterlife is where we come from: The culture of infancy in West Africa*. Chicago: University of Chicago Press.
(13) Gottlieb, Alma and Philip Graham (1994 [1993]). *Parallel worlds: An anthropologist and a writer encounter Africa*. Chicago: University of Chicago Press.
(14) Gottlieb, Alma and Philip Graham (2012). *Braided worlds*. Chicago: University of Chicago Press.
(15) Gottlieb, Alma and M. Lynne Murphy (1995). *Beng–English dictionary*. Bloomington: Indiana University Linguistics Club.
(16) Hecht, Robert M. (1983). The Ivory Coast economic “miracle”: What benefits for peasant farmers? *Journal of Modern African Studies* 12 (1), 25–53.
(17) Hellweg, Joseph (2011). *Hunting the ethical state: The Benkadi movement of Côte d’Ivoire*. Chicago: University of Chicago Press.
(18) Hellweg, Joseph (2012). Fieldsights – hot spots. A history of crisis in Côte d’Ivoire. *Cultural Anthropology Online*, June 25. www.culanth.org/fieldsights/187-a-history-of-crisis-in-cote-d-ivoire.
(19) Institute of Security Studies (2015). West Africa Report: Is Côte d’Ivoire facing religious radicalism? *Institute for Security Studies* 13. http://reliefweb.int/sites/reliefweb.int/files/resources/WestAfricaReport13.pdf.
(20) International Labor Rights Fund (2004). *The World Bank and IMF policies in Cote d’Ivoire: Impact on child labor in the cocoa industry*. Washington, DC: International Labor Rights Fund. www.laborrights.org/publications/world-bank-and-imf-policies-cote-d’ivoire-impact-child-labor-cocoa-industry.
(21) Kopytoff, Igor (1971). Ancestors as elders in Africa. *Africa* 41 (2), 128–42.
(22) Kouadio, Bertin K. (2009). *From stability to insurgency: The root and proximate causes of the September 2002 civil war in Côte d’Ivoire*. Ph.D. dissertation, Department of International Relations, Florida International University.
(23) McGovern, Mike (2011). *Making war in Côte d’Ivoire*. Chicago: University of Chicago Press.
(24) Manning, Patrick (1999). *Francophone sub-Saharan Africa, 1880–1985*. Second edition. Cambridge: Cambridge University Press.

(25) Marshall-Fratani, Ruth (2006). The war of "who is who": Autochthony, nationalism, and citizenship in the Ivoirian crisis. *African Studies Review* 49 (2), 9–43.
(26) Newell, Sasha (2012). *The modernity bluff: Crime, consumption, and citizenship in Côte d'Ivoire*. Chicago: University of Chicago Press.
(27) Rice, Xan (2008). The president, his church and the crocodiles: Côte d'Ivoire's Félix Houphouët-Boigny ruled for 33 years, dying with a dream to turn his home villa. *New Statesman*, October 23.
(28) Rodney, Walter (1975). *How Europe underdeveloped Africa*. Washington, DC: Howard University Press.
(29) Scheper-Hughes, Nancy and Carolyn Sargent (eds.) (1998). *Small wars: The cultural politics of childhood*. Berkeley: University of California Press.
(30) Stephen, Sharon (ed.) (1995). *Children and the politics of culture*. Princeton: Princeton University Press.
(31) Straus, Scott (2011). "It's sheer horror here": Patterns of violence during the first four months of Côte d'Ivoire's post-electoral crisis. *African Affairs* 110 (440), 481–89.
(32) Thonneau, Patrick, Tomohiro Matsudai, Eusèbe Alihonou, José De souza, O. Faye, J. Moreau, Y. Djanhan, C. Welffens-Ekra, and N. Goyaux (2004). Distribution of causes of maternal mortality during delivery and post-partum: Results of an African multicentre hospital-based study. *European Journal of Obstetrics and Gynecology and Reproductive Biology* 114 (2), 150–4.
(33) US Department of State, Bureau of Democracy, Human Rights and Labor (2014). Country reports on human rights practices for 2014: Cote d'Ivoire. www.state.gov/j/drl/rls/hrrpt/humanrightsreport/index.htm?year=2014&dlid=236350#wrapper.
(34) Weiskel, Timothy C. (1980). *French colonial rule and the Baule people: Resistance and collaboration, 1889–1911*. Oxford: Clarendon Press.

7 From Mogadishu to Minneapolis

Citations

The numbers in the citations below refer to the numbered references in the Sources Cited section immediately following this chapter.

Page

191 urban literacy campaign – 9; rural literacy campaign – 9

Citations and Sources Cited

192 primary school – 9; girls in education – 9; women in teaching profession – 9; refugee statistics – 32
193 Dadaab refugee camp – 33; encampment policy – 19; Somali refugee-cum-suspects – 5
194 Lewiston letter – 13; Manchester – 16; Springfield – 23
195 Islamophobia in Minnesota – 7; Halloween costume – 14; reasons for Minnesota as destination for Somali diaspora – 15; Somali businesses – 15, 29
196 *dugsi* – 28
197 communal – 22; social interconnectedness – 20; child obedience – 12
198 closing of coastal refugee camp – 8
202 vitamins to fatten children – 18; vitamins as medicine – 34
203 infibulation – 21; complications of infibulation – 21; shame over *gudniin* – 34
204 Somali women misunderstood – 34
205 increased C-sections – 21
206 future fertility – 18; deinfibulation – 18; *afartan-beh* – 1
207 special foods – 25
208 *wanqal* – 1
209 *abtiris* – 1; the travels of *Igal Shidad* – 11; *Qayb Libaax* – 2
210 pumping breastmilk – 18; nursing in Islam – 31; challenges to exclusive breastfeeding – 27
211 overweight women and breastfeeding – 4; colostrum – 6
212 toothstick – 3; "food deserts" – 24
215 statistics on autism in Somali community – 17
216 vaccinations – 35
220 spanking – 26; Black youth – 10
221 North Carolina murders – 30
222 the Prophet and men's house work – 3

Sources Cited – Chapter 7

(1) Abdullahi, M. D. (2001). *Culture and customs of Somalia*. Westport, CT: Greenwood Press.

(2) Ahmed, S. (2007). *Qayb libaax [The lion's share]*. Minneapolis: Minnesota Humanities Commission.

(3) Al-Bukhari, Muhamad ibn Ismail (1997). *The translation of the meanings of Sahih al-Bukhari: Arabic and English*. Riyadh: Dar-us-Salam Publications.

(4) Baker, J. L., Michaelsen, K. F., Rasmussen, K. M., and Sorensen, T. (2004). Maternal prepregnant body mass index, duration of

breastfeeding, and timing of complementary food introduction are associated with infant weight gain. *American Journal of Clinical Nutrition* 80 (6), 1579–88.

(5) Balakian, S. (2016). "Money is your government": Refugees, mobility and unstable documents in Kenya's Operation *Usalama* Watch. *African Studies Review* 59(2), 87–111.

(6) Barstow, M. (2012). Working towards pragmatic and sustainable exclusive breastfeeding practices among Somali mothers in Lewiston, Maine. Unpublished B.A. honors thesis, Bates College.

(7) Bigelow, M. (2010). *Mogadishu on the Mississippi: Language, racialized identity, and education in a new land*. Malden, MA: Blackwell.

(8) Canada: Immigration and Refugee Board of Canada (1999). *Somalia: The "Benadir" refugee camp including location and ethnic backgrounds of camp dwellers*. December 31. www.refworld.org/docid/3ae6ad7b64.html.

(9) Cassanelli, L. and F. S. Abdikadir (2008). Somalia: Education in transition. *Bildhaan: An International Journal of Somali Studies* 7 (7), 91–125.

(10) Coates, T. (2015, July 4). Letter to my son. *The Atlantic.* www.theatlantic.com/politics/archive/2015/07/tanehisi-coates-between-the-world-and-me/397619/.

(11) Dupre, K. (2008). *Safarada Cigaal Shidaad [The travels of Igal Shidad]*. Hershey, PA: IGI Distributors.

(12) Dybdahl, R. and K. Hundeide (1999). Childhood in the Somali context: Mothers' and children's ideas about childhood and parenthood. *Psychology and Developing Societies* 10 (2), 131–45.

(13) Ellison, J. (2009, January 16). Lewiston, Maine, revived by Somali immigrants. *Newsweek*. www.newsweek.com/lewiston-maine-revived-somali-immigrants-78475.

(14) Gilbert, C. (2013). St. Paul Police Department probe hijab costume photo. *Minnesota Public Radio News,* February 5. www.mprnews.org/story/2013/02/04/police/photo-somali-halloween-costume.

(15) Golden, S., E. Boyle, and Y. Jama (2010). Achieving success in business: A comparison of Somali and American-born entrepreneurs in Minneapolis. *CURA Reporter* 40 (1–2), 43–51.

(16) Goodnough, A. (2011, November 25). After taking refugees for years, a New Hampshire city asks for a pause. *The New York Times*. www.nytimes.com/2011/11/26/us/manchester-new-hampshire-seeks-halt-in-refugee-resettlement.html.

(17) Hewitt, A., Jennifer Hall-Lande, Kristin Hamre, Amy N. Esler, Judy Punyko, Joe Reichle, and Anab A. Gulaid (2013). *Minneapolis*

Somali autism spectrum disorder prevalence project: Community Report 2013. University of Minnesota. Minneapolis, MN.
(18) Hill, N., E. Hunt, and K. Hyrkas (2011). Somali immigrant women's health care experiences and beliefs regarding pregnancy and birth in the United States. *Journal of Transcultural Nursing* 23 (1), 72–81.
(19) Human Rights Watch (2013, January 21). Kenya: Don't force 55,000 refugees into camps. www.hrw.org/news/2013/01/21/kenya-don-t-force-55000-refugees-camps.
(20) Hurley, E., A. Boykin, and B. Allen (2005). Communal versus individual learning of a math-estimation task: African American children and the culture of learning contexts. *Journal of Psychology* 139 (6), 513–27.
(21) Johnson, E., S. Reed, J. Hitti, and M. Batra (2005). Increased risk of adverse pregnancy outcome among Somali immigrants in Washington State. *American Journal of Obstetrics and Gynecology* 193 (2), 475–82.
(22) Kapteijns, L. and A. Arman (2008). Educating immigrant youth in the United States: An exploration of the Somali case. *Bildhaan: An International Journal of Somali Studies* 4, 8–43.
(23) Larson, J. (2014, June 24). Massachusetts Mayor doesn't want more Somali refugees in his town. *Vice News*. https://news.vice.com/article/massachusetts-mayor-doesnt-want-more-somali-refugees-in-his-town.
(24) Lewis, L., L. Galloway-Gilliam, G. Flynn, J. Nomachi, L. Keener, and D. Sloane (2011). Transforming the urban food desert from the grassroots up: A model for community change. *Family and Community Health* 34 (1S), 92–101.
(25) Lewis, Toby, Jessica Mooney, and Gillian Shepodd (2009 [1996])) Somali cultural profile. Ethnomed. https://ethnomed.org/culture/somali/somali-cultural-profile.
(26) Meyers, T. (2014, September 22). Spanking isn't culture. It's a cycle of abuse. *The New York Times*. http://parenting.blogs.nytimes.com/2014/09/22/spanking-isnt-culture-its-a-cycle-of-abuse/.
(27) Minnesota International Health Volunteers (2005). Somali women's breastfeeding practices and preferences: Somali health care initiative focus group findings. http://wellshareinternational.org/.
(28) Moore, L. (2011). Research directions: Moving through languages, literacies and schooling traditions. *Language Arts* 88 (4), 288–97.

(29) Samatar, H. (2008). Experiences of Somali entrepreneurs in the Twin Cities. *Bildhaan: An International Journal of Somali Studies* 4 (9), 78–81.
(30) Talbot, M. (2015, June 22). The story of a hate crime. *The New Yorker.* www.newyorker.com/magazine/2015/06/22/the-story-of-a-hate-crime.
(31) *The Noble Qur'an* (1999). Riyadh: Dar-us-Salam Publications.
(32) United Nations High Commissioner for Refugees (2015). *UNHCR Global Trends: Forced Displacement in 2015.* http://www.unhcr.org/en-us/statistics/country/576408cd7/unhcr-global-trends-2015.html.
(33) United Nations High Commissioner for Refugees (2016). *Refugees in the Horn of Africa: Somali Displacement Crisis – Kenya.* http://data.unhcr.org/horn-of-africa/country.php?id=110.
(34) Wojnar, D. (2014). Perinatal experiences of Somali couples in the United States. *Journal of Obstetric, Gynecologic and Neonatal Nursing* 44 (3), 358–69.
(35) Wolff, E. and D. Madlon-Kay (2014). Childhood vaccine beliefs reported by Somali and non-Somali parents. *Journal of the American Board of Family Medicine* 27 (4), 458–64.

8 Quechua or Spanish? Farm or School?

Citations

The numbers in the citations below refer to the numbered references in the Sources Cited section immediately following this chapter.

Page

226 pre-colonial history and Spanish conquest of the Incan empire – 27, 42; Felipe Guamán Poma de Ayala – 27, 42, 43, 47
227 José María Arguedas – 5, 6, 7, 42; Peru's colonial history – 27, 42; history of Peru's independence and early nationhood – 19, 20, 42; Peru's first constitution – 11
228 numbers of dead and disappeared – 36; Andean communities' attitudes toward/experiences with schooling – 2, 3, 4, 9, 20, 26, 28; history of Shining Path – 23, 36, 42, 44, 45
230 meaning of "respect" for Quechua speakers in the Andes – 12, 13, 18, 22, 26, 32, 40
231 importance of "respect" in Andean childrearing and social norms – 12, 13, 21, 22, 26, 32
233 Andean Spanish – 37; life in the *puna* – 25
238 Amaru legend – 8, 43, 46, 47

239 coca leaves in Andean cosmology – 1, 24, 29
240 Andean practices of "reciprocity" – 1, 12, 14, 26, 29, 33, 37, 43, 47; sacred nature of water, mountains, all forms of life and landscape in Andean cosmology – 1, 10, 12, 29
241 reciprocity and postwar reconciliation – 45
242 Quechua greeting – 41; childbirth – 13, 17, 31
245 external womb – 12, 13, 31
246 personhood of babies and young children – 13, 34, 38
247 protective water – 13; synchronization of Catholicism with Andean cosmology – 1, 12, 13, 29; first haircut – 12, 13, 31
250 disciplining children – 13, 14, 22, 26, 39; children's household labor – 13, 15, 26, 30
251 learning by watching and helping – 14, 21, 26, 28, 35
253 communal work sessions – 1, 13, 26, 29
254 preschool in Andean communities – 2, 3
256 Andean children's aptitude for math – 13
259 raising children to be better than their parents – 26, 30

Sources Cited – Chapter 8

(1) Allen, C. (1988). *The hold life has: Coca and cultural identity in an Andean community*. Washington, DC: Smithsonian Institution Press.

(2) Ames, P., V. Rojas, and T. Portugal (2009). *Starting school: Who is prepared? Young Lives' research on children's transition to first grade in Peru*. Working Paper No. 47. Oxford: Young Lives.

(3) Ames, P., V. Rojas, and T. Portugal (2010). *Continuity and respect for diversity: Strengthening early transitions in Peru*. Working Paper No. 56, Studies in Early Childhood Transitions. The Hague: Bernard van Leer Foundation.

(4) Ansión, J. (1988). *La escuela en la comunidad campesina. Proyecto escuela, ecología y comunidad campesina*. Lima: Ministerio de Agricultura, Ministerio de Educación, FAO/ Organización de las Naciones Unidas para la Agricultura y Alimentación, COTESU/ Cooperación Técnica del Gobierno de Suiza.

(5) Arguedas, J. M. (1978). *Deep rivers*. Trans. F. H. Barraclough. Austin: University of Texas Press.

(6) Arguedas, J. M. (1985). *Yawar fiesta*. Trans. F. H. Barraclough. Austin: University of Texas Press.

Citations and Sources Cited

(7) Arguedas, J. M. (2000). *The fox from up above and the fox from down below*. Trans. F. H. Barraclough. Pittsburgh: University of Pittsburgh Press.

(8) Arguedas, J. M. and F. Izquierdo Ríos (eds.) (1947). *Mitos, leyendas y cuentos Peruanos*. Lima: Ministerio de Educación Pública.

(9) Arnold, D. and J. D. Yapita (2006). *The metamorphosis of heads: Textual struggles, education, and land in the Andes*. Pittsburgh: University of Pittsburgh Press.

(10) Bauer, B. and C. Stanish. (2001). *Ritual and pilgrimage in the ancient Andes: The islands of the sun and the moon*. Austin: University of Texas Press.

(11) Bernardo de Tagle, J. (1823). *Constitución política de la República Peruana. Sancionada por el Primer Congreso Constituyente el 12 de Noviembre de 1823*. Lima.

(12) Bolin, I. (1998). *Rituals of respect: The secret of survival in the high Peruvian Andes*. Austin: University of Texas Press.

(13) Bolin, I. (2006). *Growing up in a culture of respect: Childrearing in highland Peru*. Austin: University of Texas Press.

(14) Bolton, C. and R. Bolton (1974). Techniques of socialization among the Qolla. *Atti del XL Congresso Internazionale degli Americanisti*. Rome: International Congress of Americanists, pp. 531–39.

(15) Bolton, C. and R. Bolton (2010 [1982]). El trabajo de niños en la sociedad Andina. In R. Bolton, *La vida familiar en comunidades Andinas: Estudios antropológicos en la sierra sur del Perú*. Lima: Editorial Horizonte, pp. 243–60.

(16) Bolton, R. and E. Mayer (eds.) (1977). *Andean kinship and marriage*. Washington, DC: American Anthropological Association.

(17) Bradby, B. (2002). Local knowledge in health: The case of Andean midwifery. In Henry Stobart and Rosaleen Howard (eds.), *Knowledge and learning in the Andes*. Liverpool: Liverpool University Press, pp. 166–93.

(18) Cordero, L. (1992). *Diccionario Quichua–Castellano y Castellano–Quichua*. Quito: Proyecto Educación Bilingüe Intercultural and Corporación Editora Nacional.

(19) de la Cadena, M. (2003). *Indigenous mestizos: The politics of race and culture in Cuzco, Peru, 1919–1991*. Durham, NC: Duke University Press.

(20) García, M. E. (2005). *Making indigenous citizens: Identities, education, and multicultural development in Peru*. Stanford: Stanford University Press.

(21) García Rivera, F. A. (2005). *Yachay: Concepciones sobre enseñanza y aprendizaje en una comunidad Quechua*. La Paz, Bolivia: PINSEIB, PROEIB Andes, and Plural Editores.
(22) García Rivera, F. A. (2007). *Runa hina kay*: La educación familiar y comunitaria orientada al respeto en una comunidad Quechua. Doctoral dissertation. Mexico City: Centro de Investigación de Estudios Avanzados, Departamento de Investigaciones Educativas.
(23) Gorriti, G. (1999). *The Shining Path: A history of the Millenarian War in Peru*. Trans. Robin Kirk. Chapel Hill: University of North Carolina Press.
(24) Gose, P. (1994). *Deathly waters and hungry mountains: Agrarian ritual and class formation in an Andean town*. Toronto: University of Toronto Press.
(25) Grim-Feinberg, K. (2012). Una aventura por las punas del Perú, parts I, II, and III. *La Voz: Cultura y Noticias del Valle del Hudson* 5 (8), 6 (9), 7 (9) (June, July, and August). http://lavoz.bard.edu/archivo/index.php?year=2012.
(26) Grim-Feinberg, K. (2013). Cultural models of respectful subjectivity among primary school children in post-conflict Ayacucho, Peru: An embodied learning analysis. Doctoral dissertation, Department of Anthropology, University of Illinois at Urbana-Champaign.
(27) Guamán Poma de Ayala, F. (2009). *The First New Chronicle and good government: On the history of the world and the Incas up to 1615*. Trans. Roland Hamilton. Austin: University of Texas Press.
(28) Howard, R. (2002). *Yachay:* The *Tragedia del Fin de Atahuallpa* as evidence of the colonisation of knowledge in the Andes. In Henry Stobart and Rosaleen Howard (eds.), *Knowledge and learning in the Andes*. Liverpool: Liverpool University Press, pp. 17–39.
(29) Isbell, B. J. (1985). *To defend ourselves: Ecology and ritual in an Andean village*. Long Grove, IL: Waveland Press.
(30) Leinaweaver, J. (2008). *The circulation of children: Kinship, adoption, and morality in Andean Peru*. Durham, NC: Duke University Press.
(31) Lestage, F. (1999). *Naissance et petite enfance dans les Andes péruviennes: Pratiques, rites, représentations*. Paris: L'Harmattan.
(32) Lyons, B. J. (2001). Religion, authority, and identity: Intergenerational politics, ethnic resurgence, and respect in Chimborazo, Ecuador. *Latin American Research Review* 36 (1), 7–48.
(33) Meyer, E. (2002). *The articulated peasant: Household economies in the Andes*. Boulder, CO: Westview Press.

Citations and Sources Cited

(34) Morgan, L. M. (1998). Ambiguities lost: Fashioning the fetus into a child in Ecuador and the United States. In Nancy Scheper-Hughes and Carolyn Sargent (eds.), *Small wars: The cultural politics of childhood*. Berkeley: University of California Press, pp. 58–74.

(35) Paradise, R. and B. Rogoff (2009). Side by side: Learning by observing and pitching in. *Ethos*, 37 (1), 102–38.

(36) Peru. Truth and Reconciliation Commission (2014). *Hatun Willakuy: Abbreviated version of the Final Report of the Peruvian Truth and Reconciliation Commission*. Lima: Transfer Commission of the Truth and Reconciliation Commission of Peru. www.ictj.org/sites/default/files/ICTJ_Book_Peru_CVR_2014.pdf.

(37) Platt, T. (1986). Mirrors and maize: The concept of *Yanantin* among the Macha of Bolivia. In John V. Murra, Jacques Revel, and Nathan Wachtel (eds.), *Anthropological history of Andean polities*. Cambridge: Cambridge University Press, pp. 228–59.

(38) Silver, S. and W. R. Miller (1997). *American Indian languages: Cultural and social contexts*. Tucson: University of Arizona Press.

(39) Smith, B. (2012). Language and the frontiers of the human: Aymara animal-oriented interjections and the mediation of mind. *American Ethnologist* 39 (2), 313–24.

(40) Soto Ruíz, C. (2012). *Quechua–Spanish–English functional dictionary. Ayacucho–Chanka*, vol. 1. Lima: Lluvia Editores.

(41) Soto Ruíz, C. (n.d.). *Quechua online.* Center for Latin American and Caribbean Studies, University of Illinois at Urbana-Champaign. www.clacs.illinois.edu/quechua/exercises.aspx.

(42) Starn, O., C. I. Degregori, and R. Kirk (eds.) (2005). *The Peru reader: History, culture, politics*. Durham, NC: Duke University Press.

(43) Steele, P. R. with C. J. Allen (2004). *Handbook of Inca mythology*. Santa Barbara, CA: ABC-CLIO.

(44) Stern, S. (ed.) (1998). *Shining and other Paths: War and society in Peru, 1980–1995*. Durham, NC: Duke University Press.

(45) Theidon, K. (2013). *Intimate enemies: Violence and reconciliation in Peru*. Philadelphia: University of Pennsylvania Press.

(46) Urton, G. (1981). *At the crossroads of the earth and the sky: An Andean cosmology*. Latin American Monographs Series 55. Austin: University of Texas Press.

(47) Urton, G. (1999). *Inca myths*. Austin: University of Texas Press.

Citations and Sources Cited

9 Equal Children Play Best

Citations

The numbers in the citations below refer to numbered references in the Sources Cited section that follows these citations.

Page

261	geography – 13; population distribution – 13
261–2	relationship to Denmark –13; relationship to the European Union –16; closeness of family, valuing tradition – 13
262–3	traditional and modern subsistence, historical struggles – 13
262–4	importance of independence and family – 15, 16; changes with World War II – 49; technology and lifestyle in remote villages in the late twentieth century – 24; modern technological access, social services, economy; the continuing whale hunt – 20; practices in the whale hunt – 4, 11, 13, 48; sheep population – 6, 13; importance of wool – 13
264–5	religion in the Faroe Islands – 15, 20; diversity in religious devotion – 15, 34; religion in Denmark – 10, 50; religion and LGBT rights – 29; children born to single parents – 37
265	xenophobic attitudes in Denmark – 25, 35, 44
265–6	anti-immigrant political parties in Europe – 3, 7; mass shooting in Norway – 9, 36, 39; homogeneity in the Faroe Islands – 15; growing immigrant population 20; dropping birthrate – 20; Faroese women leaving, and the "imported bride" phenomenon – 45; international responses to immigrants – 27; Faroese attitudes on immigration – 38
266–7	closeness with neighbors, and visiting practices – 49; close family relationships – 17; the idealized concept of the Faroese childhood – 17
268	the existence and role of the maternity nurse in Denmark – 31
268–9	maternity nurses' responsibilities – 31
269	Faroese and American infant mortality rates – 43
270–1	increasing numbers of foreign brides – 45; Faroese women leaving, and the "imported bride" phenomenon – 2; marriage migration practices – 5; quality of immigrant marriages – 21; immigrant rights and resources – 28
271	LGBT marriage in Denmark – 1
272–3	recommendations regarding drinking and smoking during pregnancy – 41; Faroese drinking habits – 13, 24
273	sources of water pollution – 30, 45; the importance of avoiding whale and certain fish while pregnant – 18, 19

Citations and Sources Cited

274	immigrant education and employment – 21
275	naming laws in other societies – 22, 23; popular Faroese names – 20
276	the "hidden people" and naming practices – 8, 13, 47
277	women working part-time – 20
278	breastfeeding recommendations – 41; maternity nurse assistance with breastfeeding – 31
279–80	sleep recommendations – 40
280–1	benefits of and beliefs about babies sleeping outdoors – 26, 42; closeness among villagers and awareness of strangers – 13
281	arrest of Danish woman in New York – 32
281–2	reliance on and closeness with extended family – 13, 16, 17
284–5	children's freedom to play independently, and the concept of the idyllic Faroese childhood – 16, 17
285	birds of the Faroe Islands – 33
286	disciplining children – 17
287	the *rukka* practice – 12, 13
287–8	families' decisions to attend church, Christian practices in schools – 13
289	early school attendance – 14
289–90	educational practices, controversies, and rates of graduation – 14, 16
290	Danish attitudes about the Faroese – 49
290–1	Faroese language – 15; learning traditions in school – 14; the chain dance – 13
291	the "hidden people" – 8, 13, 24, 47
292	concept of the Faroe Islands as a "children's paradise" – 17

Sources Cited – Chapter 9

(1) Badgett, M. L. (2009). *When gay people get married: What happens when societies legalize same-sex marriage*. New York: NYU Press.

(2) BBC News (2013). Faroe Islands: Men "must import brides." *News from Elsewhere*, October 23.

(3) Blee, K. M. (2007). Ethnographies of the far right. *Journal of Contemporary Ethnography* 36 (2), 119–28.

(4) Boyd, R., G. Gigerenzer, P. J. Richerson, A. Robson, J. R. Stevens, and P. Hammerstein (2008). Individual decision making and the evolutionary roots of institutions. In E. Engel and W. Singer (eds.), *Better than conscious? Decision making, the human*

mind, and implications for institutions. Cambridge, MA: The MIT Press, pp. 325–42.
(5) Del Rosario, T. C. (2005). Bridal diaspora migration and marriage among Filipino women. *Indian Journal of Gender Studies*, 12 (2–3), 253–73.
(6) Dýrmundsson, Ó. R. (2006). Sustainability of sheep and goat production in North European countries – From the Arctic to the Alps. *Small Ruminant Research* 62 (3), 151–57.
(7) Ellinas, A. A. (2013). The rise of Golden Dawn: The new face of the far right in Greece. *South European Society and Politics* 18 (4), 543–65.
(8) Enni, J., J. P. Heinesen, J. Henriksen, S. Niclasen, and J. A. Naes (1978). Eg sat maer I heyyi. *Lesibók til 8. Skúlaár*. Tórshavn: Føroya Skulabokagrunnur, pp. 230–31.
(9) Erlanger, S. and S. Shane (2011). Oslo suspect wrote of fear of Islam and plan for war. *The New York Times,* July 23.
(10) European Commission (2010). Biotechnology report. *Special Eurobarometer 341, Wave 73.1.* Brussels: European Commission. http://ec.europa.eu/public_opinion/archives/ebs/ebs_341_en.pdf.
(11) Faroe Islands Parliament (2013). Executive order on the pilot whale drive, No. 100. July 12.
(12) Gaffin, D. (1995). The production of emotion and social control: Taunting, anger, and the *Rukka* in the Faeroe Islands. *Ethos* 23 (2), 149–72.
(13) Gaffin, D. (1996). *In place: Spatial and social order in a Faeroe Islands community*. Prospect Heights, IL: Waveland Press.
(14) Gaini, F. (2009). *Family and primary school in the Faroe Islands. Conference Paper: International Conference on Primary Education*. Hong Kong.
(15) Gaini, F. (2011). Preface. In F. Gaini (ed.), *Among the islanders of the north: An anthropology of the Faroe Islands*. Tórshavn: Faroe University Press, pp. 7–10.
(16) Gaini, F. (2011). Cultural rhapsody in shift. In F. Gaini (ed.), *Among the islanders of the north: An anthropology of the Faroe Islands*. Tórshavn: Faroe University Press, pp. 132–62.
(17) Gaini, F. (2013). *Lessons of islands: Place and identity in the Faroe Islands*. Tórshavn: Faroe University Press.
(18) Grandjean, P., P. Weihe, P. J. Jørgensen, T. Clarkson, E. Cernichiari, and T. Viderø (1992). Impact of maternal seafood diet on fetal exposure to mercury, selenium, and lead. *Archives of Environmental Health: An International Journal* 47 (3), 185–95.

(19) Grandjean, P., P. Weihe, R. F. White, and F. Debes (1998). Cognitive performance of children prenatally exposed to "safe" levels of methylmercury. *Environmental Research* 77 (2), 165–72.
(20) Hagstova Føroya (2014). *Statbank and Faroe Islands in figures.* www.hagstova.fo/en.
(21) Hayfield, E. A. and M. G. Schug (paper in preparation). Building new lives in a remote Nordic society: Immigrant experiences in the Faroe Islands.
(22) Henley, J. (2014). Icelandic girls can't be called Harriet, government tells family. *The Guardian,* June 26.
(23) Israel, D. K. (2010). Oh no, you can't name your baby THAT! *CNN*, July 3.
(24) Kaysen, S. (1990). *Far afield.* New York: Vintage Books.
(25) Kingsley, P. (2012). Something puzzling in the state of Denmark, *The Guardian*, December 21.
(26) Lee, H. (2013). The babies who nap in sub-zero temperatures. *BBC News Magazine*, February 22.
(27) Martin, P. L. (1985). Migrant labor in agriculture: An international comparison. *International Migration Review* 19 (1), 135–43.
(28) Ministry of Social Affairs (2014). *Welcome: Feel free!* [brochure concerning rights and resources for immigrants to the Faroe Island] Tórshavn: Faroe Islands.
(29) Mohr, B. (2014). Uppskotið um at loyva borgarligt hjúnaband fall. *Kringvarp Føroya* [The Faroese Broadcasting Company], March 13. http://kvf.fo/greinar/2014/03/13/uppskotid-um-loyva-borgarligt-hjunaband-fall#.V a1QJouppuZ.
(30) Monteiro, L. R. and R. W. Furness (1997). Accelerated increase in mercury contamination in North Atlantic mesopelagic food chains as indicated by time series of seabird feathers. *Environmental Toxicology and Chemistry* 16 (12), 2489–93.
(31) Newcomb, C. (2009). Breastfeeding and mothering in Denmark. *New Beginnings* 29 (5–6), 56–59.
(32) Ojito, M. (1997). Danish mother is reunited with her baby. *The New York Times*, May 15.
(33) Olofson, Silas (2014). *Birds of the Faroe Islands*. Visit Faroe Islands. http://issuu.com/visitfaroeislands/docs/birds_of_the_faroe_islands_-_englis
(34) Pons, C. (2011). The anthropology of Christianity in the Faroe Islands. In F. Gaini (ed.), *Among the islanders of the north: An anthropology of the Faroe Islands*. Tórshavn: Faroe University Press, pp. 132–62.

Citations and Sources Cited

(35) Roemer, J. E. and K. Van der Straeten (2006). The political economy of xenophobia and distribution: The case of Denmark. *Scandinavian Journal of Economics* 108 (2), 251–77.

(36) Sanchez, R. (2011). Norway's royal family lead moment of silence for terror victims. *The Telegraph*, July 25.

(37) Schug, M. G. (2012). Nordic perspectives: Attitudes about and impacts of gay marriage in Nordic societies. Public lecture for the exhibit *Diversity of the North*. Öström Exhibit Hall, Tórshavn.

(38) Schug, M. G. and E. A. Hayfield (paper in preparation). The psychology of diversity: Attitudes on immigration to the Faroe Islands.

(39) Schwirtz, M. (2011). For young campers, island turned into fatal trap. *The New York Times*, July 23.

(40) Sundhedsstyrelsen (2011). *Prevent cot death – and avoid plagiocephaly or flat head syndrome*. Copenhagen: Danish Health and Medicines Authority.

(41) Sundhedsstyrelsen (2015). *Healthy habits before, during, and after pregnancy*. Copenhagen: Danish Health and Medicines Authority.

(42) Tourula, M., A. Isola, and J. Hassi (2007). Children sleeping outdoors in winter: Parents' experiences of a culturally bound childcare practice. *International Journal of Circumpolar Health* 67 (2–3), 269–78.

(43) United States Central Intelligence Agency (2014). *The World Factbook, 2015*. New York: Skyhorse.

(44) Vinocur, J. (1997). A xenophobic weed is growing in Denmark's tidy little garden, *The New York Times*, November 17.

(45) Weaver, R. (2013). Women disappearing from the Faroe Islands. *The Copenhagen Post*, October 23.

Index

Index

Index

Index

Index

Index

Index

Index

Index

Index

Index

Index

Index

Index

Index

Index

Index

Index

Index

Index

Index

Index